FACILITATING DEEP LEARNING

Pathways to Success for
University and College Teachers

FACILITATING DEEP LEARNING

Pathways to Success for University and College Teachers

Julian Hermida, DCL

Apple Academic Press

TORONTO   NEW JERSEY

Apple Academic Press Inc.	Apple Academic Press Inc.
3333 Mistwell Crescent	9 Spinnaker Way
Oakville, ON L6L 0A2	Waretown, NJ 08758
Canada	USA

©2015 by Apple Academic Press, Inc.

First issued in paperback 2021

Exclusive worldwide distribution by CRC Press, a member of Taylor & Francis Group
No claim to original U.S. Government works

ISBN 13: 978-1-77463-322-9 (pbk)
ISBN 13: 978-1-77188-005-3 (hbk)

This book contains information obtained from authentic and highly regarded sources. Reprinted material is quoted with permission and sources are indicated. Copyright for individual articles remains with the authors as indicated. A wide variety of references are listed. Reasonable efforts have been made to publish reliable data and information, but the authors, editors, and the publisher cannot assume responsibility for the validity of all materials or the consequences of their use. The authors, editors, and the publisher have attempted to trace the copyright holders of all material reproduced in this publication and apologize to copyright holders if permission to publish in this form has not been obtained. If any copyright material has not been acknowledged, please write and let us know so we may rectify in any future reprint.

Trademark Notice: Registered trademark of products or corporate names are used only for explanation and identification without intent to infringe.

Library of Congress Control Number: 2014940040

Library and Archives Canada Cataloguing in Publication

Hermida, Julian, author
Facilitating deep learning: pathways to success for university and college teachers/Julian Hermida, PhD.

Includes bibliographical references and index.
ISBN 978-1-77188-005-3 (bound)

1. Learning. 2. Education, Higher--Study and teaching. 3. Effective teaching. I. Title.

LB1060.H48 2014	370.15'23	C2014-903268-4

Apple Academic Press also publishes its books in a variety of electronic formats. Some content that appears in print may not be available in electronic format. For information about Apple Academic Press products, visit our website at **www.appleacademicpress.com** and the CRC Press website at **www.crcpress.com**

ABOUT THE AUTHOR

Julian Hermida, DCL

Julian Hermida is Associate Professor at Algoma University's Department of Law (Sault Ste. Marie, Ontario). He was also the Chair of Algoma's Teaching and Learning Committee for several years. Julian has a very successful practice of more than 10 years of full-time teaching at all levels. Prior to joining Algoma, he taught at Dalhousie University in Halifax, Canada, where he was recognized with the 2004–2005 Award of Excellence for Teaching and Learning.

A seasoned educational developer, Julian has ample experience designing, implementing, and evaluating university-wide faculty development programs and initiatives. He has conducted educational development workshops and led seminars on teaching and learning in Canada, the United States, Europe, and Latin America. He has won several internal and external grants to fund his scholarship of teaching and learning research projects on deep learning.

Julian Hermida holds master's and doctoral degrees from McGill University's Faculty of Law. He did his postdoctoral studies at the University of Ottawa. He has also received formal education and training in higher education teaching in a unique and intensive program offered at the University of Montreal as well as in educational development programs in Canada and the United States. These include the Best Teachers Institute and Alverno College Assessment workshop, among many others.

Julian has published extensively on a wide array of teaching and learning topics. Together with his books and journal articles in the legal field, he has more than 80 publications, including several books.

CONTENTS

Disclaimer.. *ix*
Acknowledgments... *xi*
Preliminary Part: The Context ....*xv*
Introduction... *xvii*

1. The Instruction Paradigm.. 1

Part I: Deep Learning

2. The Deep Learning Process and the Construction of Knowledge 15

3. Goals 49

4. Performances 77

5. Collaborative Learning 93

Part II: Academic Skills and Deep Learning

6. Academic Reading and Deep Learning 115

7. Deep Writing.. 141

Part III: Deep Learning and Diversity

8. Inclusive Deep Learning Environments and Knowledge Modes ... 169

9. Internationalization and Deep Learning 185

10. International Students and Academic Proficiency 203

Part IV: Deep Learning and Evaluation

11. Evaluating to Learn.. 225

12. Student Evaluation of Teaching: Evaluating Deep Learning....... 253

Part V: Deep Learning and Time

13. Intensive Teaching 275

Final Part: A New Paradigm

14. The Learning Paradigm 291

Final Summary.. 303

Epilogue 309

Appendix 311

Index 339

DISCLAIMER

The names, affiliations, and certain identifying characteristics of students, teachers, and administrators whose stories are described in this book have been changed in order to protect their privacy. In addition, some of the stories are fictitious. Any resemblance to actual persons, institutions, or events is purely coincidental.

ACKNOWLEDGMENTS

I would like to thank many people who directly or indirectly contributed to the realization of this book.

I could never have written this book without the challenges, enthusiasm, and support of all my students: past, present, and future. My students have always inspired me to look for different ways to help them succeed and learn deeply. I embarked on this quest for deep learning for them. I have been teaching in different capacities, levels, institutions, and even countries ever since I started college. My thanks go to all of them, particularly my students at Algoma University, and my students at Dalhousie University, where I taught full-time for four years before accepting my position at Algoma.

I am equally grateful to my teachers. I had the privilege to study with some truly remarkable teachers at both the graduate and undergraduate levels. They have been fantastic role models. Their teaching practice has been an inspiration for me. I would like to mention Ram Jakhu and Michael Milde from McGill University, and Mario Folchi and Aldo Cocca from the University of Buenos Aires. As part of my master's degree, I took a seminar on Teaching and Learning at the University of Montreal led by Diane Labreche. This seminar awakened a passion in me for the field of teaching and learning. For this, I will be forever grateful. Merci!

As Chair of Algoma University's Teaching and Learning Committee for several years, I have developed a passion for educational development. The issues, problems, and situations that we have to deal with at the Committee have had a very positive influence in my research and practice interests. Every single member of the Committee has helped me grow as a teacher and as an educational developer. I would like to thank every member whom I have worked with, particularly those with whom I have worked the closest for several years: Deborah Woodman, Linda Burnett, Gerry Davies, Jan Clarke, Pedro Antunes and Dave Marasco.

As part of my educational development practice, I regularly give workshops and conferences in North America, Latin America, and Europe. Participants in these educational development activities have also influenced the content of this book. While I can't name all of them, I would like to mention Juan Antonio Seda from the University of Buenos Aires, Raul Farias, from FORES, Flavia Propper who was at the University of Belgrano, Juan Cayon Peña from Nebrija, Radhames Mejia of UNAPEC, and Elena Bogonez from the Autonomous University of Madrid.

Rick Myers, David Schantz, and Arthur Perlini, president, Vice President, and Academic Dean of Algoma University, respectively, have supported my educational development and teaching practice in ways, which are remarkable. They have invited me to be part of very interesting university projects, such as the block plan initiative and the university foundations program, among many others. These very challenging initiatives have helped me acquire unique experiences that are reflected in this book.

Two icons of the Scholarship of Teaching and Learning have profoundly transformed my teaching and educational development practice: John Tagg and Ken Bain. I met John Tagg at Algoma University, when he came to visit us as guest speaker for our Teaching Forum. He led a workshop entitled the "Learning Paradigm University." His presentation and conversations changed the way I see higher education. I met Ken and Marsha Bain in a teaching conference in Oklahoma in 2007. I then participated in the Best College Teachers Institute. In addition, I invited Ken Bain to be the keynote speaker at the 2010 Educational Developers Caucus conference that I organized at Algoma. Multiple references to John Tagg and Ken Bain throughout the book reflect the profound admiration I have for them and the influence they both have had in my professional life.

Florencia Carlino is a deep-learning teacher and educational developer to whom I am truly grateful for her permanent support. She organizes a very successful annual Teaching and Learning Conference at Sault College and numerous educational development activities. These conferences, workshops, and seminars have also imprinted a unique mark in the way I think about teaching and learning. Like with John Tagg and Ken Bain, the numerous stories and examples I give from Florencia's teaching practice throughout the book are a testimony of the impact of her teaching and educational development practice.

My thanks also go to Alejandro Casavalle, a drama teacher and theater director. A constructivist with a wealth of experiences and intellectual generosity, Alejandro has also left his mark in this book with many experiences from his vast teaching trajectory.

A special big thank you goes to Susan Berardini and Iride Lamartina-Lens from Pace University in New York for their support and friendship.

I am also truly indebted to Sandra Sickels from Apple Academic Press for believing in this book from the very beginning when it looked a lot different. Her encouragement made this book possible. I am equally indebted to Ashish and Rakesh Kumar. Without their support, this book would not exist.

I am also grateful to Cindy Leibfried from Shepherd Incorporated and Rakesh Kumar from AAP for proofreading the manuscript. I am also thankful to the Wishart Library's staff, particularly Anne Beaupre.

Finally, I am truly grateful to my family for their endless support. This book is dedicated to my two favorite children in the world: Mike Hermida and Lucas Hermida.

PRELIMINARY PART
THE CONTEXT

INTRODUCTION

Soon after I had finished my doctoral studies, my supervisor asked me to give two lectures to his undergraduate students. He told me that he would be absent for a week in order to participate in a conference in Europe. And since it was the beginning of the term, he did not want to cancel these classes. He wanted me to cover his classes in the following day and two days later. I already moved to another city, a few hundred miles away from my *alma mater*, as I had obtained a nontenure track teaching position in another university. So, I was hesitant at first, because that meant that I would need to make alternative arrangements with my own students. But my supervisor insisted. He told me that he had no doctoral students specializing in space law and that it would be easy for me to teach these two classes. He convinced me when he told me that he would cover all my expenses, including executive-class airfare and accommodations at a five-star hotel. That did the trick. So, I agreed to teach for him. He then told me that he would send me an email with the topics he wanted me to explain in each class. I talked to my teaching assistants (a luxury I don't have in my current university as a tenured associate professor), and they agreed to show a video and lead a discussion for me that week. A couple of hours later, I was flying in executive class for the first time in my life. As anyone who went to graduate school would know, life as a doctoral student is tough. I worked as a research assistant for my thesis supervisor for minimum wage. This salary and a small scholarship were my main sources of income. I hardly had money for food, books, and rent.

So, when I arrived at the hotel, I was truly fascinated. I spent hours at the swimming pool. Then, I tried the sauna, the Jacuzzi, and the fitness center. I even had a massage at the spa for the very first time in my life (and so far the only one). Then, I gobbled up a spectacular dinner buffet like I had never eaten in years. After dinner, I was too tired to check my email. I didn't think I would have any problem whatsoever giving a lecture on any topic of space law to a group of undergraduate students. After all, I had just finished my doctoral dissertation in space law. I had several publications in the field. I had given presentations on space law in academic conferences. I had been a research assistant for my supervisor for years. And I had aced this course as an undergraduate student. What's more, as part of my graduate studies, I had also taken advanced courses in space law. So, I decided to check my email in the morning after breakfast; I also decided I would mentally outline a lecture on the ten-minute walk from the hotel to the university. After sleeping like a baby, I had a decadent breakfast. Then, I checked my email. When I read that my supervisor wanted me to discuss the technological aspects of outer space that day and the legal background of the Outer Space Treaty on Thursday, I was shocked. I literally panicked. I did not remember anything about the technological aspects of outer space. The terms *apogee* and *perigee*, which my supervisor wanted me to explain to his students, rang a bell, but I could not remember what they meant. I had completely forgotten all about the technological aspects of outer space. Yes, I had aced this course every time I took it. And such courses always started with an explanation of these and other technological terms. But I had no idea what they were. Not knowing what to do, I walked into the classroom and briefly introduced myself. Then, almost instinctively, I asked students if they had read the chapter from the casebook on the technological aspects of outer space. Because very few students raised their hands, I told them to read that chapter for Thursday; I then went on to explain the legal background of the Outer Space Treaty, which I knew very well. After class, I ran to the library to prepare for next class. Although I managed to prepare a decent lecture on apogee, perigee, and other technical aspects in the following 48 h before the class on Thursday, I had to forget about the swimming pool, the sauna, and the Jacuzzi.

The lecture went well, or so I thought at that moment. But when I came back home, I was still shocked. I wanted to know why I had forgotten about something I had studied several times during my undergraduate and graduate years. How was it possible that I had no idea about something that I had learned at school not that long ago? What about my own students? Was I teaching them in the same way? Would they forget everything I taught them? If so, why? Is there something structurally wrong in higher education that prevents students from learning in a way that they will remember the material? Or was I alone in having done something

Introduction xix

wrong that caused me to forget? How could I teach so that my students would learn for life? What could I do so that students could transfer and apply what they learn to other situations and contexts? What could be done to change the existing teaching paradigm? I embarked on a professional life-long journey to grapple with these questions in search for answers.

At the core of these questions lie two fundamental concepts, which I ignored at that time: deep learning and surface learning. Deep learning is a committed approach to learning where learners learn for life and can apply what they learn to new situations and contexts. Surface learning is a superficial approach to learning where students use knowledge that they acquire for writing exams or papers and soon forget it. Deep learners discover and construct their own knowledge by negotiating meanings with peers and by making connections between existing and new knowledge. Surface learners receive knowledge passively from their teachers or books. We can learn deeply, write deeply, read deeply, and engage in any academic task in a deep way. Similarly, we can approach any academic task in a surface way.

One of the most shocking research findings about deep and surface learning reported in the literature in virtually every country and region in the Western world is that most university and college students approach learning in a surface way (Biggs & Tang, 2007). In other words, students forget what they learn and cannot use it meaningfully outside the setting of higher education. In any other activity, industry, or sector, this would make headlines all over the world. For example, if car manufacturers produced cars that ran for a few miles only, if planes flew only a few minutes after takeoff, or if computers stopped working after a few mouse clicks, it could not be business as usual in those industries. People would be fired; companies would be closed down, consumers would file multimillion-dollar lawsuits, and society would demand immediate changes. Fortunately, higher education is different. We have time to work on our mistakes and fix them. We have time to go back to the drawing board and teach our courses differently. But unfortunately, it takes us too long to realize that things are not working well and even longer to find a meaningful solution. In the meantime, entire cohorts of students are sent out to the world outside academia having learned only superficially.

Deep learning is the answer to higher education's performance problem. It is what helps students become active protagonists of their own learning process. It is the key to their success in their future academic and professional endeavors. Deep learning leads to the attainment of quality learning goals. It also helps the learner develop cognitively and emotionally. It enables learners to connect, apply, and transfer knowledge to a wide array of settings and to act effectively in different contexts. Committing to fostering a deep learning environment in our classes and across higher education institutions is an urgent imperative. We owe it to our students. We need to radically change our teaching practice so that all students can learn deeply and transform their lives.

One of the most powerful research findings is that we teachers play the most influential role in students'—usually unconscious – decision to take a deep approach to learning. We can create the environment and conditions that can encourage our students to approach learning in a profound way. And this is so, even if we work in institutions that are not learning oriented and that have strong structural barriers that make innovative pedagogical changes difficult.

This book aims to show what we can do to create a learning environment that encourages students to take a deep approach to learning. By deconstructing the notion of deep learning and by examining every element of the teaching and learning system, I will show you how to bring about deep learning in our teaching practice. After reading this book and engaging with the proposed activities in the practice corner, you will have the theoretically grounded and research-supported strategies and tools that are necessary to implement a deep learning environment across all classes.

ORGANIZATION OF THE BOOK

This book is divided into several parts and chapters. The preliminary part, which contains the introduction and Chapter 1, situates this book in its context. In Chapter 1, I briefly examine the prevailing paradigm in higher education. Many teachers, students, and administrators have long expressed discontent with the status quo. This discontent revolves around the fact that the Instruction-paradigm University, dominated as it is by the

Introduction xxi

lecture method, produces shallow and superficial learning instead of deep learning. The goal of that chapter is to raise awareness of the artifacts of the institutions we work at so that we can effect and implement informed changes in our classroom teaching.

Part I contains Chapters 2 to 5 and addresses the notion of deep learning and its major components. In Chapter 2, the focus will be on the answer to the Instruction-paradigm's structural problem: deep learning. I will delve into a detailed examination of the elements and factors of deep learning. Deep learning requires a series of cognitive and metacognitive interventions at both the individual and the group (social) levels so that learners can construct new knowledge that results in both a conceptual change in their cognitive structure and in their position in a community of knowledgeable peers. I follow a constructivist approach to deep learning, as this approach is understood by Schwandt and McCarty (2000), who advanced the idea that "everyone who believes the mind is active in the making of knowledge is a constructivist" (Graffam, 2003). In this sense, constructivism is a point of departure, which includes doubts, debates, criticism, and self-criticism (Carretero, 2009). Constructivism is founded upon the idea that the individual is not a mere product of the social context or his or her internal dispositions, but rather his or her own construction that is produced every day as a result of the interaction between those two factors. At the same time, my conception of deep learning is compatible with vygotskian and neo-vygotskian notions of social learning and development. It is also compatible with findings in cognitive neuroscience (Zull, 2002). Cognitive neuroscience deals with research on brain processes and structures; it also examines the role that the brain plays in the learning process (Zull, 2011).

After the analysis of the notion and elements of deep learning in Chapter 2, the rest of the chapters are about how to facilitate deep learning. I explore the goals of teaching and learning at the classroom and program levels (Chapter 3) and the ways to reach these goals through student performances (Chapter 4). Deep learning proceeds in a very special way that changes how we think about goals and objectives. It requires a change in the fundamental arrangements for teaching and learning. In particular, it requires that students formulate their own goals or, at least, play an important role in creating their own curriculum around their own interests and goals. For this purpose, we need to design activities and performances that will help them construct their own knowledge.

Learning is both an individual and a collective process. Chapter 5 deals with the social aspect of learning. Knowledge is conceived as both an individual and a social construction. At the social level, it implies either the reacculturation from one community of knowledgeable peers to another or a move from the periphery of a community to its center. Learning communities in higher education institutions facilitate this process. This entails a significant change in our role as teachers. It requires us to give up control and to become facilitators of student learning.

Becoming academically proficient in a discipline or professional field requires the mastery of some fundamental academic skills, particularly reading and writing. Despite the importance of these skills for academic success, they are generally taken for granted, and they are seldom taught explicitly at universities and colleges. Part II, which includes Chapters 6 and 7, deals with deep reading (Chapter 6) and deep writing (Chapter 7). I will explore some strategies and methods to help students learn to read deeply and to write deeply. I will also discuss how to use writing to bring about deep learning.

Part III examines the connection between deep learning and diversity. This part of the book is premised on the idea that interacting with peers from different backgrounds and cultures helps learners explore problems and questions from angles that cannot be considered when social interaction is restricted to interaction with peers from a similar background. But diversity of backgrounds alone does not automatically lead to deeper levels of learning. This only takes place if these diverse backgrounds are valued and explicitly incorporated into the teaching and learning experience. The most effective way to achieve this is through the creation of inclusive deep learning environments, where we incorporate diverse knowledge modes into our classes and we help students learn from diverse worldviews, cultural perspectives, and languages (Chapter 8). The other two essential aspects of the deep learning environment are the development of a global and international education, where students approach the content, discourse, and strategies of the academic disciplines from a global and international perspective, and the development of a plurilingual education, where students learn the academic disciplines in a plurality of languages (Chapter 9). Chapter 10 deals with one of the most significant challenges

Introduction

derived from the creation of inclusive deep learning environments: helping nonnative speaking students pursue higher education in a second or a foreign language.

Evaluation also plays a fundamental role in facilitating deep learning. Part IV includes Chapters 11 and 12 and explores evaluation from the students' and the teachers' perspectives. In Chapter 11, I analyze the notion of evaluating to learn —an approach that conceives of evaluation as an integral part of the deep learning process. I will examine the main aspects, characteristics, instruments, and subjects in every phase of the evaluating-to-learn process. I will also explore the notion of metacognition and how we can help students use metacognitive strategies to engage in reflection and self-evaluation. The emphasis of this chapter is on how we can use evaluation in order to encourage students to take a deep approach in their discovery and construction of knowledge. Chapter 12 deals with another aspect of evaluation: student evaluation of courses. Universities and colleges have been relying on student evaluation of teaching to assess the effectiveness of their faculty for decades. Teachers need meaningful feedback in order to continue improving their teaching practice. However, the predominant instruments have no correlation with student learning and are used for tenure and promotion purposes rather than to give useful information to teachers about their practice. The chapter focuses on how to create a meaningful approach to student evaluation of teaching effectiveness that assesses teaching effectiveness from a deep learning perspective, where the emphasis is not on the methods teachers use to teach their classes but on whether or not teachers help students learn deeply.

Part V consists of one chapter, which explores the connection between time and deep learning. It also advances the notion and advantages of intensive teaching formats.

The final part of the book explores the Learning paradigm, conceived as a model for higher education organizations focused on producing deep learning. Chapter 14 analyzes the main elements of the Learning paradigm and compares them to those of the Instruction paradigm. The goal of Chapter 14 is to show that creating an institutional environment that promotes deep learning is not a utopian dream. It is possible when there is a concerted effort among all main players involved in the learning enterprise, particularly, teachers, students, and administrators.

Finally, the last chapter offers a brief summary of the main ideas of this book, that is, that deep learning is the answer to higher education's performance problem and that the pathways, practices, tools, strategies, and initiatives developed in this book can foster an environment that is conducive to deep learning.

KEYWORDS

- deep learning
- higher education
- learning environment
- lecture
- student learning
- surface learning
- teaching

REFERENCES

Biggs, J.; Tang, C. Teaching for Quality Learning at University; Open University Press: Maidenhead, 2007.

Carretero, M. Constructivismo y Educación; Paidós: Buenos Aires, 2009.

Graffam, B. Constructivism and Understanding: Implementing the Teaching for Understanding Framework. Journal of Secondary Gifted Education 2003, 15.

Schwandt, T.; McCarty, L. In Seductive Illusions: Von Glasserfield and Gergen on Epistemology and Education; Phillips, D., Ed.; Constructivism in Education: Opinions and Second Opinions on Controversial Issues; Chicago University Press: Chicago, 2000.

Zull, J. From Brain to Mind. Using Neuroscience to Guide Change in Education; Stylus: Sterling, VA, 2011.

Zull, J. The Art of Changing the Brain: Enriching the Practice of Teaching by Exploring the Biology of Learning; Stylus: Sterling, VA, 2002.

CHAPTER 1

THE INSTRUCTION PARADIGM

Teaching is not something you can go into the forest and do by yourself.

— RALPH W. TYLER

CONTENTS

1.1 Introduction 2

1.2 Discontent with the Predominant Higher Education Paradigm 2

1.3 The Instruction Paradigm 5

1.4 Summary 8

Practice Corner 9

Keywords 11

References 11

1.1 INTRODUCTION

Teachers, students, administrators, and other key players have been showing a discontent with the essential goals of universities and colleges in North America and across the world. This discontent is manifested through a myriad of publications, works, reports, and even every-day conversations, which point out that higher education institutions are not producing meaningful and long-lasting learning. Instead, they are producing surface learning. In this chapter, I will briefly examine this discontent. I will also explore the main characteristics of the prevailing paradigm in higher education: the Instruction paradigm. The goal of this examination is to draw your attention to some taken-for-granted artifacts of our universities and colleges, which need to be changed if we want to create environments that are conducive to student deep learning.

1.2 DISCONTENT WITH THE PREDOMINANT HIGHER EDUCATION PARADIGM

Before the terrorist attacks of September 11, 2001, the South Tower of the World Trade Center in New York City housed some of the most sophisticated banks, law firms, insurance companies, engineering firms, government departments, investment organizations, transportation companies, architectural studios, telecommunications service providers, and management firms. Together, they employed thousands of highly successful graduates from U.S. and international universities and colleges, including the most highly recognized higher education institutions, in virtually every single discipline.

On September 11, 2001, right after the collapse of the North Tower, the South Tower began evacuation. At that time, the elevators were still operational, and the stairwells were relatively unobstructed. Some minutes later, United Airlines' Boeing 767–222 impacted the South Tower. There was a very loud and frightening thunderous sound. The building shook; the lights went out instantly. Cracks started to appear in the walls; as steam pipes exploded, sending a cloud of hot steam all over the building. There was debris falling everywhere. The heat was intense, almost unbearable. A

The Instruction Paradigm

very strong smoke inundated the building. In the upper floors, the smell of airplane fuel mixed with the smell of smoke and human panic. It was very hard to breathe. Every now and then, an elevator door opened violently to reveal the inevitable: dozens of people had been burned alive inside.

Amid this chaos, one of the stairwells was still clear. It was still possible to evacuate. Evidently, leaving the building was the only possibility to remain alive. There was no other way to survive. Strangely enough, official announcements emphatically instructed everyone to remain in their offices and not to leave a soon-to-collapse tower. Instructions were repeated incessantly over the speakers on every floor. Regrettably, most people blindly obeyed these orders. They stayed put and started to make frantic phone calls to loved ones. Even many of those who had begun evacuation returned to their offices. Only a very small minority dared to challenge these instructions and left the building to save their lives.

Alfie Kohn (2001) speculates that highly educated professionals ought to have questioned these instructions and used their reasoning abilities to find the only possible route to save their lives, which, in this case, was also the most evident and logical alternative. Kohn (2001) believes that many deaths in the World Trade Center could have been avoided if our universities and colleges had embraced a different pedagogical stance. If instead of insisting on a teaching method that stresses passive absorption of information, coupled with a hidden curriculum that conveys a message of intellectual submission to the authority, our higher education institutions had focused on helping students think for themselves and question basic assumptions, hundreds of our finest graduates would have saved their lives in one of the most tragic episodes on North American soil.

Luckily, the consequences of a poor university and college education do not usually result in such tragic events as this one. But our society still suffers the consequences of a system that is not doing what it ought to do: produce meaningful, profound, transformational, and long-lasting student learning.

Many stakeholders both inside and outside higher education institutions have been voicing their discontent with this somber situation. Employers usually complain that recent graduates are not adequately prepared to work in the white-collar job marketplace. They argue that graduates lack the necessary skills to carry out even the most basic functions; so private and public organizations have to spend millions of dollars in training their recent hires not only in specific technical aspects of their industries or activities but also in intellectual skills, which have traditionally been the exclusive territory of higher education (Millen, Greenleaf, and Wells-Papanek, 2010).

Authors have also shown their concerns about the outcomes of higher education and have voiced their frustration with university graduates who have run out of ideas to solve important societal problems and blindly insist on piecemeal solutions that fail to capture society's fundamental issues. There is widespread disappointment because not even the brightest graduates have the intellectual capacity to question the assumptions deeply engrained in today's society (Hedges, 2009).

Students also realize that their universities and colleges are not delivering the promises they have engraved in their vision and mission statements. When truly transformational learning does not occur, our universities and colleges become a bureaucratic apparatus of producing grades and degrees. So, students become disengaged with their own learning process and focus on obtaining those grades leading to degrees and job opportunities with minimum effort, without fully committing to their education (Côté & Allahar, 2007).

Teachers—from the most progressive and most prone to radical reforms to the most conservative and adverse to changes—also complain about the status quo. Teachers feel frustrated with a job that is becoming less fulfilling, because it is harder to motivate and reach out to newer generations of students. Many teachers believe that students are not interested in learning and that they only want to pass exams to get good grades and receive their degrees. Many students, in turn, think that teachers do not care about teaching them in a way that helps them transform their lives and that they are only interested in evaluating them and giving them a final grade so that students can graduate and teachers can gain tenure and promotions (Cox, 2009).

Although we all know many exceptions and strive to be exceptions ourselves, the truth of the matter is that the structure of our colleges and universities has trapped all of us in rigid compartments, which impeded us from creating the necessary environment to encourage our students to take a deep approach to learning.

The Instruction Paradigm

1.3 THE INSTRUCTION PARADIGM

Let's have a look at the characteristics of the structural foundations of higher education. In a seminal work published in Change magazine in 1995, Robert Barr and John Tagg (1995) synthesized the main shortcomings of our higher education institutions. For their analysis, they came up with two paradigms: the Instruction paradigm and the Learning paradigm. The Instruction paradigm describes the goals, attitudes, theories, and elements of the predominant universities and colleges. The Learning paradigm, which I will explore later in the book, is Barr's and Tagg's proposal to transform higher education institutions into organizations focused on learning.

The Instruction paradigm is characterized for its emphasis on teaching. Teaching is the purpose, the object, and the method of higher education institutions. The main goal of universities and colleges is to produce teaching regardless of whether this leads to student learning or not. Universities and colleges take a series of measures to ensure that teaching takes place. But they do not necessarily take similar measures to ensure that students are learning, let alone that they are learning deeply. So, for example, they hire teachers; they assign teachers to courses and classrooms, and they provide them with the resources needed to teach: boards, projectors, and computers, among others. Even the physical aspects of universities and colleges tend to privilege teaching and teachers over learning and students. Most teachers have offices, whereas undergraduate students generally do not. The classroom usually contains anonymous rows of seats for students; teachers are given the limelight in front of the classroom. Teachers are paid, whereas in most cases students have to pay tuition fees, in some cases even astronomical fees.

Although teaching may take diverse formats, the predominant pedagogy is the teacher-centered lecture. The lecture is premised on the fact that teachers are disciplinary experts who transmit their knowledge to students and that students absorb it passively. Students' main role is to take down notes of that content to reproduce it later in examinations and papers. Teachers have full control of the teaching experience. Teachers formulate the objectives, prepare their lectures, make decisions, talk for the most part in class, determine which students may ask questions or may make some comments, and evaluate their students. The origin of the lecture dates back to the beginning of modern universities—more than a thousand years ago—when it was difficult to access books and information. So, teachers were the only ones who read books and transmitted the information to their students. With ample access to information both in print and in digital form, the reason that led universities to resort to lectures no longer exists.

Teaching in the Instruction paradigm is organized around a rigid atomistic structure that consists of one-teacher-per-classroom courses, where students accumulate credits for courses chosen from a distributional curriculum, organized on the basis of disciplines and rigid departments (Hedges, 2009). This emphasis on independent disciplines fossilized in independent departments has created a disconnection between the work of academics and the fundamental questions of everyday life. Academics "rarely understand or concern themselves with the reality of the world. Works of literature are eviscerated and destroyed. They are mined for obscure trivia and irrelevant data. This disconnection between literature and philosophy on one hand and the real life on the other is replicated in most academic disciplines" (Hedges, 2009).

The Instruction paradigm has also produced "a particular, elitist vocabulary —the vocabulary of the discipline specialist, which bars access to any outsider. It destroys the search for the common good. It dices disciplines, faculty, students, and finally experts into tiny, specialized fragments. It allows students and faculty to retreat into these self-imposed fiefdoms and neglect the most pressing moral, political, and cultural questions" (Hedges, 2009). Along with disciplinary vocabulary, teachers have adopted a common language to communicate among and across departments and disciplines, which is as impenetrable and as meaningless for outsiders as disciplinary jargon. Not surprisingly, this language revolves around courses. After teaching full-time for more than ten years (and after being involved in various roles in higher education for my whole adult life) when I go to department and committee meetings, I still find it hard to understand the jargon. I hear most of my colleagues talk, and fight feverishly about things such as ECON 305, BIOL 101, ADMIN 1006, SOCI 2087, POLI 2405, and ESPA 1005. I have seen some colleagues get emotional and fight about the differences between joint enrollment and cross-

The Instruction Paradigm

listed courses. Some never stop talking about antirequisites. Others always advocate for splitting courses, and most get angry when the administration does not enforce prerequisites and corequisites. Every language has cognitive blind spots, that is, concepts for which the language does not have any terms, or does not have sufficient terms. Student learning and student transformation sometimes seem to be cognitive blind spots in the language spoken in higher education.

The Instruction paradigm also embraces an atomistic and one-sided notion of knowledge, generally presented as objective. "Knowledge is often accepted as truth legitimizing a specific view of the world that is either questionable or false" (Giroux, 1983). This has produced a kind of knowledge that is not socially important. Students do not learn how to question the fundamental assumptions of our time. They do not learn to think for themselves, challenge, and criticize the structure and foundations of our system. The hidden curriculum of the Instruction paradigm, that is, the byproduct of schooling, what is actually learned even though it is not explicitly stated in the official curriculum (Vallance, 1983)—teaches students to follow orders and play by the rules of the universities and colleges in order to survive academically.

In the Instruction paradigm, time is the same for every student, even if students have different learning styles and need different times to construct knowledge. This is so because teaching—and not learning—is of paramount importance in the Instruction paradigm. Because teachers need the same time to transmit information to students, courses can have the same duration for everyone, irrespective of their students' learning processes.

The typical Instruction-paradigm institution tends to absorb large numbers of students, particularly because student enrollment determines their funding. Even in many countries where governments provide taxpayers' money to fund universities, they do so according to the number of students registered in programs and courses. So, institutions need to be efficient in the way they deal with such large numbers of students. For this purpose, they need uniform and routine practices that apply to everyone regardless of their actual learning needs. These practices resemble a factory assembly line conveyor belt that moves students along until they graduate. In the Instruction paradigm, one of the benchmarks of success is a student graduation rate. Universities and colleges are considered successful if they can graduate the greatest number of students in the predetermined duration of their programs. In other words, they are successful if the conveyor belt does not lose any students throughout the process.

Students' experience in university and colleges is molded by all of these elements and artifacts of the Instruction paradigm. Students absorb these elements through their senses, which shape their mindsets and learning orientations (Prosser and Trigwell, 1999). Students soon realize that true learning does not really matter. They realize that they have to pass tests, write papers, and occasionally be in the classrooms and labs. They also understand that they have to respect their teachers, pay their tuition fees, and not question the fundamental structures of the Instruction-paradigm institution. They learn how to play the university and college game. All this fosters a culture of surface—including strategic—learning.

1.4 SUMMARY

Numerous studies, projects and proposals, which are as diverse as their authors and proponents, share a discontent with the status quo of colleges and universities. In one way or another, they all point out the fact that students are not learning deeply in higher education.

The Instruction-paradigm, a concept first envisaged by Robert Barr and John Tagg, captures the predominant goals, attitudes, theories, and elements of universities and colleges. The Instruction paradigm is characterized by its emphasis on teaching. Teaching is the raison d'être of higher education institutions. It is at the same time their sole purpose, object, and method. The Instruction paradigm is also characterized by a curriculum consisting almost exclusively of courses in academic or professional disciplines, which students take without actually addressing the most pressing and fundamental issues of everyday life. One of the most salient aspects of the Instruction paradigm is the preponderant role of lectures. The lecture reflects a traditional conception of knowledge as a fact, which is transmitted from teachers to students. Students' role is marginal in lectures. It mainly consists of absorbing and reproducing information. Universities and colleges today also place strong emphasis on uniform practices. They

The Instruction Paradigm

resemble a factory conveyor belt, which processes students quickly and mechanically from admission to graduation.

Most important, the Instruction paradigm is also characterized by a complete disregard for student learning, particularly deep student learning.

Educational change requires a transformation of beliefs, teaching approaches, and instructional resources, which must occur simultaneously in practice for that transformation to be meaningful (Fulham, 2001). The following chapters offer the foundations for that change. The next chapter will focus on the notion and elements of deep learning.

PRACTICE CORNER

1. Read your institution's academic plan, strategic plan, collective agreement, or other official documents. Identify all of the sections and clauses that reflect elements of the Instruction paradigm. How would you change these clauses to help move your institution away from the Instruction paradigm?

2. Think of the last class you taught. What elements of the Instruction paradigm were present? What changes can you implement to move away from the Instruction paradigm the next time you teach it? How can you make those changes without risking your job?

3. Think of your last department or committee meeting. What elements of the Instruction paradigm transpired in the discussions? Did those elements impede any changes to promote students' deep learning? If so, how?

4. Pulitzer Prize winner, Chris Hedges (2009) argues that academics "rarely understand or concern themselves with the reality of the world." Do you agree? Why or why not? If so, what changes could you introduce in your courses so that they can become more relevant for your students' lives?

5. In an age dominated by easy access to information, what is the value, if any, of traditional lectures?

6. Think of a successful learning experience, whether in a formal or informal educational context, where you learned something deeply that you apply in your personal, social, or professional life. What

did you learn? How did you learn it? Were the artifacts of the Instruction paradigm present? If so, how did they influence your learning experience?

7. Remember or watch Peter Weir's 1989 film *Dead Poets Society*. What elements of the Instruction paradigm does John Keating rebel against? What elements of the Instruction paradigm, if any, does he embrace?

8. On May 24, 2013 in *The View*, an ABC show the hosts debated then New York mayor Michael Bloomberg's remark that some students do not need to pursue higher education and should learn a trade instead. Watch a short clip entitled "Should Mediocre Students Skip College?" posted on YouTube by ABCTheView (if the copyright holder has made that video available in your country) and read Bloomberg's remarks widely available online. What do you think of Bloomberg's position? Do you agree or do you disagree? Why? What do you think of the arguments debated in *The View*? Do you agree or do you disagree? Why? Are there any elements of discontent with the Instruction paradigm? If so, can you identify them? For those of you who cannot watch the clip, imagine arguments in favor of and against Bloomberg's opinion.

9. In a well-known study, Richard Arum and Josipa Roksa (2011) conclude that "American higher education is characterized by limited or no learning for a large proportion of students." What do you think the authors mean by "limited or no learning"? What type of learning do they refer to? Do you agree with this conclusion? Why or why not? If so, why do you think this happens? If you are not from the United States, do you think that these conclusions also apply to higher education institutions in your country? Why or why not?

10. The vocabulary of the Instruction paradigm is very peculiar. Think of everyday words and phrases such as *final exam, deadline,* and *fail.* What images do they evoke? Can you think of other words or phrases used in the Instruction paradigm institution that evoke similar images? Can you think of any replacement terms that might be more effective?

KEYWORDS

- **academic disciplines**
- **courses**
- **departments**
- **distributional curriculum**
- **hidden curriculum**
- **instruction paradigm**
- **lecture**
- **surface learning**
- **teaching**
- **uniform practices**

REFERENCES

Bain, K. What the Best College Teachers Do; Harvard University Press: Cambridge, MA, 2004.

Bain, K.; Zimmerman, J. Understanding Great Teaching. Peer Review 2009, 11, 9.

Arum, R.; Roksa, J. Academically Adrift. Limited Learning on College Campuses; The University of Chicago Press: Chicago, 2011.

Barr, R.; Tagg, J. From Teaching to Learning – A New Paradigm for Undergraduate Education. Change 1995, 13.

Biggs, J.; Tang, C. Teaching for Quality Learning at University; Open University Press: Maidenhead, 2007.

Côté, J.; Allahar, A. Ivory Tower Blues: A University System in Crisis; University of Toronto Press: Toronto, 2007.

Cox, R. The College Fear Factor: How Students and Professors Misunderstand One Another. Harvard University Press: Cambridge, 2004.

Fulham, M. The New Meaning of Educational Change; Teachers College Press and Toronto: Irwin Publishing Ltd: New York, 2001.

Giroux, H. Theory and Resistance in Education: A Pedagogy for the Opposition; Bergin & Garvey: South Hadley, MA, 1983.

Hedges, C. Empire of Illusion: The End of Literacy and the Triumph of Spectacle; Random House: Toronto, 2009.

Kohn, A. September 11. Rethinking Schools 2001.

Light, R. Making the Most of College: Students Speak Their Minds; Harvard University Press: Cambridge, MA, 2001.

Millen, E.; Greenleaf, R.; Wells-Papanek, D. Engaging Today's College Students: What All College Instructors Need to Know & Be Able to Do; Greenleaf Papanek Publications: Newfield, ME, 2010.

Miller, J. The holistic curriculum; OISE Press, Inc: Toronto, 20001.

Perkins, D. Making Learning Whole. How Seven Principles of Teaching can Transform Education; Jossey-Bass: San Francisco, 2009.

Prosser, M.; Trigwell, K. Understanding Learning and Teaching: The experience in higher education; Open University Press: Buckingham, 1999.

Ramsden, P. Learning to teach in higher education; Routledge: London, 1992.

Sanjurjo, L.; Vera, M. T. Aprendizaje significativo y enseñanza en los niveles medio y superior; Homo Sapiens: Rosario, 1994.

Shulman, L. Teaching as Community Property. Essays on Higher Education; Jossey-Bass: San Francisco, 2004.

Tagg, J. The Learning Paradigm College; Anker Publishing Company: Bolton, MA, 2003.

Tussman, J. Experiment at Berkeley Oxford University Press: New York, 1969.

PART I
DEEP LEARNING

CHAPTER 2

THE DEEP LEARNING PROCESS AND THE CONSTRUCTION OF KNOWLEDGE

The most important form of learning is that which enables us to see something in the world in a different way.

— JOHN BOWDEN AND FERENCE MARTON

Learning is change.

— JAMES ZULL

CONTENTS

2.1 Introduction 17
2.2 Origin of Deep Learning and Other Similar Concepts 18
2.3 Notion of Deep Learning 19
2.4 Analysis of the Elements and Factors of Deep Learning 20
2.5 Motivating Problem and Cognitive Conflict 21
2.6 Connections between New Knowledge and Prior Knowledge
Structures 24
2.7 Non-Arbitrary and Substantive Connections 25
2.8 Higher-Order Cognitive Skills, Competences, and Processes 26
2.9 Collective Negotiation of Meanings 28
2.10 The New Knowledge and the Zone of Proximal Development 29
2.11 Conceptual Change 30
2.12 Perry's Stages of Development 32
2.13 Changes in or Across Communities of Knowledge 35
2.14 Evaluation and Metacognitive Reflection 35
2.15 Safe and Motivating Environment 36
2.16 Summary 41

Practice Corner... 41
Keywords 44
References.. 44

2.1 INTRODUCTION

With their obsessive focus on teaching and lecturing, the Instruction-paradigm institutions have given rise to a culture of surface learning, neglecting to help students learn meaningfully and for life. Deep learning is the solution to this problem. Deep learning is an enthusiastic and committed approach to learning. It is a process of discovery and construction of new knowledge in light of prior cognitive structures and experiences, which can be applied to new problems and in different situations (Tagg, 2003). Deep learning entails a "sustained, substantial, and positive influence on the way students act, think, or feel" (Bain, 2004). A deep approach to learning results in better-quality learning and profound transformation (Tek Yew, 2005). Deep learning produces learning that lasts a lifetime. In contrast, surface learning involves a dispassionate approach to learning. The surface learner is not concerned with understanding (Bain and Zimmerman, 2009). Information acquired is usually lost after examinations; there is no profound transformation or knowledge construction.

In this chapter, I will develop the notion of deep learning. I will break down and analyze every element of deep learning as well as the factors and processes that contribute to produce an environment that is conducive to deep learning. Although based on the studies first carried out by Marton and Säljö (1976), my conception of deep learning is broader, as it embraces the most important and compatible aspects of other conceptions of learning, which regard learning as superior and transformational.

Some authors point to the existence of a third category of learning, which they refer to as strategic (Ramsden, 1979). The strategic learner is the one who learns the rules of the academic game and acts accordingly. For example, the strategic learner is the one who comes to class, raises his or her hand to ask a question with a few words that will sound educated, and gives the teacher what he or she expects without engaging in a process of construction of knowledge. Strategic learners focus on obtaining good grades with the minimum necessary effort. The strategic learner is a kind of surface learner. Thus, I will treat this type of learning within the general category of surface learning.

2.2 ORIGIN OF DEEP LEARNING AND OTHER SIMILAR CONCEPTS

The notion of deep learning arose in the 1970's with a research study conducted at the University of Gothenburg, Sweden. Marton and Säljö asked students to read an article written by a professor of education on some proposed university reforms in Sweden. They told students that they would ask them some questions about the text once they finished reading it. Marton and Säljömet with the students and asked them open-ended questions to assess their approach to reading and their understanding of the text. Additionally, they specifically asked the students how they had gone about studying the text (Bowden and Marton, 2000). Marton and Säljö(1976) report that while reading the text, some students simply identified isolated facts mentioned in the text, which they believed the researchers would ask them about during the interview, and memorized those facts. These students could not make any connections between these facts. They even failed to see any connection to their realities. Another group of students tried to understand what the author was saying, focused on the underlying meaning of the text, and sought to integrate the different facts mentioned in the text. The first group of students focused on the surface level of the text, whereas the second one adopted a deeper approach. From this experience, Marton and Säljöcame up with the notions of surface and deep approaches to learning. Similar research was replicated and expanded in Europe and Australia during the subsequent decades (Entwistle, 1998; Entwistle and Ramsden, 1983; Gibbs, 1992; Ramsden, 1992; Trigwell and Prosser, 1991).

Although the distinction between deep and surface approach to learning is relatively new, the idea that teaching and learning may be merely superficial or may be transformational in the lives of students is quite an old proposition. This idea has adopted different names—albeit with some different implications—throughout the history of education. Even Aristotle made references to profound knowledge and transformation (Shulman, 1997). Table 2.1 lists the main contemporary conceptions of transformational and profound knowledge and their proponents.

The Deep Learning Process and the Construction of Knowledge 19

TABLE 2.1 Main contemporary conceptions of transformational knowledge.

Concept of profound/transformational learning	Authors
Deep learning: a profound understanding of the underlying meaning of a text and the integration of the different facts mentioned in a text.	Ference Marton and Roger Säljö(1970).
Meaningful learning: a process of attributing meaning to new knowledge by making nonarbitrary and substantive connections between new and prior knowledge that produces conceptual change in the learner's cognitive structure.	David Ausubel (1963; 1978).
Transfer of principles and attitudes: the learning of a general idea instead of a basic skill and the recognition of problems, situations, and examples as specific cases of the general idea.	Jerome Bruner (1966; 1977).
Teaching for Understanding: the possibility of doing a variety of thought-provoking tasks with a topic, such as generalizing, explaining, finding evidence, applying to new situations, and solving problems.	David Perkins (2009), Tyna Blythe (1998).
Learning that lasts: an ongoing process that contributes to the development of the person. This idea of learning is conceived as an integration of learning, development, and performance.	Marcia Mentkowski (2000).
Transformative learning: the process of producing change in a frame of reference by incorporating new information to the existing frame of reference. This process involves thoughts, feelings, and dispositions.	Jack Mezirow (1997).
Effective learning: a constructive, cumulative, self-regulated, intentional, situated, and collaborative process of knowledge and meaning building. Effective learning enables learners to acquire adaptive expertise or competence.	De Corte (2010).
Autonomous learning: a process of learning and developing competences that generates an agency capacity, that is, a feeling of empowerment and autonomy. This enables learners to apply and transfer knowledge to a wide array of diverse personal, professional, and social experiences	Joan Rué (2009).

2.3 NOTION OF DEEP LEARNING

Deep learning is a process of permanent knowledge construction. It takes place when a learner faces an exciting problem or question, which creates a cognitive conflict derived from social interaction with peers that the learner feels motivated to solve. To do so, the learner makes nonarbitrary and substantive connections between new knowledge arising from the problem or question (which must be within the learner's zone of proximal development) and his or her existing cognitive structure. While making these connections individually and together with peers, the learner must access higher-order cognitive and metacognitive skills, processes, and competences, which engage the frontal, integrative cortex of the brain. If adequately and intrinsically motivated by playing the whole game of the discipline in a safe and nonthreatening environment, the learner will change his or her cognitive structures (Piaget's accommodation) so as to resolve the problem. In so doing, the learner will incorporate the new knowledge into his or her cognitive structure (Piaget's assimilation), which will produce a conceptual change, that is, a new schema or the modification of an existing one. The learner will be able to use and apply this knowledge to new and unfamiliar situations and see the connections to a larger framework. From a biological point of view, the conceptual change implies a physical change in the neuronal networks of the learner's brain. At the same time, at the social level, this process implies one of the following changes: a reacculturation from one community of knowledgeable peers to another (Bruffee, 1999), or a movement from the periphery of a community of knowledgeable peers to the center, where the learner achieves full participation by performing the roles and functions that experts display in the community (Lave and Wenger, 1991). For deep learning to occur, there must also be an ongoing evaluation and self-evaluation of the learning process and an awareness of this movement and the resulting conceptual change (Piaget, 1969).

2.4 ANALYSIS OF THE ELEMENTS AND FACTORS OF DEEP LEARNING

Let's break down the notion of deep learning into its main elements, and let's discuss each one. Table 2.2 summarizes the main aspects of deep learning and the main requirements of each aspect.

The Deep Learning Process and the Construction of Knowledge   21

TABLE 2.2 The deep learning process.

Deep Learning Process	
Elements	**Requirements**
Problem, question, or situation.	Problem, question, or situation must be interesting for the learner.
Cognitive conflict.	It must derive from social interaction.
Non-arbitrary and substantive connections between new knowledge arising from the problem or question and the learner's existing cognitive structure.	New knowledge must be within the learner's zone of proximal development.
Higher-order cognitive and metacognitive competences.	Individual abstract thinking and collective negotiation of meanings.
Intrinsic motivation to solve the cognitive conflict.	Playing the whole game of the discipline or professional field.
Safe and nonthreatening environment.	Adequate workload.
	Enjoyable atmosphere.
	No negative factors, e.g., stereotyping and discrimination.
Conceptual change.	Change in the neuronal networks of the learner's brain.
Modification of the cognitive structure to solve the problem or to answer the question.	Progress through developmental stages.
Changes in or across communities of knowledge.	Social interaction.
	Negotiations.
	Learning communities.
Evaluation.	Information.
	Initial, simultaneous, and retrospective evaluation of the deep learning process and awareness of this movement and the resulting conceptual change.
Metacognition.	General and specific metacognitive categories.

2.5 MOTIVATING PROBLEM AND COGNITIVE CONFLICT

The first step in the deep learning process is the creation of a problem, situation, or question that students find exciting to solve or answer (Bain, 2004). This problem or question must include new information or new knowledge that creates a cognitive conflict. A cognitive conflict generates an imbalance in the learner's knowledge structures (Pozo, 2008). This is produced when the learner's cognitive structure does not coincide with, or cannot explain, the new knowledge, or cannot explain it in a coherent way. To solve the conflict, the learner creates responses, asks questions, investigates, and discovers until the learner constructs knowledge that restores that balance (Carretero, 2009, Pozo, 2008). Ken Bain (2004), who refers to a cognitive conflict as an expectation failure, describes it as a situation in which the attempt to explain the new knowledge by means of the existing cognitive structures leads to faulty expectations. He argues that "an expectation failure is usually created from some sort of intellectual challenge or cognitive dissonance" (Bain, 2004). The rationale of the expectation failure or cognitive conflict lies in the fact that human beings tend to learn from mistakes better than from achievements (Dewey, 1910).

We need to know the cognitive structures of our students in order to create cognitive conflicts whereby students face situations that they cannot solve using their existing knowledge structures. The default student attitude to a problem or situation is to adopt a surface approach by ignoring the conflict, or by trying to make it fit somehow within their existing cognitive structures (Bain, 2004). For example, in Aesop's fable, the fox tried to grab some grapes that were hanging from a high branch. He jumped, but he could not reach the grapes. He backed up and jumped again. He made several attempts to reach the grapes, but he was not successful. Then, he gave up and convinced himself that the grapes were sour. Trying to get the grapes is a conflict (albeit not an academic one) that the fox tried to solve, as he presumably did in other circumstances (jumping to get lower hanging fruit). Instead of trying a different approach (getting a ladder, climbing up a tree, or stepping on a big rock), the fox ignored the conflict by thinking the grapes were not worth getting. He did not try to modify his preconceived idea that jumping is the only way to get things that are quite high. Such outcomes result because we all have a tendency to try to understand new information in terms of existing knowledge (Bain, 2004). But students can instead take a deep approach to learning if they modify their cognitive structures while working to solve the problem or situation. For this to occur, learners must actually care that their cognitive structures cannot help them deal with the situation or problem. Students must be motivated enough to try to solve the problem. Otherwise, they will not modify their existing mental paradigms.

Vygotsky (1978) understands that a cognitive conflict is produced because of the learner's interaction with the social context. For example, while interacting with peers who are at different levels of cognitive development or who have different cognitive structures, the individual learner will face a conflict that he or she will not be able to solve without modifying his or her knowledge structure. In the example of the fox and the grapes, probably the fox failed to change his mental models of reality because the cognitive conflict did not arise from, and did not even have, a collective instance. From a pedagogical point of view, we can design situations that will promote the creation of a cognitive conflict by proposing that students work in small groups to solve a problem or answer a question. Groups must be made up of students with a wide array of diverse backgrounds and developmental phases. This interaction with students in different developmental phases will help produce the cognitive conflict.

Some constructivist scholars postulate that the learner's cognitive structure may change also as a result of an analogy and not only in cases of cognitive conflict. They recognize, however, that the literature has paid considerably less attention to analogies than to cognitive conflicts (Carretero, 2009; Duit, 1991). When prior knowledge is fragmented or not deeply anchored, an analogy may help produce a conceptual change in the learner's knowledge structure. When knowledge is organized around theories or when it is consolidated, the only possibility to produce conceptual change is through cognitive conflicts. The analogy pursues learning of an unknown content from a series of projections, structural or functional, that are established over another (analogous) known content (Carretero, 2009). We learn new content based on known content with which the new one shares some structural or functional elements. There are three main types of analogies: (i) simple, (ii) enriched, and (iii) extended. The simple analogy compares the target object with an analogous and known concept. The enriched analogy is more explanatory. It provides the grounds or conditions for the similarity of the analogous concepts. The extended analogy either compares the target object with several known analogous concepts or contains a combination of simple and enriched analogies (Duit, 1991). Analogies can produce new knowledge when used appropriately by students, as they help students make connections between prior knowledge—the analogous concept or experience—and new knowledge. The most effective analogies are the ones that students themselves generate (Harrison and Treagust, 2006). But also analogies is effective only if teachers are fully aware of:

- "the suitability of the analogy to the target for the student audience and the extent of teacher-directed or student-generated mapping needed to understand the target concept;
- an understanding that an analogy does not provide learners with all facets of the target concept and that multiple analogies can better achieve this goal;
- an appreciation that not all learners are comfortable with multiple analogies because the epistemological orientation of some is to expect a single explanation for a phenomenon" (Harrison and Treagust, 2006).

2.6 CONNECTIONS BETWEEN NEW KNOWLEDGE AND PRIOR KNOWLEDGE STRUCTURES

The deep learner engages in a spiral process of permanent knowledge construction, where he or she interrelates actively with the target object, that is, the new knowledge created by the problem the learner is grappling with. Human beings do not act upon reality directly but through their cognitive structures. Thus, while trying to solve the problem or situation that created the cognitive conflict, the learner engages in a process of relating and connecting the new knowledge arising from the problem or situation to some specifically relevant aspect of his or her cognitive structure. This may be an experience, an image, an already meaningful symbol, a concept, or a proposition that exists in the learner's cognitive structure. From the information received from the external world, the learner selects only what is relevant for the activated, existing knowledge, and discards the irrelevant. Then, from this selected information, the learner makes abstractions and generalizes its meaning (Carretero, 2009). In biological terms, a learner receives input from the outside world through the brain's sensory cortex. This input is transmitted to the back integrative cortex, which integrates sensory information to create images and meaning. Then,

The Deep Learning Process and the Construction of Knowledge 25

the frontal integrative cortex analyzes these images, solves the problem, and comes up with a solution. Finally, the motor cortex carries out the solution to the problem by acting out, writing, or speaking the solution to the problem (Zull, 2002). For example, if, while reading this paragraph, you try to connect its main idea to your personal experience as a learner, then you are making a connection between a new idea, that is, the deep learner's connection between prior and new knowledge, and an experience that is already part of your knowledge structure, for example, what you do as a learner when trying to learn something that interests you in a way that will last forever. You will also extract the main idea from this paragraph that activates that prior experience and discard the rest. To give a further example, imagine a reader who is a bilingual Mexican immigrant who completed her elementary school in the United States. Such reader may have related the ideas in this paragraph to the way she used to connect everything she saw at school with the way her family did things while living in Mexico. She will probably associate the ideas of this paragraph with concepts, theories, and principles of cross-cultural experiences. Another reader, a drama teacher, who usually emphasizes corporeal and emotional learning over intellectual learning, may be connecting the idea of deep learning to the way he acts on the stage and teaches drama. While doing so, he may be adapting the notion of deep learning to a notion that includes feelings, emotions, and bodily memory. In both cases, the readers will be discarding a lot: words, sentences, and examples that are not relevant to the activated knowledge. The readers will be making generalizations about the concepts in this paragraph and will remember the generalizations they made from the connections they were able to make.

2.7 NON-ARBITRARY AND SUBSTANTIVE CONNECTIONS

In order for the connections between new and prior knowledge to produce deep learning, learners must relate new knowledge to some specifically relevant existing aspect of the learners' cognitive structures. Some learners take the whole new concept as a point of departure; others focus on parts of the concept, breaking them apart to restructure them in unique ways (Mentkowski, 2000). In all cases, the connections may not be irrelevant, superficial, or whimsical. For example, if while reading an academic text on the taxation of imported goods by Organization for Economic Co-operation and Development (OECD) countries, the reader focuses on the fact that the font used by the author resembles the font of a children's book he used to read when he was in elementary school, this connection will be irrelevant to produce deep learning on any aspect of the taxation of foreign goods. A more relevant connection in this case would be to compare the gist of the academic text with the taxation regime used in colonial South American countries, if the reader is familiar with that regime.

2.8 HIGHER-ORDER COGNITIVE SKILLS, COMPETENCES, AND PROCESSES

This connection between new and prior knowledge employs higher-order cognitive skills, competences, and processes. These include critical analysis, synthesis, problem solving, extrapolation, theorization, comparison, contrast, and application to new situations. So, to continue with previous examples, the Mexican reader will be doing comparisons while making connections; the drama teacher will be extrapolating aspects of a notion to another one. From a biological point of view, all of these functions are carried out in the front integrative cortex of the brain (Zull, 2002).

Learning is a consequence of thinking, and "knowledge comes on the coattails of thinking. As we think about and with the content that we are learning, we truly learn it" (Perkins, 2002). There are many lists and taxonomies that help us classify these skills, competences, and processes. Bloom's taxonomy is the most widely used set of cognitive skills. The higher levels of Bloom's taxonomy (application, analysis, synthesis, and evaluation) may help promote deep learning (Bloom, 1984). Similarly, Biggs and Tang (Biggs and Tang, 2007) classify these competences as those that merely help increase knowledge, which they refer to as quantitative and those that help deepen understanding, which are qualitative in nature. Quantitative competences include identifying, doing simple procedures, enumerating, describing, listing, combining, and doing algorithms, among others. Qualitative competences include comparing, contrasting, explaining causes, analyzing, relating, applying, theorizing, generalizing,

The Deep Learning Process and the Construction of Knowledge 27

hypothesizing, and reflecting. Quantitative competences usually lead to superficial learning whereas qualitative ones may lead to deep learning (Biggs and Tang, 2007). Table 2.3 summarizes Biggs' SOLO taxonomy. Appendix II contains an example of how to implement the SOLO taxonomy for the assessment of traditional evaluation instruments.

TABLE 2.3 Bigg's SOLO taxonomy*.

Level	Key competences
Unistructural	Memorizing, copying, matching, identifying, and recognizing.
Multistructural	Classifying, listing, describing, and reporting.
Relational	Applying, analyzing, comparing, concluding, and transferring.
Extended abstract	Inventing, creating, theorizing, and hypothesizing.

*Biggs and Tang (2007).

These taxonomies are illustrative of the kinds of competences that students may employ in their learning process. They should not be taken in isolation from the rest of the principles, factors, and conditions that help create an environment conducive to deep learning. Neither should they be considered as static because one competence may activate higher-order cognitive skills in one circumstance, and that same competence may involve a lower-order skill in another circumstance. For example, Biggs and Tang (2007) consider writing as a very basic competence. If used merely to record the first thing that comes to the learner's mind, it will probably engage a lower-order skill that will lead to superficial learning. As I will show in a later chapter, if used in certain ways, writing can have powerful effects on learning. At the same time, whereas theorizing is usually considered a higher-order competence, a learner may generate a very simple and naïve theory that will not necessarily lead to deep learning.

Another example of the fact that the taxonomies should not be given an excessive importance other than as a guide to help us encourage students to employ higher-order competences is the excessive emphasis they place on critical thinking and the consequent devaluing of other ways of thinking, including System 1 thinking. System 1 refers to quick mental reactions and almost instinctive thinking. We have little control over System

1 thoughts. System 2 deals with elaborate mental activities and thought processes. Most of our thoughts, ideas, and perspectives come from System 1. In many cases, "System 2 often endorses or rationalizes ideas and feelings that were generated by System 1" (Kahneman, 2011). Despite the importance of System 1 thinking, taxonomies tend to consider it as a low competence. Thus, it plays a marginal role in university and college teaching, when, in fact, it should be promoted and encouraged along with System 2 thinking. Also, in acting, for example, the actor must start from his or her visceral, instinctive response to the text and "must reject intellectual choices at the beginning of his or her work" (Guskin, 2003). This leads to deep learning in drama. All this shows that the taxonomies are useful only to guide teachers to promote students' connections in a very general way.

2.9 COLLECTIVE NEGOTIATION OF MEANINGS

Jean Piaget (1969) focused his constructivist theory of learning on the individual interaction with new knowledge, which produces a process involving assimilation and accommodation. Critics of Piaget's postulates criticize the lack of emphasis on the social context. Lev Vygotsky—a Soviet scholar and another founding father of constructivism—adopted a position that focused on the importance of the social context as determinative of conceptual change. For Vygotsky (1978), knowledge is a social and cultural product. All higher-order cognitive processes, for example, communication, language, and reasoning, are first acquired in a social context and are later internalized (Carretero, 2009). In Vygotsky's words: "every function in the child's cultural development appears twice: first, on the social level, and later, on the individual level; first, between people (interpsychological) and then inside the child (intrapsychological)" (Vygotsky, 1978). We have the capacity to reflect and think, that is, to employ higher-order cognitive and metacognitive processes and competences on an individual basis, because we have internalized social conversations (Vygotsky, 1978). In this respect, learning is not an individual activity, but rather a social activity. It is clear that learners learn more effectively when they do so in a collaborative context with their peers and have the opportunity to negotiate meanings with peers and to reflect individually (Carretero, 2009).

The Deep Learning Process and the Construction of Knowledge 29

Knowledge is a social construct, a consensus among the members of a community of knowledgeable peers (Bruffee, 1999). Human thought is social in its origins, functions, forms, and applications. In this line, "membership in a knowledge community means everything we do is unhesitatingly correct or incorrect according to the criteria agreed to within that local community, the community we belong to" (Bruffee, 1999). Because knowledge is a social consensus among members of a certain community, who construct it interindependently by conversing with one another, deep learning must include an instance for the collective negotiation of meanings. Students need to construct and reconstruct knowledge by engaging in conversations with their peers. In order to be effective in producing conceptual change, this collective negotiation of meanings needs to include recourse to higher-order cognitive processes, skills, and competences. Neuroscience confirms that the learning process includes a collective instance, which is produced through the activation of mirror neurons. Mirror neurons are considered intelligent cells that help us understand and interact with others (Iacoboni, 2005). The same neurons that activate when an individual carries out an activity also activate when the individual observes someone else do that activity. "Thus, the mirror system transforms visual information into knowledge" (Rizzolatti and Craighero, 2004).

2.10 THE NEW KNOWLEDGE AND THE ZONE OF PROXIMAL DEVELOPMENT

There is a level of effective development, which is what the learner can do independently and a level of potential development, which is constituted by what the individual is capable of doing with the help of other adults or more capable peers. Vygotsky referred to this distance between effective development and potential development as the "zone of proximal development." Learning takes place when students can construct knowledge by advancing through their zone of proximal development.

Vygotsky's notion of the zone of proximal development was further elaborated by other scholars. For example, Ausubel (1978) postulates that for meaningful learning to occur, the target knowledge must be potentially meaningful, which he refers to as "potentially meaningful material." This implies that the target material must be relatable to the learner's cognitive structure on a nonarbitrary and nonverbatim basis (Ausubel, 1978). Similarly, Krashen (1981) advanced the input hypothesis for second language acquisition. This hypothesis posits that a second language learner who is at a certain level of language development—referred to as "level i" must receive comprehensible input that is at "level i+1" (Cantiello and Fabricant, 1987). In Krashen (1991)'s own terms, "we acquire [a language] only when we understand language that contains structure that is 'a little beyond' where we are now."

Vygotsky's position that more knowledgeable others (teachers, mentors, coaches, or even peers who have a deeper knowledge than the learner) help advance cognitive development has led to the theory of situated learning and legitimate peripheral participation (Lave and Wenger, 1991). Situated learning theory claims that learning is not an individual cognitive activity, but rather a social practice, which takes place as the learner accesses participating roles usually associated with experts within communities of practitioners. In this respect, learning is "a process by which newcomers become part of a community of practice" (Lave and Wenger, 1991). In this process, "the mastery of knowledge and skills requires newcomers to move toward full participation in the sociocultural practices of a community" (Lave and Wenger, 1991).

From a pedagogical perspective, in order to help students construct deep learning, we must start from the students' prior knowledge and must advance through the construction of meaningful learning toward the learning goals. These must be in the zone of proximal development. If the new material is too complex, students will not be able to attribute any meaning. If it is too simple, students will not feel the need to revise and change their knowledge structures (Carretero, 2009). Because learning is a continuing process, we need to help students continually move the zone of proximal development forward (Tagg, 2003).

2.11 CONCEPTUAL CHANGE

The most important aspect of deep learning, and the one that distinguishes it from other forms of learning, is that it produces conceptual change.

The Deep Learning Process and the Construction of Knowledge

Conceptual change is a change in the learner's cognitive structure. Through the interaction with new knowledge, learners come to incorporate that knowledge into their cognitive structures and change that knowledge and their knowledge paradigms forever. Piaget (1969) explained this process of conceptual change by means of the assimilation and accommodation principles. Individuals receive continuous stimuli from the environment, which causes disequilibrium. Individuals will assimilate that stimulus and incorporate it into their previously existing cognitive structures. This process, known as assimilation, is subjective, because human beings tend to modify experience or information to fit it in with preexisting beliefs. But continuous stimuli from the environment cause disequilibrium, as the cognitive structures that individuals use to respond to these stimuli are not useful any more. Thus, there is an adaptation process, that is, the individual tries to assimilate the new knowledge to the existing cognitive structures that he or she has and accommodates such structures to the new situations. Accommodation involves altering existing schemas, or ideas, as a result of new information or new experiences. New schemas may also be developed during this process. This tension between assimilation and accommodation produces cognitive crises due to the contradictions and incompatibilities between schemas that the individual constructed or because one or more of the properties of the objects are resistant to being interpreted with the available strategies. Assimilation and accommodation are two complementary processes that produce learning (Sanjurjo and Vera, 1994).

From a biological point of view, learning produces a physical change in the brain. The brain contains billions of neurons, which receive and transmit information in the form of chemical or electric signals to other neurons through synapses. These synapses, that is, the connections between neurons, form neuronal networks that wire the brain by building up on other neuronal networks. Synapses are formed in the brain in response to experiences and learning (Zull, 2002). There is "a neuronal network in our brain for everything we know" (Zull, 2002). A conceptual change resulting from a deep learning process forms unique connections between neuronal networks (Bransford et al., 2008). The conceptual change is a change in neuronal connections: "more connections, stronger connections, different connections, or even fewer connections" (Zull, 2002).

The conceptual change is not simple or immediate. The learner goes through a series of intermediate phases in which he or she changes his or her ideas about the new phenomenon, but these changes do not yet constitute the learner's final conceptual change. The process of change is very important for learning and not just its product or result (Carretero, 2009). There are some conditions for the existence of conceptual change. First, the existing intuitive idea must be weakened, that is, the learner must realize that this idea may no longer explain a situation or solve a problem that the learner cares about (Bain, 2004). Second, the new conception must be intelligible, initially plausible, and fructiferous. An intelligible conception means that it makes sense and is meaningful for the learner, who must understand the new conception. Initial plausibility refers to the fact that the learner must regard the new concept as correct, which permits it to explain reality in a valid way. The new conception must solve the problems that the prior conceptions did not solve. It must also be consistent with other well-established beliefs that the learner holds. A new conception is fructiferous if it is an instrument with the capacity to explain future problems and to suggest new approaches to new phenomena and not simply to the present situation or problem, which the learner is trying to grapple with (Carretero, 2009).

2.12 PERRY'S STAGES OF DEVELOPMENT

Closely associated with conceptual change is the notion that higher education students go through different developmental stages as they progress through their university and college years. Students develop cognitive structures and ways of thinking that evolve as a consequence of conceptual changes.

Piaget (1969) introduced the idea of cognitive development. His studies focused on children; he did not delve into the analysis of university students. Piaget's understanding of child development was premised on the fact that development necessarily precedes learning. In contrast, Vygotsky (1978) argued that social learning precedes development. Thus, an individual's epistemological beliefs are created socially (Magolda, 2002). This has significant pedagogical implications. According to Vygotsky's

The Deep Learning Process and the Construction of Knowledge 33

postulates, students will move from one stage of cognitive development to the next through the creation of cognitive conflicts.

William Perry (1970) elaborated a theory of cognitive development specifically focused on university students. He found that students adopt different epistemological positions with respect to knowledge and learning. Perry identified the following four stages of cognitive development:

- **Dualism**: Students see the world in absolute terms and knowledge as one whole, where things are either right or wrong, true or false, or good or bad. The authority that the teacher represents is the repository of this knowledge, which he or she transmits to the students. Students view the teacher as always right. Students feel upset when they have to work in small groups to discuss a situation or solve a problem. They want their teachers to tell them what they need to know. Their ideal classroom format is the lecture, where the teacher gives them the knowledge they need, and they take down notes, which they will memorize and repeat the day of the exam. They feel that listening to other students' opinions is a waste of their time.

- **Multiplicity:** Students now begin to understand that knowledge is a matter of opinion and that any opinion is valid. They incorporate the idea of uncertainty. Their favorite classroom format is the open discussion, where they can offer their opinions. They feel upset when teachers restrict their freedom by imposing constraints to their work, such as instructions to write papers and limitations on their in-class assignments. They do not appreciate that these constraints come from the disciplines. They feel that anything goes.

- **Contextual Relativism**. Students recognize that every discipline has distinctive objects, methodologies, language, theories, and principles. Students are aware of the context, constraints, and possibilities that academic disciplines provide. They now use the methods and elements of the disciplines. During this stage, the learners become active constructors of meaning. They see knowledge as relative and contextual. They feel comfortable when they can use the discipline to produce new knowledge.

- **Commitment within Contextual Relativism**. Students adopt a commitment within their disciplines. They use the disciplines in a variety of settings both inside and outside the university or college. They apply the disciplines to solve problems in their everyday lives. Few university students reach this development stage during their undergraduate studies.

William Perry's theory suffered criticism because he focused mainly on male students. An important body of literature that took into account gender differences (e.g., Belenky et al., 1986/1997, Duell and Schommer-Aikins, 2001; Hofer and Pintrich, 2002; Magolda, 2002) elaborated upon Perry's research. In this line, Belenky and her colleagues came up with a classification of cognitive development experienced by female university students. These stages are: (i) silence, (ii) received knowing, (iii) subjective knowledge, (iv) procedural knowledge, and (v)constructed knowledge. These categories do not fundamentally differ from the ones Perry described for male students. Epistemological beliefs are not determined— at least exclusively by gender (LaFrazza, 2005). Thus, Magolda (2002) asserted that "developmental trends were similar for men and women, males interestingly adopted more impersonal and individualist ways of knowing, while women adopted more personal and interindividualist ways of knowing" (LaFrazza, 2005). The main contribution of research focused on female cognitive development is the fact that females have a way of knowing that is related to their self-concept. Women's epistemological assumptions are integral to how they perceive themselves and the world around them (Belenky et al., 1986/1997). Changes in self-knowledge precede understanding of themselves in relation to knowledge and truth. This development marches toward a vision where a female student sees herself as a constructor of knowledge (Hofer and Pintrich, 1997).

Another phenomenon closely connected to cognitive development deals with nonnative speakers, such as international students taking courses at universities and colleges where English is the language of instruction (Louis, 2002). Whereas students who are native speakers usually need a period of four years to become academically proficient in a discipline (the duration of most undergraduate programs in North America and other parts of the world), nonnative speakers of English need a period of five to seven years, provided they are already academically proficient in that discipline in their first language. Otherwise, this period can even be somewhat longer (Slocum, 2003).

The Deep Learning Process and the Construction of Knowledge 35

2.13 CHANGES IN OR ACROSS COMMUNITIES OF KNOWLEDGE

Deep learning implies changes either across communities of knowledgeable peers or inside one's community. The first type of possible change involves the renegotiation of meanings within the knowledgeable community the learner comes from and the negotiation of meanings in the new community (Bruffee, 1999). The second possible result of the learning process embraces a move from the periphery of a knowledge community to its center, where the learner achieves full participation by performing the roles and functions that experts display in the community (Lave and Wenger, 1991).

2.14 EVALUATION AND METACOGNITIVE REFLECTION

Deep learning requires the learner to reflect about his or her learning process and the resulting conceptual and social changes. The conceptual change is not simple or immediate. The learner goes through a series of intermediate phases in which he or she changes his or her ideas about the new phenomenon, but these changes do not yet constitute the learner's final conceptual change (Carretero, 2009). The learner must be able to reflect about these intermediate changes as well as the change in the cognitive structure. At the same time, the learner must reflect about his or her reaccultaration from one community of knowledgeable peers to another or the move from the periphery of a community of knowledgeable peers to the center.

Piaget (1969) argues that the learner must be aware of the properties of objects (empirical abstraction) and the actions and knowledge applied to the objects (reflective abstraction). The learner must also be aware of the restructuring of the cognitive structure.

This metacognitive reflection about the learning process must satisfy some conditions in order to be effective. First, learners must recognize their initial conceptions. Because most of these conceptions are implicit, the learner must reflect about them and get to explain them. Second, the learner must evaluate his or her conceptions and beliefs in light of the new conceptions that are being learned. Third, the learner must decide whether or not he or she will restructure his or her initial conceptions (Carretero, 2009).

From a pedagogical perspective, we need to provide students with information about their learning processes (evaluation) and create opportunities for students to receive information from multiple sources, including peers, disciplinary experts, professionals, and other relevant members of the community of knowledgeable peers. More specifically, we need to help students engage actively in this metacognitive process. For this purpose, we need to know students' prior cognitive structures, the intermediate changes that the students go through, and the resulting conceptual changes (Carretero, 2009).

2.15 SAFE AND MOTIVATING ENVIRONMENT

The creation of a safe and motivating teaching and learning environment is a fundamental aspect of the deep learning process. Learners learn more profoundly when they enjoy what they do. They need a stress-free atmosphere to engage in the complex cognitive competences that the process demands. Neuroscience also confirms the connection between emotion and learning and the importance of a stress-free environment. There is a very strong connection between the frontal cortex, which is responsible for abstract thinking and other higher order cognitive competences, and the amygdala, which is the emotion hub of the brain (Zull, 2002). "Emotion is probably the most important factor for learning. Our feelings determine the energy with which we begin new challenges and where we will direct that energy. The actions we take are determined by how we feel and how we believe those actions will make us feel" (Zull, 2011). A stressed environment produces too much adrenaline, which ends up obstructing the functions of the frontal cortex and in extreme cases even reducing the size of the cerebral cortex (Meaney et al., 1988).

Several factors contribute to the creation of a teaching and learning environment. These include "faculty-student interaction, the tone instructors set, instances of stereotyping or tokenism, the course demographics, student-student interaction, and the range of perspectives represented in the course content and materials" (Ambrose et al., 2010).

I once conducted a very simple experiment with my own classes. I compared the results of a traditional criminal law course and the same course on criminal law entirely taught through popular culture. In both courses, I explored the same criminal law topics, I had the same goals, and students did the same activities. The only difference was that in the second course, I exemplified criminal law issues through the analysis of films, TV shows, songs, and commercials. This created a relaxed and fun atmosphere, which my students and I really enjoyed. I compared the results attained by students in this course to those in the criminal law course taught without recourse to popular culture. The results show that students learned more deeply in the course with the more enjoyable atmosphere than in the traditionally taught course (Hermida, 2013).

Intrinsic motivation plays a fundamental role in the creation of a safe and enjoyable environment. Intrinsic motivation takes place when students learn because they want to, because they see the importance of learning for their own personal growth as human beings. A teaching and learning environment that emphasizes learners' independence and choice is conducive to intrinsic motivation.

One of the most powerful ways to generate intrinsic motivation is by helping students play the whole game of the discipline (Perkins, 2009). Students are motivated when they can actively participate in all aspects of the discipline through authentic performances and activities.

Another issue to take into account is to prevent the creation of a negative environment; as this generally leads to surface learning. There are several factors that contribute to generate a stressful and negative teaching and learning environment. One of these factors is a very heavy workload,which students perceive as unmanageable (Prosser and Trigwell, 1999). A negative environment also occurs when the environment is influenced by extrinsic motivation. This takes place when learning is geared by a system of rewards and punishments. Students do not try to learn because it is important for their lives, but because they are threatened with punishment or stimulated with rewards. Rewards come in different forms, usually associated with high grades. But they also include credit for the course, a diploma or degree, a job offer, a scholarship, honors, inclusion in the dean's list, or any other academic prize. Punishment includes low grades, failing the course, academic probation, and the loss of fellowships. Students will do what they need to get the rewards at the minimum cost for them, that is, they will study without fully committing to learning. Once the extrinsic factor disappears, students lose their motivation to continue, so they tend to abandon the learning enterprise altogether (Tagg, 2003).

Two other factors that generate a negative environment are stereotyping and discrimination. Although overt discrimination and stereotyping are rarer today than a few decades ago, subtler forms of stereotyping, such as stereotype threat, and discrimination are common in some higher education institutions. Stereotype threat is a phenomenon that takes place when people are reminded of their gender or race when these are associated with culturally shared stereotypes suggesting negative academic performance. In those cases, the performance of such students on certain tasks is more likely to conform to the stereotype (Handelsman, Miller, and Pfund, 2007). Steele and Aronson (1995) introduced this concept when they noticed that African American undergraduate students did worse than white students when they were reminded of their race just before completing an academic task. When there was no emphasis on race they did as well or even better than white students. Similar results occurred with other minority groups (Nguyen and Ryan, 2008). For example, Asian female students were given a questionnaire before doing a math assignment. Some students received a questionnaire that focused on Asian ethnicity; other students received a questionnaire that focused on gender; a third group of students received a questionnaire that focused on neither. In the United States, it is a popular stereotype that Asian students are good at math. A similarly popular stereotype is that males are better than females in math. Results show that those students who were reminded of their Asian background performed better than the other groups. Students who received the questionnaire that focused on gender performed the worst (Shih, Pittinsky and Ambady, 1999).

Another factor that hinders the creation of a safe environment is a relatively new and subtle discriminatory phenomenon that occurs in some colleges and universities in North America. In the name of multiculturalism, some universities favor one single minority group over all other minority groups through often well-intentioned diversity initiatives, which tend to grant privileges to a minority group that has been traditionally considered

The Deep Learning Process and the Construction of Knowledge

to have been oppressed by the dominant majority group in the geographical area where the university is located. In many cases, the oppression has disappeared or substantially diminished, at least when compared to the oppression and disadvantaged conditions currently experienced by other minority groups. Members of the favored minority group are seen as "sainted victims" and are perceived as good regardless of historical facts and actual individual behaviors. At the same time, the needs of other minority groups are ignored (Younkins, 2007). Minority groups that have been equally or—in some cases even more badly repressed both in the past and in the present—feel doubly victimized by this policy. In many cases, this attitude is carried over to the classroom where readings, content, examples, and projects revolve around the favored minority group and/or the majority group. These actions exacerbate the problems of neglected minority students.

Even in relaxed, enjoyable, nondiscriminatory, and nonstereotyping learning environments, challenging and changing longstanding beliefs may cause learners to experience emotional trauma (Bain, 2004). So, a safe classroom environment needs to make sure that students receive the support which they need as they abandon a community of knowledge to enter a new one.

Table 2.4 outlines some strategies to engage students and to create a motivating learning environment.

TABLE 2.4 Creating a motivating learning environment.

Know your students' interests, likes, concerns, and backgrounds.
Design interesting problems and questions for students to solve or answer.
Help students see the connections between the problem or question and their personal and social lives.
Make sure the problem or question is within the students' zones of proximal development, that is, a bit more difficult than their present level.
Create a relaxing atmosphere in the classroom.
Foment intrinsic motivation, that is, encourage students to want to learn and to realize the significance of learning for their own personal growth.
Help students play the whole game of the academic discipline or professional field.
Do not implement a system of rewards and punishments to influence student learning.

40   Facilitating Deep Learning

TABLE 2.4 *(Continued)*

Give students freedom to choose learning goals, the performances to achieve those goals, and the way to reflect upon the attainment of those goals.

Help students deal with the emotions that they experience throughout the learning process.

Help students reflect about the learning process and provide effective feedback.

Avoid stereotyping your students.

Prevent discrimination.

Be aware of stereotype threat, that is, refrain from reminding students of their gender, race, and background when these are associated with negative academic performance.

Do not favor any group over all other groups.

Treat every student and every group of students equally.

Include diverse worldviews and cultural perspectives into your course.

Help students develop academic skills, competences, and practices. Help students become academically proficient in the official language of instruction and in, at least, another language.

Teach from diverse knowledge modes.

Do not create a heavy workload that students may perceive as unmanageable.

Communicate course expectations clearly.

Be fair.

Recognize that some students may have special needs or may be in special circumstances.

Be mindful of the needs of students with learning disabilities.

Foment cooperation among students.

Create learning communities.

Encourage students to construct knowledge and negotiate meanings through social interaction with peers.

Include diverse teaching and learning activities that cater to different students.

Vary students' performances.

Design authentic and meaningful student performances.

Recognize the importance of helping students acquire and develop the discourse of the academic discipline or professional field.

Be mindful of the needs of nonnative speaking students.

The Deep Learning Process and the Construction of Knowledge 41

2.16 SUMMARY

A fixation with teaching and an obsessive emphasis on lectures have given rise to superficial learning across Instruction-paradigm universities and colleges. Deep learning is the key to changing this problem. Deep learning is both an individual and a social process. It is the result of individual and collective interactions. For deep learning to occur, the learner must face an exciting problem or question, which gives rise to a cognitive conflict derived from interaction with peers, and that the learner feels motivated to solve. To do so, the learner must make nonarbitrary and substantive connections between new knowledge arising from the problem or question and his or her cognitive structures through recourse to higher order cognitive and metacognitive competences.The new knowledge that the learner grapples with must be within the learner's zone of proximal development. If adequately and intrinsically motivated, the learner will change his or her cognitive structure through a process of accommodation and assimilation. This will produce two interrelated phenomena. At the individual level, the learner will produce a conceptual change. From a biological point of view, this change will imply a physical transformation of the neuronal connections in the learner's brain. At the social level, there will be a reacculturation from one community of knowledgeable peers to another or a movement from the periphery of a community of knowledgeable peers to the center. Deep learning also requires an awareness of this movement and the resulting conceptual change.

The next chapters expand and elaborate on the main aspects of the deep learning process. The goal of the rest of the book is to show you how to facilitate deep learning. Chapter 3 explores students' goals in the quest toward deep learning.

PRACTICE CORNER

1. Think of a class you currently teach. Design a situation or problem that your students will not be able to solve by using their existing cognitive structures. How can you ensure that the situation or problem is within your students' zone of proximal development?

What will you do to help students connect the new knowledge to their existing knowledge structures and experiences? What kind of connections can you help your students make? What instances of collective negotiation of meaning will you plan?

2. You have been asked to prepare a teaching orientation workshop for new faculty. One of your main learning goals is that workshop participants demonstrate appreciation for deep learning. What teaching and learning activities can you think so that participants will develop appreciation for the importance of deep learning?

3. James Zull (2002), a renowned biology professor and educational developer, who has studied the relation between learning and the brain, argues that there is a strong connection between reasoning centers (frontal cortex) and the emotion centers (amygdala) in the brain. He claims that "emotions tend to overpower cognition" and that "our emotions influence our thinking rather than our thinking influences our emotions." Zull concludes that this is so because there are more neuronal "connections that run from the amygdala to the cortex than the other way." What implications do you think this has for teaching? What specific actions and strategies can we take in our classes in light of these findings? How can we help students develop positive emotions in their learning processes?

4. David Perkins (2009) argues that helping students play the whole game of the discipline leads students to engage in their learning processes. How can you re-create the whole game—or a junior version—of your discipline given the limiting resources and the institutional constraints of your institution? What can you do in your classes to help students play that whole game?

5. Think of the last student whose work you evaluated. In what stage of Perry's cognitive development is that student? What clues do you have? Can you think of specific examples of that student's behavior that show his or her stage of cognitive development? What challenges can you create to help that student progress toward the next stage?

6. Remember or watch the film *Stand and Deliver* (1988) directed by Ramón Menéndez. Do students learn calculus deeply or superficially? Can you identify instances of deep and/or surface learning?

The Deep Learning Process and the Construction of Knowledge   43

What is the students' motivation? How does Jaime Escalante teach his students? Are there any cognitive conflicts? Can you spot a conceptual change in the students?

7. Imagine you are asked to teach a first-year foundation course entitled "Introduction to College Success." This course aims at helping students develop skills and strategies for academic success. Students learn note-taking skills, exam strategies, study and communication skills, time and stress management skills, and goal-setting and organizational skills. You want to create a cognitive conflict for your students. What problems or situations can you think of that can lead to a cognitive conflict?

8. Think of the last group activity or project in one of your courses. Can you identify any instance of stereotype threat? If so, what changes can you introduce next time to minimize this phenomenon?

9. John Tagg (2003) and James Zull (2002), among many other authors, argue that grades constitute extrinsic motivation, which ultimately leads to surface learning as opposed to intrinsic motivation. Intrinsic motivation takes place when students learn because they see the importance of learning for their own personal growth. Reflect about the following quote from the book *On Your Own*, written by then Princeton University student Brooke Shields (1985): "I love to challenge myself –I'm always trying to reach some goals that I've set for myself. And achieving good grades is one of them. [...] After much hard work I've reached my goal; I've met my challenge." Can these two seemingly opposed ideas be reconciled? Is it possible that good grades can become an intrinsic motivating factor under certain circumstances? Or are grades always an extrinsic reward? Do grades have any value for students' deep learning process? Or are grades mostly a way of complying with accreditation requirements?

10. Listen to the song "Wonderful World" by Sam Cooke. What instances of surface learning can you identify in the song? Now change the lyrics (and keep the same music) to reflect the story of a deep learner in a similar context.

KEYWORDS

- changes in or across communities of knowledge
- cognitive conflict
- cognitive development
- collective negotiation of meanings
- competences and processes
- conceptual change
- deep learning
- evaluation
- higher-order cognitive skills
- learning environment
- metacognition
- motivating problem
- motivation
- new knowledge
- non-arbitrary and substantive connections
- prior knowledge
- SOLO taxonomy
- zone of proximal development

REFERENCES

Ambrose, S.; Bridges, M.; DiPietro, M.; Lovett, M.; Norman, M. How Learning Works: Seven Research-Based Principles for Smart Teaching; Jossey-Bass: San Francisco, CA, 2010.

Ausubel, D. In defense of advance organizers: A reply to the critics. Review of Educational Research 1978, 48, 251.

Ausubel, D. The Psychology of Meaningful Verbal Learning; Grune and Stratton: New York, 1963.

Ausubel, D.; Novak, J.; Hanesian, H. Educational Psychology: A Cognitive View; Holt, Rinehart and Winston: New York, 1978.

The Deep Learning Process and the Construction of Knowledge

Bain, K. What the Best College Teachers Do; Harvard University Press: Cambridge, MA, 2004.

Bain, K.; Zimmerman, J. Understanding Great Teaching. Peer Review 2009, 11, 9.

Barr, R.; Tagg, J.From Teaching to Learning –A New Paradigm for Undergraduate Education. Change 1995, 13.

Belenky, M.; Clinchy, B.; Goldberger, N.; Tarule, J. Women's ways of knowing: The development of self, mind, and voice; Basic Books: New York, 1997.

Biggs, J.; Tang, C.Teaching for Quality Learning at University; Open University Press: Maidenhead, 2007.

Blythe, T.; and Associates. The teaching for understanding guide; Jossey-Bass: San Francisco, CA, 1998.

Bransford, J.; Brown, A.; Coocking, R. Mind and Brain in The Jossey-Bass Reader on The Brain and Learning; Jossey-Bass: San Francisco, 2008.

Bruffee, K. Collaborative Learning: Higher Education, Interdependence, and the Authority of Knowledge, 2nd ed.; The John Hopkins University Press: Baltimore and London, 1999.

Bruner, J. The Process of Education; Harvard University Press: Cambridge, MA, 1977.

Bruner, J.Toward a Theory of Instruction; Harvard University Press: Cambridge, MA, 1966.

Cantiello, M.; Fabricant, H. Natural-Communication Methodology: An up-to-date Guide to the Teaching of English as a Foreign and Second Language; Ediciones Braga: Buenos Aires, 1986.

Carretero, M. Constructivismo y Educación; Paidós: Buenos Aires, 2009.

De Corte, E. In search of effective learning environments for self-regulation in mathematics;EARLI SIG18 Educational Effectiveness; 2010, p. 25.

Dewey, J. How We Think; Heath and Co: Lexington, Mass: DC, 1910.

Duit, R. On the role of analogies and metaphors in learning science.Science Education 1991, 75, 649.

Entwistle, N. In Improving teaching through research on student learning; Forest, J., Ed.; University teaching: international perspectives; Garland Publishing: New York, 1998.

Entwistle, N.; Ramsden, P. Understanding student learning; Croom Helm: London, 1983.

Gabriel, K. Teaching Unprepared Students: Strategies for Promoting Success and Retention in Higher Education; Stylus Publishing: Sterling, VA, 2008.

Gibbs, G.Improving the quality of student learning; Technical and Educational Services: Bristol, 1992.

Guskin, H. How to Stop Acting; Faber and Faber: New York, 2003.

Harrison, A.; Treagust, D. In Teaching and learning with analogies friend or foe; Aubusson, P., Harrison, A. and Ritchie, S., Eds.; Metaphor and analogy in science education; Springer: Netherlands, 2006; pp. 11.

Hermida, J. Teaching Law through Popular Culture, 3rd Annual Popular Culture Association of Canada, Niagara Falls, Canada, 2013.

Hofer, B.; Pintrich, P. Personal epistemology: The psychology of beliefs about knowledge and knowing; Erlbaum: Mahwah, NJ: Erlbaum, 2002.

Iacoboni, M. Neural mechanisms of imitation.Current Opinion in Neurobiology 2005, 15, 632.

Kahneman, D. Thinking Fast and Slow; Doubleday Canada: Toronto, 2011.

Krashen, S. Principles and Practice in Second Language Acquisition; Prentice-Hall International Ltd: London, 1981.

LaFrazza, G. Domain Specificity of Teachers' Epistemological Beliefs about Academic Knowledge, The Florida State University College of Education, 2005.

Lave, J.; Wenger, E. Situated learning: Legitimate peripheral participation; Cambridge University Press: Cambridge, 1991.

Light, R. Making the Most of College: Students Speak Their Minds; Harvard University Press: Cambridge, MA, 2001.

Magolda, M. In Epistemological reflection: The evolution of epistemological assumptions from age 18 to 30; Hofer, B., Pintrich, P., Eds.; Personal epistemology: The psychology of beliefs about knowledge and knowing; Erlbaum: Mahwah, NJ, 2002.

Marton, F.; Säljö, R. On Qualitative Differences in Learning — 1: Outcome and Process."British Journal of Educational Psychology 1976, 46, 4.

Marton, F.; Säljö, R. On Qualitative Differences in Learning — 2: Outcome as a function of the learner's conception of the task. British Journal of Educational Psychology 1976, 46., 115.

Meaney M; Aitkin, D.; Bhatnagar, S.; Van Berkel, C.; Sapolsky, R. Postnatal Handling Attenuates Neuroendocrine, Anatomical and Cognitive Impairments Related to the Aged Hippocampus. Science 1988, 283, 766.

Mentkowski, M.; Associates Learning that lasts: Integrating learning, development, and performance in college and beyond. Jossey-Bass: San Francisco, 2000.

Mezirow, J. Transformative Learning: Theory to Practice. New Directions for Adult and Continuing Education 1997, 74, 5.

The Deep Learning Process and the Construction of Knowledge

Perkins, D. Making Learning Whole. How Seven Principles of Teaching can Transform Education; Jossey-Bass: San Francisco, 2009.

Perry, W. Forms of Intellectual and Ethical Development in the College Years: A Scheme; Hold, Rinehart and Winston: Troy, Mo, 1970.

Piaget, J. The Psychology of intelligence; Routledge: London, 1968.

Pozo Municio, J. I. Aprendices y maestros; Alianza: Madrid, 2008.

Prosser, M.; Trigwell, K. Understanding Learning and Teaching: The experience in higher education; Open University Press: Buckingham, 1999.

Ramsden, P. Learning to teach in higher education; Routledge: London, 1992.

Ramsden, P. Student Learning and Perceptions of the Academic Environment. Higher Education 1979, 8.

Rizzolatti, G.; Craighero, L.The Mirror Neuron System.Annual Review of Neuroscience 2004, 27, 169.

Rué, J. El Aprendizaje Autónomo en Educación Superior; Narcea: Madrid, 2009.

Sanjurjo, L.; Vera, M. T. Aprendizaje significativo y enseñanza en los niveles medio y superior; Homo Sapiens: Rosario, 1994.

Shields, B. On Your Own; Villard Books: New York, 1985.

Shulman, L. Professing the liberal arts. In Education and democracy: Re-imagining liberal learning in America; Orrill, R., Ed.; College Board Publications: New York, 1997.

Slocum, S. ESL Strategies. Facilitating Learning for Students Who Speak English as a Second Language; Alverno College: Milwaukee, 2003.

Tagg, J. The Learning Paradigm College; Anker Publishing Company: Bolton, MA, 2003.

Tek Yew, L. Adoption of deep learning approaches by final year marketing students: A case study from Curtin University Sarawak. In The Reflective Practitioner, Proceedings of the 14th Annual Teaching Learning Forum, Perth, Murdoch University, 3–4 February 2005.

Trigwell, K.; Prosser, M. Improving the quality of student learning: the influence of learning context and student approaches to learning on learning outcomes. Higher Education 1991, 22, 251.

Vygotsky, L. Mind in Society: The Development of Higher Psychological Processes; Harvard University Press: Cambridge, MA, 1978.

Zull, J.From Brain to Mind. Using Neuroscience to Guide Change in Education; Stylus: Sterling, VA, 2011.

Zull, J. The Art of Changing the Brain: Enriching the Practice of Teaching by Exploring the Biology of Learning; Stylus: Sterling, VA, 2002.

CHAPTER 3

GOALS

Goal setting means continual striving—never letting up on yourself.

— BROOKE SHIELDS (1985)

CONTENTS

3.1	Introduction	50
3.2	Terminology	50
3.3	Outcomes and Accountability	51
3.4	Goals and Deep Learning	53
3.5	Goals and the Unschooling Movement	55
3.6	Goals and Oblique Learning	57
3.7	The Goals of Learning	58
3.8	Constructive Alignment	60
3.9	Goals and Curriculum	61
3.10	Traditional Approaches to Curriculum Development	62
3.11	A Deep Learning-Oriented Conception of Curriculum	65
3.12	Summary	69
	Practice Corner	70
	Keywords	73
	References	73

3.1 INTRODUCTION

The deep learning process necessitates a change in the fundamental arrangements for teaching and learning. It requires that students play a central role in the design of their own curriculum and the formulation of their own goals based on their own interests and needs.

This chapter deals with the goals of teaching and learning. It begins with a clarification of the notion of learning outcomes, which has been the predominant approach to goals for the last few years. For this purpose, I will briefly contextualize the predominant learning outcomes approach and explore its negative consequences for the learning process. Then, I will analyze an alternative to the predominant notion of learning outcomes, which aims at fostering the construction and discovery of knowledge. This is premised on the belief that the fundamental goal of the teaching and learning process is to produce deep learning, that is, to help students discover and construct knowledge that they will be able to apply to different contexts and to connect to other knowledge and ideas. Goals affect both specific courses or other teaching and learning units and the whole program. In order to examine the role of goals at the program level, I will examine some perspectives on curriculum development.

3.2 TERMINOLOGY

Governments and higher education administrators, together with some scholars, have embraced the notion of learning outcomes to advance assessment and accountability initiatives that have little to do with student deep learning. The conception of learning outcomes that help improve the learning process differs from the notion of learning outcomes that prevails in higher education practice and literature. In order to differentiate the deep learning approach to outcomes from the predominant notion of outcomes, which focuses on accountability rather than learning, I will refer to the objectives for student deep learning as "goals" or "learning goals" instead of as "learning outcomes" (Blythe, 1998; Gimeno Sacristán, 2009).

Goals

3.3 OUTCOMES AND ACCOUNTABILITY

In the last few decades, the assessment movement took over and influenced higher education in the United States and other Western nations. The assessment movement focuses on accountability, credit-based curriculum, and quality assurance. It regards degrees and diplomas as commodities, which may be exchangeable in the marketplace. In order to meet job market requirements and pressured by accreditation agencies, universities and colleges adopted institutional outcomes that express what students are intended to have learned at the end of their higher education studies. These outcomes are based on the attributes of the ideal university or college graduate. Higher education administration tends to require teachers to teach for and assess these outcomes in every course (Biggs and Tang, 2007). These outcomes are not aimed at improving the quality of the teaching and learning process. They simply aim at facilitating the commoditization of degrees and diplomas. Furthermore, authors and faculty have long noticed that the outcome-based education model has been imposed dogmatically; those who want to work along alternative avenues have been ostracized in academia (Gimeno Sacristán, 1986; Stenhouse, 1971).

The European Union recently created the European Higher Education Area (EHEA), after a long negotiation process initiated with the Bologna Declaration signed on June 19, 1999. This immense area now includes 47 countries—even many states that are not members of the European Union, such as Russia and Norway. The EHEA adopted several significant reforms, including the adoption of an overarching framework for qualifications in the EHEA and national qualification frameworks. The former is based on three cycles (bachelor, master, doctorate), generic descriptors for each cycle based on learning outcomes and competences, and credit ranges in the first and second cycles. The national frameworks set forth "what learners should know, understand and be able to do on the basis of a given qualification as well as how learners can move from one qualification to another within a system." The European notion of learning outcomes is inherited from the conception that predominates in the U. S. assessment movement (Rué, 2007).

Similarly, Australia adopted the *National Protocols for Higher Education Approval Processes* in October, 2007. The National Protocols aim to ensure consistent criteria and standards across Australia in the recognition of new universities, the operation of overseas higher education institutions in Australia, and the accreditation of higher education courses to be offered by non self-accrediting institutions (Australian Government, n/d). The National Protocols and the Learning and Teaching Performance Funding embrace the assessment of learning outcomes as a key indicator of excellence in teaching and learning.

In Canada, Ontario adopted general degree-level expectations as part of its Quality Assurance Framework, which all Ontario universities have to follow for the approval and review of new and existing programs, respectively. Provincial authorities require all university programs to adopt learning outcomes in consonance with these degree-level expectations. Other Canadian provinces took similar measures.

Learning-outcome-based education, as well as the similar notion of competence-based education, has been criticized on a number of grounds. First, it is a harmful proposition that endangers the construction of learning, as it reduces learning to what is demonstrable and assessable, which leaves out a lot. For example, I recently witnessed a discussion that revolved around the goal of passion in an architecture program. A colleague held that one of her goals is to instill a sense of passion for learning architecture in all her students. Her disciplinary colleagues objected to this on the grounds that passion cannot be demonstrated. They challenged her to come up with standards for her students to demonstrate that they are passionate for the discipline. Because she was able to come up only with general and vague standards, her colleagues urged her to abandon this goal for other outcomes that are demonstrable. The same can happen with other very important objectives of our teaching, such as the development of student confidence to embark on certain activities, interest, commitment, and self-esteem. These are factors that we can understand, appreciate, and feel the presence of. Any experienced teacher can tell whether their students are interested in or committed to the discipline, but they cannot easily demonstrate these qualities empirically. So, reducing learning goals to what is demonstrable reduces the spectrum of learning opportunities.

Second, outcome-based education has also been criticized, because it infringes upon academic freedom. Teachers have to adapt the content and outcomes of their teaching to outcomes set externally at the institutional,

Goals 53

regional, national, and supranational levels. Teachers have less flexibility to decide what their students can learn. And students have no say in what they can learn, either. Furthermore, this model tends to reduce the significance of the aims of education and to downplay the importance of what actually happens in the classroom (Stenhouse, 1971).

Third, outcome-based education conceives of education as an efficient and technical exercise rather than as a process aimed at producing deep student learning. It is not focused on improving teaching and learning in the classroom. The main concern of the model is technical and not pedagogical (Gimeno Sacristán, 2009). For example, accrediting agencies and higher education administrations compile long lists of learning outcomes and verbs to formulate those outcomes. Then, teachers have to use those verbs in the formulation of the learning outcomes. Teachers who do so are rewarded and considered effective regardless of whether they actually help students achieve deep learning. Those who decide to use other approaches to formulate goals are punished. In Europe and North America, this system has upset many teachers who are not familiar with how to formulate learning outcomes (Rué, 2007). A growing industry of self-proclaimed specialists emerged to help higher-education institutions reform their programs, adopt outcome-based education, and assess these outcomes. This focus on accountability tainted the notion of learning outcomes with a mantra of efficiency and technicalities, which divorced them from the actual learning process.

3.4 GOALS AND DEEP LEARNING

In many cases, goals can orient our learning process. If we face a problem or situation that we cannot solve or deal with, we may experience a need to be able to reach a solution to our problem or situation. This becomes our goal, which will orient our tasks to attain it. So, for example, I wanted to include ideas from Russian and Soviet scholars in this book, particularly vygotskian and neo-vygotskian. I speak conversational Russian, but I am not familiar with specific linguistic and pedagogical vocabulary. Thus, I decided to improve my knowledge of Russian so as to be able to read Vygotsky and other authors in Russian for this book. I watched shows discussing educational programs on TV and on the Internet. I started to read university websites to acquire some specific vocabulary and talked to a student of mine, Sasha, who was born and educated in Russia. In conversations with Sasha about his everyday life, I picked up a lot of vocabulary that later helped me to understand Vygotsky in Russian. So, my goal was to improve the level of my command of Russian. I directed a series of activities toward reaching this goal. Sometimes, while searching for pedagogical materials in Russian on the Internet, I came up with information about sports and films. Although I did spend some time reading and watching these materials, my objective kept me back on track, which is very valuable, as I have a tendency to procrastinate when I surf the web.

The concept of goals is very simple to grasp, and setting goals is a relatively simple process. Blythe (1998) defines the notion of goals, which she refers to as understanding goals, as "the concepts, processes, and skills that we most want our students to understand. They help to create focus by stating where students are going. They are usually phrased as statements and questions." Blythe (1998) differentiates between unit-long understanding goals, which focus on "what we want students to get out of their work with a particular generative topic" and overarching understanding goals or throughlines, which "specify what we want our students to get out of their work with us over a course of a semester or year" (Blythe, 1998).

Students can assume and bring to the learning process two different types of goals: performance goals and learning goals. The objective of performance goals is to do better than other students, get better grades, and receive more recognition than others. The aim of learning goals is to understand and master new knowledge (Tagg, 2003). Performance goals invariably lead to surface learning, whereas learning goals may be conducive to deep learning, particularly when students themselves are involved in formulating their own learning goals. Tagg (2003) recognizes that if students were completely free to choose their goals, they would probably choose to play video games or to make money. So, Tagg advocates for helping students see the connections between what the universities and colleges offer and students' own intrinsic interests.

Goals 55

3.5 GOALS AND THE UNSCHOOLING MOVEMENT

The unschooling movement, initiated by John Holt in the 1960's and 1970's, is based on the premises that all children—and adults for that matter—want to learn and that they will learn if given the freedom to pursue their interests naturally without the constraints of the Instruction—paradigm school (Holt, 1995). In Holt's words, "children are by nature smart, energetic, curious, eager to learn, and good at learning; they do not need to be bribed and bullied to learn; they learn best when they are happy, involved, and interested in what they are doing; they learn least, or not at all, when they are bored, threatened, humiliated, frightened." In her Princeton University thesis, Brooke Shields (1987), who does not necessarily subscribe to the unschooling movement, argues that "children don't view the world about them with preconceived notions. [...] They look at the world with open eyes, and without references." Similarly, in his study of what the best college students do, Ken Bain (2012) has found that one common feature of most successful higher education students is that they rediscover the curiosity of childhood. These students had a passion for something while they were growing up, such as taking pictures, building LEGOs®, or taking care of animals. While pursuing higher education studies, these successful students find ways of connecting their studies with that passion and building upon it.

In unschooling settings, the learner is in charge of his or her own education (Taylor, 2007). The learner is the curriculum, the one who decides what and how to learn (Miller, 2001). The learning process in the unschooling movement imitates real-life learning. Unschooling learning is learning while we live and pursue our interests in a natural, constraint-free process. Students learn in the real world. They interact with other peers, objects, elders, and models (Illich, 1970). Students discover knowledge and set their own learning goals. They learn at their own pace. They enjoy learning and learn how to learn. The unschooling class is organic and internal (Holt, 1972). It grows out of the needs and abilities of the students. This view of learning is supported by neuroscience studies that argue that the search for meaning is innate in human beings and in other animals (Caine Learning Institute, 2005). For example, rats that were offered a cage-free environment, full of challenging obstacles, objects to play with, and the presence of other rats demonstrated an increase in the size of the cerebral cortex when compared to rats which were isolated in cages with regimented tasks (Diamond et al. 1964).

Unschooling education is not an education without teachers. It is an education without teachers who are the center of the system. The role of teachers in the unschooling class is that of a resource, someone who is there to help learners as they progress in the discovery and construction of their own knowledge. The relationship of each student to the teacher and to the class changes all the time (Holt, 1972). In the unschooling movement, all goals are permitted. There are no limits. Students have freedom to set their own goals, even if that means to play video games. The unschooling movement understands that even with such nonacademic goals, students will certainly face some problems that they will not be able to solve by themselves. Sooner or later, these problems will lead students to have to grapple with academic issues. For example, a Spanish-speaking student's interest in video games may lead him or her to learn about computer programming, English, algorithms, and the history of the Middle Ages to design an online video game.

Adults also behave like this when they are free from artificial constraints. For example, like many others, after the September 11 incidents, I became very interested in learning about security, terrorism, the root causes of terrorism, and the political and military responses to terrorism. I had never taken a course on security in my undergraduate or graduate education. So, I decided to learn about this. For this purpose, I read some books and journal articles. I also conversed with some colleagues about these issues. I talked to my friends about what they thought about terrorism and its causes. I incorporated this topic in some of my classes and discussed it with my students. I even wrote an article about terrorism in the aviation field. I wrote when I felt the need to write, usually after having read an interesting article or book, or after teaching a particularly challenging class. Some sort of teaching was involved, too, as I attended several academic conferences where I learned from presentations. But I learned without—formal—teachers, courses, curriculum, credits, grades, and transcripts. Learning emerged from my personal interests, not from formal, traditional schooling. I pursued my own path in the construction of knowledge without external constraints and artificial conditions. Freedom to pursue learning also meant adapting learning to my own styles, time frame,

Goals 57

and possibilities. It took me a long time to fully understand this topic, not an academic semester or whatever time period it takes others to learn. Without artificial constraints, I felt free to learn and progress at my own pace.

3.6 GOALS AND OBLIQUE LEARNING

There are many behaviors that do not have a clear goal, and meaningful learning may still result from these behaviors. For example, research on the brain shows that there is a type of learning that is implicit. Implicit learning means that human beings are capable of learning information without being aware that they are learning. The brain can process information, but we are not necessarily conscious of this process. This can be sensed when we find some facts, people, faces, rules, or even topics familiar, but we do not know how we came to know them (Blakemore and Frith, 2008). Whether this implicit learning can amount to deep learning is something that requires further research. But the point is that an exclusive focus on goals may leave out many opportunities for meaningful learning that were not part of the original goal. John Kay (2011), a UK economist, offers the notion that in many cases learning is achieved from oblique approaches and that most of our goals, particularly those that are complex and incommensurable, are pursued indirectly. A successful example of oblique learning from my experience is my discovery of whole-foods, plant-based, and nutrient-dense healthy eating. Two years ago, I decided to go on a diet to lose some weight. That was my goal. So, I read several books on weight loss and dieting. I once came across Dr. Fuhrman's (2003) *Eat to Live book*. After reading it, I decided to read his *Super Immunity* book (Fuhrman, 2011) and then Campbell's (2006) *The China Study*. These books led me to a pathway of healthy eating, which I continued even after achieving my desired weight. I now follow a very healthy whole-foods, plant-based, and nutrient-dense regimen. My intended goal was to lose weight. But I have achieved not only that goal but also a more powerful one that is learning to eat healthily. I achieved this latter goal in an indirect way, without ever consciously intending to achieve it. As Kay (2011) notes, "obliquity is the idea that goals are often best achieved when pursued indirectly. Obliquity is characteristic of systems that are complex, imperfectly understood, and change their nature as we engage with them." According to Kay (2011), we find out about these complex goals in the process of achieving other—indirect or oblique—goals. Frank Smith (1988) goes even further and argues that the most meaningful learning is neither intended nor oblique—it is incidental, that is, "we learn when learning is not our primary intention." Smith illustrates his point with the example of children who learn to speak their first language because they want to achieve certain other goals such as getting food. Their purpose is to eat, not to learn a language. So, offering students the possibility to pursue different goals may lead to the attainment of other, nonintended goals

Let me tell you a story of a student to illustrate this point. Rachel was a business major. She took a business course, in which she had to create a company and present it to the whole class. She designed a new online dating company. While working on her project, she learned about flaws in the immigration system. She identified issues involving the sponsoring of prospective spouses and partners. She became particularly interested in the phenomena of marriages of convenience and spousal abuse of sponsored partners. In the following semester, she took courses in psychology, deviance, and gender violence. She wanted to understand why abuse took place and how the immigration system could be fixed in order to prevent abuses. Although she submitted a very sound business proposal for the online dating company, she never implemented it. Instead, she developed a very strong interest in abuse suffered by sponsored spouses and partners. She became a strong advocate for immigration reforms and against transnational abuse. She finished her major in business, and then went on to achieve a master's degree in human rights. She developed her interest and knowledge in this new field only indirectly and obliquely while working on some other project. She had the freedom and opportunity to explore in the business class, which led her to find her own true goals and interests.

3.7 THE GOALS OF LEARNING

The goal of learning is a capability, which has both a general and a specific aspect (Marton, Runesson and Tsui, 2004). The general aspect deals with the nature of the capability and includes analyzing, classifying, comparing,

Goals 59

contrasting, or judging. The specific aspect of learning deals with the content of what is being learned, for example, Art Deco architecture, the notion of crime, the history of sexuality, the formation of neuronal networks in the human brain, Italian neorealist films, or the expression of desires and wishes in Spanish. The general aspect of learning is the indirect object of learning and the specific aspect of learning is the direct object of learning (Marton et al., 2004). Teachers focus on both the general and specific aspects of learning. This is the intended object of learning. As Marton et al. (2004) note:

> "What is important for students, however, is not so much how the teacher intends the object of learning to come to the fore, but how the teacher structures the conditions of learning so that it is possible for the object of learning to come to the fore of the learners' awareness. What the students encounter is the enacted object of learning, and it defines what is possible to learn in the actual setting. [...] What is of decisive importance for the students is what actually comes to the fore of their attention, that is, what aspects of the situation they discern and focus on. [...] What they actually learn is the lived object of learning, the object of learning as seen from the learner's point of view, that is, the outcome or result of learning" (Marton et al., 2004).

In some cases, the teacher's intended object of learning may coincide with the lived object of learning. But in many other cases, it does not. So, when designing and teaching a class, it is important to look at the intended teaching and learning goals from the students' perspectives. We should try to imagine how our students' backgrounds, worldviews, and prior educational experiences shape their perceptions of the intended object of learning and other learning situations (Prosser and Trigwell, 1999). "Adjusting the context to afford changes in students' perceptions may be an important strategy in improving learning" (Prosser and Trigwell, 1999). Let me illustrate this phenomenon with an example from a colleague in a Film Studies Department. She intended students to learn about the common social and cultural themes in Lucrecia Martel's first three films (*The Swamp*, *The Holy Girl*, and *The Headless Woman*). After showing the films in class, my colleague asked students to identify and discuss common social and cultural aspects in all three films and to argue whether they constitute a trilogy from this perspective. Most students discussed the unique and carefully planned sound design in all three films, the ubiquitous presence of swimming pools in all of the films, the anticipation of *The Holy Girl*'s theme in *The Swamp* through a song about Dr. Jano (the main character in *The Holy Girl*), and the anticipation of *The Headless Woman*'s theme in *The Holy Girl* through a story about a confusing automobile accident (the main plot in *The Headless Woman*). These issues are signs of a deep understanding of the films. They show that students may have achieved instances of deep learning. But students' lack of interest and familiarity with Salta's society and geography led them to ignore references to societal hierarchical issues, family conflicts, and the role of the landscape in shaping these three stories, which is what my colleague had actually intended students to learn about.

Table 3.1 illustrates the goals of learning and their connection to student learning.

TABLE 3.1   Goals of learning.

		Teacher's focus	Actual student learning
General aspect of learning: nature of the capability as well as cognitive processes, competences, and skills	Indirect object of learning	Intended object of learning	Lived object of learning (students' perception of the object of learning)
Specific aspect of learning: content	Direct object of learning		

3.8   CONSTRUCTIVE ALIGNMENT

The relationship between goals, performances, and evaluation gives rise to two different teaching models: constructive alignment and misalignment. In the aligned model, the goals coincide with student performances and with the evaluation of the attainment of those goals. In the misaligned model, the goals do not coincide with student performances and/or with evaluation. For example, suppose that a sociology teacher wants his students to critically analyze the labeling theory. The teacher lectures about this theory in class. He critically examines all aspects of the labeling theory and provides students with many examples. Then, the teacher asks

Goals

61

students to write a research essay to critically examine labeling theory in the context of crime. Here, the goal and the evaluation are aligned. They both focus on students' critical analysis of the labeling theory. But the activities that the teacher has chosen are not consistent with the goal and evaluation. The activities require students to listen passively to someone else—the teacher—doing the critical analysis. Thus, this course is not aligned. Research studies show that most university and college courses are misaligned (Biggs and Tang, 2007).

John Biggs proposes aligned teaching to foster a deep approach to learning. In aligned teaching, there is maximum consistency throughout the system and each component supports the other. Biggs (1999) conceptualizes constructive alignment as a "fully criterion-referenced system, where the objectives define what we should be teaching, how we should be teaching it; and how we could know how well students have learned it." There are two basic premises to constructive alignment. First, the teacher aligns the planned learning activities with the goal and the evaluation. Second, students construct meaning from what they do to learn.

Although aligning a course is important and may help students adopt a deep approach to learning when all of the components of the teaching and learning system (intended learning goals, teaching and learning activities, and evaluation) are aimed to encourage deep learning, other factors also influence the lived object of learning. These other factors include students'prior experiences, students' situations, students' approaches to learning, and students' perceptions of their learning situation (Prosser and Trigwell, 1999). Additionally, a rigid emphasis on constructive alignment may preclude opportunities for oblique and incidental learning. Constructive alignment helps students take a deep approach to learning when the teacher also designs opportunities for students to explore goals and develop interests other than those directly or expressly intended.

3.9 GOALS AND CURRICULUM

Goals play a role at both the unit—course in the terminology of the Instruction-paradigm university—and the program levels. The setting of goals at the program level is connected to curriculum theory and practice.

62 Facilitating Deep Learning

I will examine the traditional approaches to curriculum development and then an approach to curriculum development that aims at fostering deep learning.

3.10 TRADITIONAL APPROACHES TO CURRICULUM DEVELOPMENT

Any of us who has ever participated in or witnessed a department meeting discussing changes to the curriculum must have noticed that exchanges concerning curriculum planning and design are often agitated and tense. Derek Bok, former president of Harvard University, argues that this is due to the fact that the principal role of curriculum discussions is to "protect traditional faculty prerogatives at the cost of diverting attention away from the kind of inquiry and discussion that are most likely to improve the process of learning" (Bok, 2006). Bok further argues that the focus on course content usually neglects a pedagogical debate on how to teach courses:

> It is relatively easy to move courses around by changing curricular requirements. It is quite another matter to decide that methods of pedagogy should be altered. Reforms of the latter kind require much more effort. Instructors have to change long-standing habits and master new skills for which many of them have little preparation. To avoid such difficulties, faculties have taken the principle of academic freedom and stretched it well beyond its original meaning to gain immunity from interference with how their courses should be taught. In most institutions, teaching methods have become a personal prerogative of the instructor rather than a subject appropriate for collective deliberation (Bok, 2006).

In some cases, debates about curriculum may reflect a tension between the established, senior faculty members who cling to traditional pedagogies, classic content, and traditional conceptions of education and newer faculty members who have no investment in the past (Renner, 1995).

There are several approaches to curriculum development in the traditional Instruction-paradigm university. These include the conception of curriculum as product, process, and praxis. The product approach to curriculum derives from the works of Tyler and Bruner. Ralph Tyler (1949),

Goals   63

one of the pioneers in curriculum development thought, conceived of the curriculum as a tangible document that had to be implemented in the classroom. Tyler proposed four principles for the development of curricula in educational institutions. These four principles are: (i) the formulation of goals, (ii) the selection of learning experiences, (iii) the organization of learning experiences, and (iv) the evaluation of the goals. Tyler (1949) sees the selection of goals as a matter of value choices made by the educational institution. For this selection, he recommends a multitiered process of elimination of unimportant objectives. The first screen to carry out this elimination is the institutional mission. Those objectives that are not significant for the school mission must be discarded. The second screen is connected to the psychology of learning. Tyler (1949) suggests the selection of goals that are feasible, educationally attainable, specific, connected, and coherent.

Tyler's ideas dominated the curriculum development approach in higher education institutions for several decades. It still influences the practice and methodology of curriculum development even when teachers and administrators approach curriculum development from other perspectives (Howard, 2007). This methodology conceives of education as a technical exercise. Teachers—usually acting through their disciplinary departments—set the objectives, make a plan, implement it, and measure the outcomes (Smith, 1996 and 2000). Jerome Bruner (1960) proposed to focus on the identification of basic structures in the disciplines as the essential aspect of curriculum design. The basic structures are the fundamental concepts and principles of a discipline. Bruner proposed the adoption of a spiral curriculum wherein students are taught these basic ideas at the beginning of their studies; and then they come back to these ideas in successive courses. For example, the typical introduction course offers an overview of the main aspects of the discipline. Upper-year courses in the same discipline elaborate upon these concepts so that students can get a more specific and complete understanding.

Curriculum as a process focuses on the interactions that take place in the classroom. Curriculum as process is "an attempt to communicate the essential principles and features of an educational proposal in such a form that it is open to critical scrutiny and capable of effective translation into practice" (Stenhouse, 1975). The curriculum process includes three main phases: planning, empirical study, and justification. Planning includes selection of the content and the teaching methods to teach that content. Empirical study refers to the evaluation of the progress of teachers and students, and justification deals with the explicit formulation of curricular goals so that curriculum can be reviewed and evaluated (Stenhouse, 1975).

An elaboration of curriculum as a process, the praxis perspective on curriculum focuses on a commitment to deal with the fundamental issues of human life, such as oppression, discrimination, power, and ethnocentrism. It places these fundamental issues at the forefront of the teaching practice so that teachers and students can examine and renegotiate them (Smith, 1996 and 2000).

All of these conceptions about curriculum development and practice have in common that they rely on courses and content. They are documents and processes about disciplines and topics, which do not take into account learners' specific and unique needs. Teachers and departments develop curricula that are the same for every student, regardless of their needs, existing abilities, and knowledge (Lattuca and Stark, 2009). Therefore, students perceive the curriculum as—an arbitrary—collection of courses that they must take and pass in order to graduate. The emphasis on individual courses does not permit students to see the whole picture. These notions of curricula also reflect a conception of Level 2 teaching that predominates in universities and colleges. The curriculum revolves around what teachers do rather than focusing on what students learn or need to learn (Tagg, 2003).

Additionally, this emphasis on content has given rise to an unjustified link between curriculum reputation (at both the program and course levels) and content. According to Maryellen Weimer (2002), this fallacy holds that "the more content there is and the more complicated that content is the more rigorous and therefore the better the course and its instructor are." This emphasis on course content has been proved to be ineffective (Whitehead, 1929) and to lead to surface learning (Prosser and Trigwell, 1999). Additionally, when universities and colleges implement government-mandated learning outcomes in this context of curriculum fragmentation focused on content, "the assessment procedures for measuring students' learning are often narrow, rigid, or at a surface level—using, for example, simplistic right-or-wrong quiz questions or isolated behavioral checklists.

Goals 65

So even where applied, learning outcomes have had a somewhat checkered past with every mixed reviews and levels of successes or satisfaction in higher education" (Hubbal and Gold, 2007). Additionally, focusing on content and subject matter expertise is usually done to the detriment of academic skills and competences that students will need throughout their careers. Content in and of itself will probably become outdated and irrelevant soon after students graduate.

3.11 A DEEP LEARNING-ORIENTED CONCEPTION OF CURRICULUM

A deep learning approach to curriculum "has its pedagogical roots in constructivism and context-based learning theories and places emphasis on learning communities, curriculum cohesion and integration, diverse pedagogies, clearly defined learning outcomes, and the scholarship of curriculum practice," which has to be conceived of, negotiated, adopted, and assessed in a scholarly fashion (Hubbal and Gold, 2007). Fundamentally, a deep learning approach to curriculum conceives curriculum as what students do in order to learn. And what students do may or may not include taking courses. Like in unit-level goals, the unschooling movement offers a perspective on curriculum that focuses on student learning and facilitates learning by shifting the emphasis away from traditional courses and the traditional role of teachers. Students acting individually and socially formulate their own curriculum while interacting with each other and with the world around them without the constraints of formal courses, traditional teachers, summative evaluations, and organized activities. The student becomes the curriculum. He or she decides what and how to learn (Miller, 2001). Students set their own goals. Students even discover the learning goals while engaging in learning experiences. This can take them to places no one—neither teachers nor students—imagined.

The unschooling movement's perspective on curriculum and curriculum development reflects real life learning outside the artificial constraints of the Instruction-paradigm university's artifacts. Although the unschooling movement's perspective on curriculum development may sound too radical for many, it is an approach that many of us follow for our own faculty development after we finish our doctoral studies and accept positions at universities and colleges. For example, although I did take courses on education and teaching and learning during both my formal undergraduate and graduate studies, after finishing my formal education, I learned by myself most of what I know now about teaching and learning. When I started to teach full time, I was not happy with many aspects of my teaching practice, which I could not act upon with the resources I developed during my formal education. My education was very successful. I graduated from top schools. But I needed to have new resources, new lenses to understand and improve my teaching practice and my students' learning. So, I started to read, talk to my colleagues, and do action research. I did not have clear objectives other than improving teaching in a very general way. While in the process of reading, attending conferences, and participating in workshops, I came up with questions and topics I wanted to learn more about. For example, I came across Kenneth Bruffee's work while trying to find out how to improve student small-group work. I unconsciously set the goal of learning more about nonfoundational approaches to knowledge. This, in turn, led me to other problems. I occasionally took some courses. I attended presentations by teachers and educational developers. I embarked on research projects based on ideas that I took from the literature, presentations, and conferences. I implemented the results of these research projects into my classroom, evaluated those results, and changed them. I also wrote a lot to contribute to the conversations among teachers and educational developers. I even facilitated many workshops, seminars, and courses on teaching and learning. I learned deeply from all these experiences. I negotiated meanings and constructed knowledge with members of the teaching and learning community. I gradually moved into the community as another active member. This process was not predefined in any document. This process was not constrained by artificial time limits. It took me years, not eight semesters segmented in 90-minute classes twice a week. This process did not need formal summative evaluations and grades. Many activities were judged by peers, such as every paper I submitted to a conference or manuscripts I sent to journals. I also sought feedback from the participants who attended my workshops and presentations. But I was the one who evaluated every step in the learning process and the whole learning process itself. Some of you may think that this is

Goals   67

possible because of my extensive formal education. I would claim that it is possible despite my formal education. The unschooling movement's approach to curriculum development is the natural way we learn. We are constantly engaged in a multitude of activities. We learn when we face a situation or a problem that we cannot deal with or solve. We negotiate meanings with our peers and reflect on the problem or situation by connecting it to our own experiences until we change the way in which we see the problem. In this process, we receive information and feedback in different ways and reflect upon the process itself. The unschooling movement gives us the theoretical framework to help our students set their own goals and to pursue learning directly and obliquely.

Table 3.2 summarizes the main differences between a deep learning approach to curriculum and traditional conceptions of curriculum. Table 3.3 lists the types of syllabi that are used in courses that promote a deep learning environment and those that are used in traditional Instruction-paradigm courses. Appendix I contains an example of a promising syllabus.

TABLE 3.2 Deep learning approach vs. traditional approaches to curriculum.

	Deep Learning Approach to Curriculum	Traditional approaches to curriculum
Goal	Student learning.	Teaching.
Formulation of curriculum	Students.	Teachers.
Learning goals	Open. Discovered by students while interacting socially.	Predetermined.
	Some goals may be negotiated with teachers.	
Role of students	Central.	Marginal.
	Constructors of their own knowledge	Receptors of knowledge conveyed by teachers.
Role of teachers	Marginal.	Central.
	Designers of learning environments and experiences.	Conveyors of knowledge.
Degree of freedom	Ample freedom.	No freedom.
		System of rewards and punishments.

TABLE 3.2 *(Continued)*

	Deep Learning Approach to Curriculum	Traditional approaches to curriculum
Resources	Anything that helps students learn deeply.	Lectures.
Main artifacts	Social interaction with peers.	Courses.
Degree of flexibility	Flexible.	Rigid.
Evaluation	Reflection. Metacognition.	Summative evaluation and grades.
Theoretical foundations	Constructivism. The Unschooling movement.	Tyler. Brunner.

TABLE 3.3 Types of syllabi.

Syllabus	Content	Characteristics
Minimalist syllabus	List of basic information only.	It creates a high-anxiety environment.
Content-based syllabus	Focus on information and content. Lists of topics and readings.	It reduces learning to content.
Graphic syllabus (Linda Nilson, 2007)	Graphic representation of the course. Topical organization of the course. Focus on content.	It aims at attracting students' attention. It is premised on the belief that text syllabi are not attractive for students.
Outcomes-based syllabus	Intended learning outcomes and student goals. Course objectives. Relation between course and program learning outcomes. Constructive alignment.	It claims to be student-centered, but its focus on technical issues does not promote student deep learning. It is too rigid. No room for oblique and incidental learning.
Demanding syllabus	Students' obligations in the course. Course policy. Course objectives. Evaluation. Penalties.	Extrinsic motivation. Based on a system of rewards and punishment.

Goals 69

TABLE 3.3 *(Continued)*

Syllabus	Content	Characteristics
Maximalist syllabus	Coverage of every aspect of the course.	Rigid. Lack of freedom.
	Inclusion of all the information that students need for the course.	No room for improvisation.
		No room for oblique and incidental learning.
	Detailed course policy.	
	Explanation of topics.	
	Main theories, principles, methods, and other aspects of the discipline.	
	Glossary of terms.	
Learning-centered syllabus	Resources to help students in their learning processes.	It helps students navigate the course.
	Reading guides.	It helps students reflect upon their learning processes.
	Links to useful information.	
	Learning and study tools.	It promotes deep learning.
	Metacognitive categories.	
The promising syllabus (Ken Bain, 2004)	A promise to students about the course.	Engaging.
	An invitation to the performances that will fulfill the promise.	Intrinsic motivation.
		It promotes deep learning
	A conversation about the learning process.	

Based on Petkanas, B. The Course Syllabus: A Report, 2005.

3.12 SUMMARY

Higher education administrators and governments in North America and Europe have been placing the adoption of learning outcomes at the forefront of the curriculum. This has led to a rise in a technical—and bureaucratic—practice that has little to do with deep learning. Students need to be able to formulate their own curriculum around their interests and goals and to actually engage in a series of activities and performances in order to construct their own deep learning. This may lead to oblique learning, a phenomenon that takes place when learning is achieved indirectly while pursuing other goals. The unschooling movement offers an interesting

70   Facilitating Deep Learning

framework to help our students set their own goals and attain deep learning. It is also important to be aware of the role of the lived object of learning, that is, the object of learning as seen from the learner's point of view, as in many cases it is students' perception of their situation in the learning context that influences their—deep or surface—approach to learning.

The traditional approach to curriculum development focuses on courses, content, and subject matter expertise. In contrast, a deep learning approach to curriculum focuses on what students do in order to learn, which may or may not include courses.

The next chapter deals with the ways to reach deep learning goals: performances.

PRACTICE CORNER

1. Watch the video *The Five-Minute University* widely available online. If Father Guido Sarducci hired you to teach your discipline at the Five-Minute University, what big questions would you like your students to answer? What skills will your students need to answer that question? How will you encourage your students' interest in those questions and skills?

2. In a department meeting, the dean says that according to new governmental policy, the department needs to adopt learning outcomes for its major and include these learning outcomes in all course syllabi. You disagree with the dean's objective behind this mandate, but you also see this opportunity to move from a curriculum and courses focused on content to a curriculum and courses focused on the goal of achieving deep learning. What can you do (and say in the meeting) so as to achieve this objective?

3. John Kay (2011) argues that in some cases, researchers find out about what they are trying to do in the process of doing. Simple models, such as those advocated by the assessment movement, cannot help achieve complex goals. Do you agree with John Kay's argument? Why or why not? Compare John Kay's ideas and John Holt's unschooling postulates. Are there any similarities? Are there any differences? Is the unschooling movement the best approach

Goals 71

to implement John Kay's ideas? Can they be implemented in traditional courses? If so, how? John Kay (2011) also argues that the pursuit of some complex goals is achieved obliquely through indirect goals. How can you translate this into your own courses? Think of some complex goals in your field and design some strategies for students to achieve these goals. Can you plan the achievement of indirect goals? How can you foster a culture of free exploration of goals in your courses?

4. Suppose you teach a course on human sexuality. Your intended goal is to change your students' attitudes toward homosexual and transgender individuals. All of your students are heterosexuals, and most are homophobic. What teaching and learning activities can you design to achieve this goal? What assessment strategies can you think of to evaluate the achievement of this goal?

5. All of your colleagues in your department at a large state university think that the best way to improve the department's program is by looking into the programs of Ivy League and other reputable universities and adopting those programs. They reason that if these institutions are regarded as offering the best programs, the department should not reinvent the wheel and simply import these programs. Are there any flaws in this argument? Are there better ways to develop your own curriculum? What steps can you design to come up with a curriculum that will help your own students achieve deep learning in your program? What instances of resistance can you anticipate? How can you overcome this resistance?

6. Loretta and Les Jervis (2005) argue that constructive alignment is a "marriage between a straight jacket of obsessive alignment, rigid preset learning outcomes and philosophical confusion." They further argue that curriculum alignment reflects a behaviorist approach rather than a constructivist perspective. What do you think about these arguments? What is the value of constructive alignment? What are the disadvantages, if any, of constructive alignment? Can aligned teaching help promote deep learning? If so, how?

7. Remember or watch Randal Kleiser's (1980) film *The Blue Lagoon*. Analyze Richard's and Emmeline's learning in light of the

unschooling movement. What are their goals? Can you identify any instances of deep learning? If so, what leads to Richard's and Emmeline's deep learning? Can you identify examples of oblique and indirect learning? How can you incorporate some elements of the unschooling movement into your own courses without risking your position?

8. Prosser and Trigwell (1999) recount the perceptions of two students they interviewed after they finished a course on physics. One of the students told these researchers that she thought that the professor only lectured and all that she did was to take down notes from the lecture and from what the professor wrote on the blackboard. The other student in the same course emphasized how the professor tried to make them think and discuss the topics in small groups by looking at the reasons behind the issues discussed. How is this possible? How can two students in the same course have completely different perceptions of what happened in the course? What factors influence students' perception of the same experience? What does this finding tell us about our own courses? What can we do to ensure that our students will perceive the learning goals as we intend them?

9. Design a professional development plan to improve your teaching practice. Include short-term, mid-range, and long-term goals. Be as specific as possible. Effective development goals are those that deal with a relevant area of your teaching practice. Think of goals that you can accomplish. Link your goals to the activities that will help you get there. Give room for oblique and incidental learning.

10. Quinn Cummings (2012), who homeschooled her daughter, writes "I remember that I spent weeks and weeks trying to teach Alice how to tie her shoes. Then, one afternoon at a playdate, a four-year old friend taught her how to do it perfectly. I was less qualified to educate my child than someone who had to be reminded not to lick the class guinea pig." How can you explain this learning incident in light of the unschooling postulates? How can you explain it in light of Vygotsky's theories? What is Quinn Cummings role, if any, in this learning event?

KEYWORDS

- accountability
- actual student learning
- assessment
- constructive alignment
- curriculum
- deep learning
- deep-learning conception of curriculum
- goals
- goals of learning
- learning outcomes
- oblique learning
- outcome-based education
- praxis
- process
- product
- syllabus
- traditional approaches to curriculum
- types of syllabi
- unschooling movement

REFERENCES

Australian Government. Department of Education, Employment and Workplace Relations. http://www.deewr.gov.au/HigherEducation/Programs/StudentSupport/NationalProtocols-forHEApprovalProcesses/Pages/default.aspx(accessed Aug. 12, 2013).

Bain, K. What the Best College Students Do; The Belknap Press of Harvard University Press: Cambridge, MA, 2012.

Bain, K. What the Best College Teachers Do; Harvard University Press: Cambridge, MA, 2004.

Biggs, J.; Tang, C. Teaching for Quality Learning at University;Open University Press: Maidenhead, 2007.

74 Facilitating Deep Learning

Blakemore S.J.; Frith U. The Learning Brain: Lessons for Education; Blackwell Publishing: Oxford, 2005.

Campbell, T. C.; Campbell, T. M.The China Study. Startling Implications for Diet, Weight Loss and Long Term Health; Benbella Books: Dallas, 2006.

Cummings, Q.; The Year of Learning Dangerously: Adventures in Homeschooling. Perigee Books: New York, 2012.

Diamond M. C.; Krech D.; Rosenzweig, M. R. The effects of an Enriched Environment on the Rat Cerebral Cortex. J. Comp. Neurol. 1964, 123, 111–119.

Fuhrman, J. Eat to Live: The Amazing Nutrient-Rich Program for Fast and Sustained Weight Loss; Little, Brown and Company: New York, 2003.

Fuhrman, J. Super Immunity: The Essential Nutrition Guide for Boosting Your Body's Defenses to Live Longer, Stronger, and Disease Free; Harper Collins: New York, 2011.

Gimeno Sacristán, J. Educar por competencias, ¿qué hay de nuevo?; Morata: Madrid, 2009.

Gimeno Sacristán, J. La Pedagogía por Objetivos: Obsesión por la Eficiencia; Morata: Madrid, 1986.

Hubbal, H.; Gold, N. The Scholarship of Curriculum Practice and Undergraduate Program Reform: Integrating Theory into Practice. In Curriculum Development in Higher Education: Faculty-Driven Processes and Practices; Wolf, P.; Christensen Hughes, J. Eds.; Jossey-Bass: San Francisco, 2007.

Kay, J. Obliquity: Why Our Goals Are Best Achieved Indirectly; Penguin Press HC: East Rutherford, NJ, 2011.

Lattuca, L. R.; Stark, J. S. Shaping the College Curriculum. Academic Plans in Context; Jossey-Bass: San Francisco, 2009.

Marton, F.; Runesson, U.; Tsui, A.The Space of Learning. In Classroom Discourse and the Space of Learning; Marton, F. Tsui, A., Eds.; Lawrence Erlbaum Associates: Mahwah, NJ, 2004.

Nilson, L. B. *The Graphic Syllabus and the Outcomes Map: Communicating Your Course.*An Francisco: Jossey-Bass, 2007.

Petkanas, B. The Course Syllabus: A Report, 2005. http://www.wcsu.edu/celt/syllabus.asp (accessed Aug 13, 2013).

Prosser, M.; Trigwell, K. Understanding Learning and Teaching: The experience in higher education; Open University Press: Buckingham, 1999.

Renner, K. E. The New Agenda for Higher Education. Choices Universities Can Make to Ensure a Brighter Future; Detselig Enterprises: Calgary, 1995.

Goals

Rué, J. Enseñar en la Universidad. El EEES como reto para la Educación Superior; Narcea: Madrid, 2007.

Shields, B. On Your Own; Villard books: New York, 1985.

Shields, B. The Initiation. From Innocence to Experience: The Pre-Adolescent/Adolescent Journey in the Films of Louis Malle, Pretty Baby and Lacombe Lucien,B.A. Thesis, Princeton University, Princeton, NJ, 1987.

Smith, F, Joining the Literacy Club. Further Essays into Education; Heinemann Educational Books: London, 1988.

Stenhouse, L. *An Introduction to Curriculum Research and Development; Heinemann: London,*1975.

Stenhouse, L. Some Limitations of the Use of Objectives in Curriculum Research and Planning. Paedagogica Europaea. 1971, 6, 73–83.

Tagg, J. The Learning Paradigm College; Anker Publishing Company: Bolton, MA, 2003.

Whitehead, A. The Aims of Education and Other Essays; The Free Press: New York, 1929.

CHAPTER 4

PERFORMANCES

For the things we have to learn before we can do them, we learn by doing them.

— ARISTOTLE

CONTENTS

4.1 Introduction 78
4.2 Performances 78
4.3 Frameworks for Student Performances 79
4.4 Dialogue 79
4.5 Questions 81
4.6 Problem-Based Learning 82
4.7 Student Teaching 84
4.8 Teaching with Your Mouth Shut 85
4.9 Out-of-Class Performances 86
4.10 Whole Learning 87
4.11 Summary 88
Practice Corner 88
Keywords 90
References 90

4.1 INTRODUCTION

The deep learning process calls for the design of activities and performances that help students discover and construct their own knowledge. Students need to engage in authentic and meaningful performances that emulate the activities that members of the communities of knowledgeable peers that they aspire to join routinely carry out.

This chapter explores the ways to achieve deep learning goals: performances. First, I will analyze the characteristics of student performances that help attain deep learning goals. I will also examine some general frameworks that foster these types of performances. This is not an inventory of different student activities. Rather, it is an analysis of general categories of performances, which may be implemented in a multitude of class activities and class contexts.

4.2 PERFORMANCES

Students need to actively engage in a series of activities in order to discover and construct knowledge. These activities are performances or actions that students carry out. In order for these performances to produce a motivating learning environment conducive to deep learning, performances have to be frequent, continual, connected, and authentic (Tagg, 2003). These activities or performances must be visible and meaningful to others. Activities that have significance only in the classroom are not helpful in promoting deep learning. Examples of performances that are meaningful outside the confines of the classroom include producing a play, writing a letter to a newspaper editor, building a shelter, writing a book, constructing a website, designing an application for a smartphone, healing an animal, or giving advice to a multinational corporation. It is important for students to be engaged in authentic activities, which is the kind of work that people do in situations outside school settings (Tagg, 2003). Listening passively to lectures does not qualify as authentic. Neither does writing a paper based on lectures for the teacher to read. People do not listen to lectures and do not have to write papers about theories discussed by a teacher outside academia.

Performances 79

While engaging in authentic activities, students should be playing the whole game of their discipline (Perkins, 2009). For example, in a sociology course, students can do sociological research where they apply sociological research methods to deal with a certain societal problem instead of doing an activity where they simply discus articles or textbook chapters dealing with research methods used by sociologists. So, the teaching and learning activities that are effective are those that professionals, scientists, scholars, and experts carry out in their everyday professional lives.

These performances include the following components (Shulman, 1997):

- Activity: students should actively engage in tasks, particularly experimentation, inquiry, writing, dialog, and questioning.
- Reflection: the activity alone is insufficient for learning; "we do not learn by doing; we learn by thinking about what we are doing." (Shulman, 1997).
- Collaboration: working cooperatively with colleagues deepens the understanding of ideas.
- Passion: deep learning needs an emotional commitment to ideas, processes, and activities; and
- Community: the learning processes should occur within learning communities.

4.3 FRAMEWORKS FOR STUDENT PERFORMANCES

I will analyze some general frameworks for student performances that promote deep learning and that cut across a wide array of disciplines and interdisciplinary fields. These are not simple classroom activities. They are comprehensive approaches that underlie a myriad array of diverse activities. They all have in common that they offer an active, independent, and authentic role for students and the possibility to create an environment conducive to deep learning. Some of these approaches are embedded within larger educational philosophies.

4.4 DIALOGUE

Paulo Freire, a Brazilian educator whose ideas extended throughout the world, espoused his Pedagogy of the Oppressed in the 1970s. Freire's

(1970) pedagogy is a general theoretical framework that attempts to explain the role, structure, and objectives of education. It is not a classroom method. Freire (1970) analyzes the characteristics of mainstream education, which he refers to as the banking education. It consists of an "act of depositing, in which the students are the depositories and the teacher is the depositor." The main goal of this system is to perpetuate oppression and domination of the oppressed. The teacher, who represents the oppressor, acts as a clerk, who knows everything; the students know nothing. In this role, teachers help to dehumanize their students. The clerk teacher teaches, thinks, and is the subject of the learning process. In contrast, the students listen passively, are taught, and are the objects of the learning process (Freire, 1970).

Freire (1970) proposes a different approach to education, which he terms as *liberation education*. Its main goal is to achieve liberation from oppression. In order to attain this goal, Freire proposes the pedagogy of the oppressed. Instead of lectures where the teacher deposits knowledge onto students' minds, the predominant teaching method in liberation education is the dialog, where teachers and students teach each other and learn together by "posing the questions of human beings in their relations with the world" (Freire, 1970). This dialog has the word at its core, which has two fundamental dimensions: action and reflection. Freire postulates that reflecting on cognizable objects and acting upon reflection lead to liberation. This pedagogy also places teachers and students on the same hierarchical level, which is characterized by horizontal and noncompetitive relations (Torres, 1995). Students and teachers engage in dialogs and learn from each other. In these dialogs, students and teachers ask the fundamental, big-picture questions about humankind. Freire (1970) assigns teachers the role of revolutionary leaders who engage in dialogs and actions to liberate the oppressed from domination and oppression. This dialog is not merely a conversation or discussion about readings or lecture topics between teachers and students. It is not a tutorial, either. Freire's dialog is a more profound approach to teaching and learning. It is a radical deconstruction and reconstruction of fundamental ideas. It is a dialog that teachers foment so that students will take ownership of these fundamental ideas. In order to be effective, the dialog must lead to actions that aim at transforming reality. For example, Jaime Escalante, the famous high school teacher whose

Performances 81

practice was immortalized in Ramón Menéndez's 1988 film *Stand and Deliver*, employed Freire's dialogs with his students to discuss stereotyping, domination, and oppression in his advanced calculus class. This dialog included students' parents, grandparents, siblings, and friends. It was a dialog that helped transform students' reality and perceptions of themselves.

4.5 QUESTIONS

Questions play a fundamental role in the process of construction of knowledge. Questions identify holes in our knowledge structures and help us make connections with prior experiences and knowledge (Bain, 2004). Questions also contribute to the construction of what Ausubel (1978) refers to as relevant anchorages. Questions may also produce a cognitive conflict. If students care enough to answer a challenging and motivating question, that question can produce an expectation failure, which can trigger the learning process.

Bain (2004) goes even further and claims that "we cannot learn until the right question has been asked." Emerging adults (Searight and Searight, 2011) show a tendency not to ask questions because of peer pressure. In the Western culture, particularly in North America, some young adult students regard the asking of questions as an admission of ignorance rather than as a sign of learning. So, they prefer to remain silent than to ask a question—even a superficial one. Other young adult students in North America feel that if a student asks questions in class, he or she is asking questions only to look smarter than the rest. So, these students exert subtle pressure, as a result of which the student may end up not asking any more questions.

Bain (2004) identifies a related problem: students are not in charge of asking substantive questions in higher education. It is the teacher that usually decides on the topics, content, and materials to discuss. We could create spaces for students to pose their own questions throughout their learning processes. Several teaching methods can be used in the classrooms that embrace dialogs and questions. These methods will only be effective if they include and respect all the identified elements of the deep learning process. For example, the Socratic method can help in this direction when properly used. The Socratic method is generally associated with the method that predominates in North American law schools, as perpetuated in James Bridges's 1973 film *The Paper Chase*. But this use of the method has little to do with the true spirit of the Socratic method.

> [This method is a shared] dialog between teacher and students in which both are responsible for pushing the dialog forward through questioning. The dialog facilitator asks probing questions in an effort to expose the values and beliefs which frame and support the thoughts and statements of the participants in the inquiry. The inquiry progresses interactively; and the teacher is as much a participant as a guide of the discussion. Furthermore, the inquiry is open-ended. There is no predetermined argument or terminus to which the teacher attempts to lead the students (Reich, 2003).

The following are essential components of the Socratic method:
- Questions are used to examine the values, principles, and beliefs of students.
- The focus is on fundamental questions about how we ought to live.
- The classroom environment is characterized by "productive discomfort."
- The goal is to demonstrate complexity, difficulty, and uncertainty (Reich, 2003).

A variation of the Socratic method is student-based inquiry, where students discover and construct knowledge by asking their own questions and seeking answers. This helps students learn the methods of inquiry of the disciplines they are trying to master. The learning process can be stimulated when student-based inquiry is carried out in small groups, and students have access to the resources they need to work on the questions (Vella, 2008).

4.6 PROBLEM-BASED LEARNING

Another method that encourages students to engage in dialogs that are conducive to a deep learning process is problem-based learning, or PBL. PBL is a process where groups of students work with authentic—or simulated—problems (Barrows and Wee Keng Neo, 2007). In their attempt to solve these problems, students engage in a process of discovery and creation of knowledge. They apply what they already know to the analysis and solution of the problem. Students further seek, acquire, and use a wide array of resources to grapple with the problem. For this purpose, they do research, discuss their findings, and learn about issues that are needed to solve the problem. Students immerse themselves in discussions about solutions to the problem with their group members. Then they determine a solution and communicate it to the rest of the class. The rest of the class gives them feedback, which the students may incorporate into a revised solution of the problem (Barrows and Wee Keng Neo, 2007).

Perkins (2009) suggests that working on the hard parts of a discipline is important, provided students also get the big picture from the start. PBL is an effective method that permits students to focus on both the big picture and the hard parts. For example, Florencia Carlino, a Spanish language teacher with a doctoral degree in education, immerses students in the Spanish language from the beginning. She recognizes that native English speakers sometimes have problems with reading scientific articles published in Spanish. In one of her class activities, she asks students to figure out the best diet for different types of patients (e.g., athlete, child, healthy adult, obese adult, etc.) according to nutrition principles developed in articles authored by well-known Latin American nutritionists, such as Alberto Cormillot and Máximo Ravenna. Students focus on charts, pictures, and tables to figure out the meaning of these articles. At the same time, a series of questions that patients ask students shifts the attention to very specific parts of the articles and the language that Florencia wants their students to grapple with. This approach is also consistent with Ausubel's position that practice "increases the stability and clarity, and hence the dissociability strength, of the emerging new meanings in cognitive structure" (Ausubel, 1968).

As with questions, the main disadvantage of PBL is that teachers pose the problems. So, students do not learn how to find problems. We see this phenomenon when we teach graduate students. Many brilliant students have a hard time finding a research problem to work on for their theses. They generally have a very good knowledge of the whole discipline, but they have not been educated to find problems. An alternative approach to structuring PBL in the class is to ask a group of students to create a problem for another group to solve. Finding and writing problems for others to solve are also meaningful performances that may lead to deep learning.

4.7 STUDENT TEACHING

Many of us who have been teaching for a few years recognize that we have learned more and more profoundly about our discipline by teaching rather than by spending years as students in formal higher education. Teaching the discipline to our students forces us to think of the discipline's big picture and small details at the same time. It makes us anticipate questions and analyze potential problems. It encourages us to think of different ways of communicating the same ideas to reach a diverse population of students (Perkins, 2009). It helps us see new angles of and entry points to the discipline. Teaching encourages us to read new authors and to discover new ideas in known texts.

Encouraging our own students to teach something to real learners (other than their fellow students in the course) is a meaningful experience that helps students approach the discipline in a deep way and apply what they learn to other settings. Shulman (1997) argues that "every undergraduate who is engaged in liberal learning should undertake the service of teaching something they know to somebody else." For example, a colleague asked his social psychology students to identify a real (small) problem outside academia. He then asked them to do research based on the theories and principles they analyzed in class to try to come up with a solution. Then, students had to present their research findings in the community and try to convince relevant community stakeholders to implement the proposed solution, which they had to negotiate with community members. In this context, a group of students visited a youth criminal justice corrections facility. They noticed that some of the members were isolated and detached. They wanted to see if the notion of mindfulness could be applied to that context and if it could improve the lives of inmates. Mindfulness is an approach to life that is characterized by a state of being fully present in the present moment (Siegal, 2007). Students wanted to conduct a research project with youth inmates by giving them a pet to take care of. Students expected that taking care of the pet would help inmates achieve a state of mindfulness. The most difficult aspect of this project was to convince correctional authorities of the value of mindfulness. Students made a presentation to correctional officers. They prepared a video showing some examples of positive results derived from mindfulness. They also discussed

Performances

the advantages and disadvantages of this approach with correctional officers. Finally, they agreed to let students carry out this project—albeit on a very limited basis. Correctional authorities permitted inmates who wanted to participate in this experience to take care of an abandoned pet. Those young people who agreed showed a remarkably positive change in their behavior compared to those who did not want to adopt a pet. This activity provided students with the possibility of transferring their learning to a real-life situation and to teach the benefits of an approach and practice to people outside academia. Students not only taught the benefits of this theory, but they also applied the theory, research methods, and examples that they had discussed and learned about in class.

4.8 TEACHING WITH YOUR MOUTH SHUT

Teaching with your mouth shut is an approach that encourages students to engage in productive dialogs that foster motivating and deep learning environments. It shares many of the features of problem-based learning and the Socratic method. But it may be used with a variety of activities. Teaching with your mouth shut is not a method but a philosophy of teaching and learning. Donald Finkel (1999) developed this approach, which he contrasts with traditional teacher-centered teaching. In the traditional approach, teachers teach mainly by telling students what they are supposed to know; students are expected to listen passively. In teaching with your mouth shut, students do the talking. They discuss their readings, solve problems together, engage in discussions, and even write together. Finkel (1999) suggests extending this dialog to writing. He recommends the adoption of a community of writers, where students talk to each other not only in the classroom but also through the exchange of written texts.

Finkel (1999) further suggests the adoption of inquiry-centered teaching to implement the teaching-with-your-mouth-shut framework. This consists of the investigation of a problem or question, complemented with the reading and discussion of books in an inquiring spirit.

The teaching with your mouth shut approach can be adopted with several other formats and pedagogical methods. For example, a few years ago, I had to teach two sections of a course entitled Culture, Rights, and

Power. So, I carried out an action-research program to test Finkel's ideas. I taught one section as a traditional lecture, where I did most of the talking. Students' role was limited to taking notes and asking questions, which I answered extensively. In the second section, I made a point of not speaking throughout the whole term, which is taking Finkel's method to the extreme. Finkel does not advocate for teachers to keep their mouths shut literally. This is a metaphor for giving students an active role. Still, I knew that if I spoke, sooner or later, I would end up speaking too much. So, I imposed on myself the prohibition to talk in class. I only allowed myself to speak with students in this section in my office during my office hours to talk about serious problems if they arose. I made it clear that I did not want to discuss content or methodology. So, students had to figure out a method for teaching the course. The only limitation that I set was that they were not supposed to become traditional lecturers. Students decided to divide in 8 groups of four to five members. Each group selected one or two topics from the course syllabus and taught those topics over one class. This course—like the first section—met once a week for a three-hour period. Students presented the materials in different ways. Most included student-centered activities, such as role-playings, debates, mock trials, games, collective writing, film discussions, and collective research projects. Students even designed the evaluation tasks. I must admit that students in both sections had taken a course with me the previous year, so they were familiar with a student-centered approach. I analyzed the evaluations between students in Sections 1 and 2 carefully. In this evaluation, I focused not only on the grades, but also on signs of deep learning. Section 2students clearly outperformed those in Section 1.

4.9 OUT-OF-CLASS PERFORMANCES

Many students identify their out-of-class experiences, such as being involved in a research project with a teacher, participating in a school play, or playing varsity sports, as some of the most important aspects of their education (Light, 2001). Some students even believe that they learn more from conversations with their peers in dorms than from years of formal education with top-notch professors (Bruffee, 1999; Perry, 1970).

Performances 87

Whereas we carefully plan student activities in class, we seldom plan or coordinate their out-of-class activities. Given the fact that meaningful and significant student learning takes place out of class, we could also design learning environments that help students learn deeply outside of the confines of the classroom walls. For example, we could actively and systematically involve all of our students, particularly undergraduate, in research programs. We could also encourage them to attend conferences, prepare and participate in film debates and book clubs, visit museums, and participate in the activities that members of the knowledgeable communities of peers that we want them to join regularly participate in.

4.10 WHOLE LEARNING

David Perkins (2009) advances a series of principles (some of which I have discussed before) that are applicable to a wide array of active, student-centered activities. These principles are: (i) playing the whole game of the discipline; (ii) making the game worth playing; (iii) working on the hard parts; (iv) playing out of town; (v) uncovering the hidden game of the discipline; (vi) learning from the team and the other teams; and (vii) learning the game of learning. These principles can inform many activities. For example, some of my colleagues from the biology department regularly take students to a research facility in another state (playing out of town) so that students can engage in actual research (playing the whole game). Students spend a few weeks in the summer in that research facility with their teachers. They live in bungalows; they eat there, and they organize fun activities (making the game worth playing). The research facility is relatively isolated. So, they spend all of their time there. Students do research and discuss their methods and findings among themselves and with their teachers (working on the hard parts). Teachers act as their mentors, give them feedback about their research processes, and help them reflect about their progress and the discipline. Students also make presentations to teachers and students from the university associated with that research facility and attend presentations from these students (learning from the team and the other teams). Being immersed in actual biological research for several weeks permits students to get remarkable insight into the discipline (uncovering the hidden game of the discipline).

4.11 SUMMARY

Our role as educators is to facilitate the deep learning process by encouraging students to engage in the performances that scholars and professionals carry out in the communities that students aspire to join. A series of performances, such as Freire's dialog, Bain's questions, Finkel's teaching with your mouth shut, Barrows' problem-based learning, Shulman's student teaching, Light's out-of-class performances, and Perkins's whole learning, offer concrete opportunities for us to help students pursue their interests, discover their goals, and construct deep learning.

The next chapter deals with the social aspect of learning and the non-foundational nature of knowledge.

PRACTICE CORNER

1. Watch or remember *How I Met Your Mother's* "Field Trip" episode (2011, S7 E 5) directed by Pamela Fryman. In this episode, Ted Mosby, who teaches architecture 101, wants to take his class on a field trip to a construction site to inspire students to become architects. Ted discusses his plans with his friend Barney. Barney tells Ted that you are not supposed to 'Stand and Deliver' an intro course. What do you think Barney means by this reference to Ramón Menéndez's 1988 film? Do you agree? Why or why not? Is a field trip to a construction site a meaningful and authentic performance for students of architecture? Why or why not? What other performances can you think for Ted Mosby's students?

2. Freire proposed the dialog as the main pedagogy to achieve liberation education. This consists of asking fundamental questions concerning humankind. Think of a course you are teaching or one that you have recently taught. How can you adapt this pedagogy to your course? What specific student performances can you think of to implement in your course?

3. Watch or remember *Friend's* episode entitled "The One Where Joey Loses His Insurance" (1999, S6 E 4) directed by Gary

Halvorson. In this episode, Ross prepares to teach his very first class on sediment flow rate theories for the paleontology department. He has planned a lecture and wants to read from his notes. His friend Joey reluctantly listens to Ross and advises to include jokes and pictures of "naked chicks" (sic). What do you think of Ross's decision? What do you think of Joey's suggestion? What would you do differently if you were Ross? What performances can you think of for Ross's class?

4. Think of a course you are currently teaching or a course you have recently taught. How can you implement Finkel's teaching with your mouth shut approach? What student performances can you design to implement this approach?

5. The first and last classes of any course are very important. We usually think of the first class and prepare carefully for it. We do not tend to give the same careful thought to the last class. Think of a course you are currently teaching or a course you are going to teach soon. What student performances can you design for the last class?

6. Remember or watch Mike Newell's (2003) *Mona Lisa*. Focus on the scenes when Katherine Anne Watson finds out that her students have read the entire textbook for the very first class. On the following class, Katherine decides to launch a discussion about art and its connections to life. What do you think of this strategy? What other student performances can you design for Katherine's students?

7. Think of a course you are currently teaching or a course you have recently taught. How can you implement the playing-out-of-town concept given the existing resources at your institution? What out-of-class performances can you design to complement the in-class performances of this course?

8. Suppose you are asked to lead a workshop on teaching and learning for new faculty members at your university or college. You want the workshop participants to master the notion of deep learning. What authentic and meaningful performances can you design for the workshop participants?

9. For many of our students, particularly the digital natives, social media plays a central role in their lives. Think of a course you are teaching or one that you have recently taught. What meaningful

and authentic performances can you think of that involve social media?

10. Remember or watch Susan Seidelman's 2013 film *The Hot Flashes*. Focus on Nurse Morrey's lecture on menopause. Beth does not seem to be engaged. If you were the lecturer, what performances can you think of to motivate your audience to learn about menopause deeply? What performances can you design so that your audience will change their attitude toward menopause?

KEYWORDS

- dialogue
- framework for student performances
- out-of-class performances
- Pedagogy of the Oppressed
- performance
- problem-based learning
- questions
- student teaching
- teaching with your mouth shut
- whole learning

REFERENCES

Bain, K. What the Best College Teachers Do; Harvard University Press: Cambridge, MA, 2004.

Barrows, H.S.;*Wee Keng* Neo, L. Principles and practice of a PBL; Pearson Prentice Hall: Singapore, 2007.

Finkel, D. Teaching With Your Mouth Shut; Boynton/Cook Publishers: Portsmouth, NH, 1999.

Light, R. (2001) Making the *Most of College*: Students Speak Their Minds. Cambridge, MA: Harvard University Press.

Perkins, D. Making Learning Whole. How Seven Principles of Teaching can Transform Education; Jossey-Bass: San Francisco, 2009.

Reich, R. The Socratic Method: What it is and How to Use it in the Classroom. Speaking of Teaching [Online] 2003, 13, http://ctl.stanford.edu/Newsletter/Fall2003 (accessed Aug 12, 2013).

Searight, B.; Searight, H.The Value of a Personal Mission Statement for University Undergraduates.Creative Education,2011,313–315.

Shulman, Lee S. (1997). Professing the liberal arts. In *Education and democracy:Re-imagining liberal learning in America*; Orrill, R., Ed.; College Board Publications: New York, 1997.

Siegal, D. J.*The Mindful Brain: Reflection and Attunement in the Cultivation of Well-Being.* W.W. Norton and Company: New York, 2007.

Tagg, J. The Learning Paradigm College; Anker Publishing Company: Bolton, MA, 2003.

Vella, J. On Teaching and Learning: Putting the Principles and Practices of Dialogue Education into Action; Jossey-Bass: San Francisco, 2008.

Whitehead, A. The Aims of Education and Other Essays; The Free Press: New York, 1929.

CHAPTER 5

COLLABORATIVE LEARNING

If you have an apple and I have an apple and we exchange these apples, then you and I will still each have one apple.

But if you have an idea and I have an idea and we exchange these ideas, then each of us will have two ideas.

— GEORGE BERNARD SHAW

CONTENTS

5.1 Introduction 94
5.2 Foundational Knowledge Perspective 94
5.3 Non-Foundational View of Knowledge: Social Construction 95
5.4 Knowledge and Language 96
5.5 Authority and Foundational Knowledge........................... 98
5.6 Situated Learning and Discourse 100
5.7 Deep Learning and Social Interaction 102
5.8 The Institutional Level: Learning Communities.............. 103
5.9 Classroom-Level Pedagogical Implications 105
5.10 Students' Attitude to Collaborative Learning 106
5.11 Summary... 107
Practice Corner... 108
Keywords 110
References.. 110

5.1 INTRODUCTION

Learning is both an individual and a collective process. The deep learning process requires instances of individual and collective reflection. And it results in changes at the individual and collective planes. Knowledge plays a central role in the deep learning process. Learners construct knowledge, they relate new knowledge to existing knowledge structures; and they negotiate with peers.

The aim of this chapter is to examine the social aspect of learning and the nature of knowledge. I will begin with an examination of the predominant knowledge epistemology in current higher education institutions. Then, I will analyze an alternative conception of knowledge: the nonfoundational approach, which understands knowledge as a social, collaborative construction. I will then explore the notion of learning communities and some ideas to implement collective instances of negotiation of meanings at the classroom level. This chapter is premised on the fact that knowledge is a social construction, and learning entails both an individual and a collective process.

5.2 FOUNDATIONAL KNOWLEDGE PERSPECTIVE

The traditional or foundational notion of knowledge conceives of knowledge as something absolute, as a fact that exists out there in the world and that the individual mind can apprehend. Under this conception, knowledge so captured by the human mind can be transmitted from one person to another. In the classroom, teachers can cover it, explain it, and transmit it to students through lectures and other similar teaching methods. Students can receive knowledge by listening to lectures, summarize it by taking notes, and reproduce it in papers, reports, presentations, and exams. Teachers can also evaluate students' reception of knowledge and measure how much knowledge students retain.

Knowledge authority is grounded on some universal truth, such as sound reasoning. In ancient civilizations, knowledge was located in God. Those who were closer to God, the clergy, were the ones who were regarded as the highest knowledgeable authorities. In modern times, scientists and other researchers are

Collaborative Learning 95

considered to be closer to that universal truth. They are invested with knowledge authority, as knowledge is deemed to be discovered through the scientific method and the methods used in social sciences that derive—directly or indirectly from the hard sciences (Bruffee, 1999).

The foundational perspective on knowledge is based on a male approach to knowing (Cross, 1998). Males tend to conceive knowledge as objective, impersonal, and detached. Men tend to look for evidence to support their arguments and beliefs.

This foundational epistemology is the conception of knowledge that predominates in the Instruction-paradigm university, which is structured around a teacher who is considered the expert and students who need to learn from the experts by attending lectures and reproducing the expert's knowledge (Tagg, 2003). A foundational conception of knowledge, with its emphasis on expert discovery and transmission to novices, does not promote the sophisticated processes required for deep learning. The emphasis on transmission and expertise merely gives rise to surface learning.

5.3 NON-FOUNDATIONAL VIEW OF KNOWLEDGE: SOCIAL CONSTRUCTION

At the other side of the epistemological spectrum, there is another view of knowledge—the nonfoundational perspective—that considers knowledge as social construction, that is, as the result of the consensus among communities of knowledgeable peers. This nonfoundational epistemology derives from Thomas Kuhn's (1970) thesis on the revolution in scientific paradigms. Kuhn argued that changes in paradigms arise from conversations about and negotiations of meanings among members of a scientific community. The same process takes place for maintaining knowledge. Members of knowledgeable communities are immersed in an ongoing conversation to negotiate meanings and justify beliefs (Bruffee, 1999). For example, for centuries and even millennia there was a consensus among most civilizations that the Earth was flat. There are historical records showing that some astronomers recognized that the Earth was spherical, which date as far back as to Pythagoras in the sixth century BC. But for most people, even astronomers and geographers, the Earth was flat. The members of these communities interdependently constructed a notion of the Earth as flat. Those who followed Pythagoras's spherical conception were not members of these communities. They were members of a different community of knowledgeable peers. Whether the Earth is spherical, flat, or has another shape is irrelevant for the communities of knowledgeable peers. It is the consensus that counts. "Knowledge is not absolute and universal. It is local and historically changing. We construct it and reconstruct it, time after time, and build it up in layers" (Bruffee, 1999). This does not mean that there may not be changes within a community or that members may not exit communities. Communities may negotiate new meanings and abandon certain beliefs—even their most central. But this process is again a collective negotiation of meanings that results in a new consensus. Members who cease to adhere to consensus leave their original communities to join others. For example, Alejandro Casavalle, a renowned stage director and drama teacher, fully subscribed to "method acting," a pedagogy developed by Lee Strasberg based on Stalinavsky's principles and theories. Casavalle even participated in Lee Strasberg's Theatre Institute in New York. But a few years after he returned to his hometown from New York, he distanced himself from some aspects of method acting, particularly after getting in contact with other acting teachers and directors from Europe. So, perhaps unconsciously, he began participating in conversations, fora, congresses, and theater festivals with directors and teachers who adhered to other methods. In his classes now, Casavalle does not follow method acting (or, at least, not every aspect of the method) and follows an acting approach that members of this new group also adhere to.

Most students leave—or renegotiate the meanings in—some of their original communities of knowledgeable peers when they enter the university or college setting. In most cases, they gradually distance themselves from beliefs and ideas long held in their original communities to take part in new ones (Bruffee, 1999).

5.4 KNOWLEDGE AND LANGUAGE

Under the nonfoundational perspective, knowledge is social communication, which is carried out through linguistic and paralinguistic discourse

Collaborative Learning

negotiated by and shared among members of knowledgeable communities. Each knowledgeable community has its own distinctive language and paralanguage. Without the distinctive language and paralanguage of the community, members are unable to negotiate meanings, justify beliefs, and construct knowledge in that community of knowledgeable peers (Bruffee, 1999). Discourse is an essential aspect of learning. We engage in discourse in order to create and validate knowledge. Discourse is "a dialog devoted to assessing reasons presented in support of competing interpretations, by critically examining evidence, arguments, and alternative points of view" (Mezirow, 1991). In other words, we need to master the language—and the system of paralinguistic symbols—of the knowledgeable community in order to construct knowledge. We see this, for example, when we try to discuss some teaching and learning aspects with our colleagues who are not interested in teaching and learning issues. Some faculty members are only interested in doing research in their own base disciplines and see teaching as an obligation that they want to get out of the way as soon as possible to go back to their disciplinary research. Although they are highly educated and proficient in English—or whatever other language they speak—they lack the vocabulary to think about teaching and learning issues. I remember that when I gave a teaching demonstration for my current position, I wanted to engage in a conversation with a member of the hiring committee about my teaching demonstration. I talked about constructive alignment, cognitive conflicts, metacognition, contextual relativism, conceptual change, and even teaching and learning activities. He looked at me as if I was speaking in a foreign language. He often stopped me to require clarification. At one point, he even asked me, "What do you mean by teaching and learning activities?" I thought that maybe he did not follow John Biggs and preferred to follow David Perkins's terminology and referred to class activities as "performances of understanding." So, I gave him an explanation of the differences and similarities between Biggs's and Perkins's conceptions. I later learned that his questions aimed at something even more basic. For him, teaching is giving lectures that students have to reproduce in final exams. He honestly did not understand what I was saying. This means that we belonged to different knowledge communities. His community does not have the vocabulary—the language—that mine has. So, we do not share the same knowledge or vocabulary. Neither he nor I is correct or incorrect. Neither community is better than the other. We are both right in our own communities and according to the standards negotiated among the members of our communities. "No one is a relativist locally. Locally, we are all foundationalists. By definition, membership in a knowledge community means everything we do is unhesitatingly correct or incorrect according to the criteria agreed to within that local community, the community we belong to" (Bruffee, 1999).

5.5 AUTHORITY AND FOUNDATIONAL KNOWLEDGE

Under the nonfoundational perspective, knowledge is not something that can be transmitted from an expert to novices, from teachers to students, as there is no knowledge out there waiting for the human mind to apprehend. Knowledge is communication; as such it is not subject to transmission— only to negotiation and renegotiation. In this respect, knowledge authority does not lie in the expert. It is justified in the consensus negotiated by members of the community. For example, our authority as teachers does not come from knowing the content of our discipline or by doing research in the discipline but from central participation in the community of knowledgeable peers in our base disciplines as well as in the community of teacher scholars or the academic community of our universities or colleges.

The nonfoundational model of knowledge is closer to the way females approach knowledge. Cross (1998) refers to this approach as "connected learning," where knowledge is considered a connected conversation in a learning community. Unlike males, females are not concerned with looking for evidence to support arguments and claims. They are interested in seeing the connections and experiences that lead to ideas. Table 5.1 summarizes the main differences between nonfoundational and foundational conceptions of knowledge.

Collaborative Learning

TABLE 5.1 Foundational vs. non-foundational knowledge.

Foundational view of knowledge	Non-foundational view of knowledge
Knowledge is something absolute; it is a fact.	Knowledge is social construction.
Knowledge is objective, impersonal, and detached.	
Knowledge is something that the individual mind can apprehend.	Knowledge is the result of the consensus among communities of knowledgeable peers.
Knowledge is absolute and universal.	Knowledge is local and historically changing.
Knowledge can be captured by the human mind and can be transmitted from one person to another.	Knowledge is the result of consensus from collective negotiations of meanings.
In the classroom, teachers cover it, explain it, and transmit it to students.	Students move from a community of knowledgeable peers to another one, or they move from the periphery to the center within a community of knowledge.
	Knowledge is communication. It is not subject to transmission. It is negotiated.
Students receive knowledge passively and reproduce it.	Knowledge is social communication carried out through linguistic and paralinguistic discourse negotiated by and shared among members of knowledgeable communities.
	Students need to master the language—and the system of paralinguistic symbols—of the knowledgeable community in order to construct knowledge.
Teachers can also evaluate students' reception of knowledge and measure how much knowledge students retain.	Knowledge is not measurable.
Teachers as experts and students as novices.	Teachers' authority comes from central participation in the community of knowledgeable peers in their base disciplines and in the community of teacher scholars.
	Knowledge is justified in the consensus negotiated by members of the community.
Experts discover knowledge.	Members of knowledgeable communities converse and negotiate meanings within their communities.
	Knowledge is constructed and built up in layers.
Male approach to knowledge.	Female approach to knowledge.
Men tend to look for evidence to support their arguments and beliefs.	Females tend to be interested in seeing the connections and experiences that lead to ideas.
Instruction paradigm.	Learning paradigm.

Based on Bruffee, K. Collaborative Learning: Higher Education, Inter-dependence, and the Authority of Knowledge, 2nd ed.; The John Hopkins University Press: Baltimore and London, 1999.

5.6 SITUATED LEARNING AND DISCOURSE

Deep learning implies—geographical—changes either across communities of knowledgeable peers or inside one's own community. The first type of possible changes entails a reacculturation from one community of knowledgeable peers to another (Bruffee, 1999). The second implies moving from the periphery of a community to the center (Lave and Wenger, 1991).

The first possibility involves a process of moving from one community of knowledge to another. College and university teachers help students leave—or renegotiate meanings of—their original communities to join the academic community of a certain discipline or profession. They do so by helping students acculturate in the linguistic and paralinguistic discourse of the academic community that they try to join. In this process, students do not necessarily come from the same communities of knowledgeable peers (Filene, 2005). This has significant implications for our teaching practice. Students may hold diverse beliefs, principles, traditions, and even vocabulary.

Notice that different negotiations take place in the process of social construction of knowledge (Bruffee, 1999). These include the following:

- Negotiation among members of a community of knowledgeable peers: peers engage in normal discourse to reinforce and reify the beliefs, standards, language, and principles of the community. Frank Smith (1988) refers to communities of knowledge as literacy clubs and argues that learning takes place when we perceive ourselves as members of the club.
- Negotiation at the boundaries among knowledge communities: different communities negotiate meanings in a language that is not their own. They adapt their discourse so that it may be understood by the other community of knowledge.
- Negotiation at the boundaries between communities and outsiders who want to join them: a teacher adapts and translates the discourse

of the community his or her students aspire to join. For teachers, students' discourse is nonstandard; and for students, teachers' discourse is also nonstandard (Bruffee, 1999). The reason is that students and teachers belong to different communities of knowledge. Yves Chevallard (1985), a professor from Université d'Aix-Marseille II, argues that this discourse translation gives rise to a phenomenon that he refers to as didactic transposition. Didactic transposition is the transition from the language (academic knowledge) of the learning community of knowledgeable peers of a certain discipline to the language used to teach and learn in the community of peers that takes place in the classroom (taught knowledge). This transposition is a social construction negotiated by members of different learning communities (academics, disciplinary organizations, professors, government, university administration, faculty associations, and other organizations) who define what is to be taught in the classroom. This negotiation takes place in a virtual space known as noosphere (Chevallard, 1985).

The second possible consequence of deep learning at the social level involves moving from the periphery or margins of a community of knowledge to the center, where the learner achieves full participation by performing the roles and functions that experts display in the community (Lave and Wenger, 1991). The center of the community of knowledgeable peers is occupied by routine or classic experts, that is, those experts who know the rules, routines, and procedures of their discipline or profession and are highly respected for their expertise and professionalism (Hatano, 1982). The most prominent and central role is occupied by adaptive experts, that is, those experts who, on top of their—routine—expertise, can also rewrite the rules of the game. They can understand why their routines, rules, and procedures work, they can change them when necessary, and they can invent new ones to solve new problems when the existing routines, rules, and procedures are ineffective (Hatano and Inagaki, 1986).

When students transition from their original communities to join academic and disciplinary communities of knowledge, they do so gradually. They observe the way their teachers talk, question, respond, and think. They also observe written disciplinary conventions. They interact with their peers. They negotiate meanings within this community and construct knowledge. Eventually, they move to the center as they adopt the linguistic and paralinguistic language of the experts in the community. They embrace the beliefs, ideas, methods, and principles of the learning community. Usually this takes place when students reach Perry's (1970) state of commitment within contextual relativism state or Magolda's (2002) constructed knowledge.

5.7 DEEP LEARNING AND SOCIAL INTERACTION

Whereas knowledge is social—that is, a social construction—learning is both an individual and a collective enterprise. Learning requires individual cognitive and metacognitive processes, which result in individual—as well as collective—changes (Ausubel, 1978; Bruner, 1997; and Piaget, 1972). But learning also needs and entails social interaction and negotiation of meanings. "We learn together by analyzing the related experiences of others to arrive at a common understanding that holds until new evidence or arguments present themselves" (Mezirow, 1991).

Social influence in the construction of knowledge is seen at every step of the learning process. But so are individual actions, practices, competences, skills, and processes. In order to identify these individual and collective aspects of learning, it is useful to recall some key aspects of the notion of deep learning. Deep learning requires nonarbitrary and substantive connections between new knowledge and existing prior knowledge that activate higher-order cognitive processes and skills. These processes are possible because we converse with others. These connections are both individual and social in nature. First, there is a collective negotiation of meanings through the use of higher-order cognitive processes. Peers carry out this negotiation by analyzing, critiquing, comparing, contrasting, applying, theorizing, evaluating, and discussing. Second, there is also a process of individual reflection, which also includes these higher-order cognitive processes, that is, analysis, critique, comparison, contrast, application, theorization, evaluation, and discussion. Higher-order thoughts are continuations of these conversations in our minds. Individually, we can resort to these cognitive processes, because we have internalized the conversations with others. If we do not have the opportunity to interact with others and use higher-order cognitive skills in these social interactions,

Collaborative Learning 103

then we cannot use them individually. "Every function in our cultural development appears twice: first, on the social level, and later, on the individual level, that is, first between people and then inside" (Bruffee, 1999). But, both social and individual instances are essential for the construction of deep learning.

As discussed earlier, deep learning also requires a cognitive conflict, that is, a situation or problem that an individual is unable to deal with or resolve with his or her existing cognitive structure. Cognitive conflict is produced socially. It is the interaction with our peers who operate in different zones of development that leads to problems that we cannot solve individually with our existing knowledge structure (Vygotsky, 1978). The deep learning process results in a conceptual change, which is an individual result—triggered by social interaction—with consequences at the collective level. Deep learning also requires an awareness of this restructuring or conceptual change, which in turn needs both individual and collective reflection.

5.8 THE INSTITUTIONAL LEVEL: LEARNING COMMUNITIES

The best way to adopt a nonfoundational approach to knowledge in universities and colleges is through the creation of learning communities that gives students an active role in the creation of knowledge and the collective negotiation of meanings. A learning community is a group of students and teachers who associate themselves for a common purpose: learning. In learning communities, students can negotiate their meanings interdependently by conversing with other students and teachers. In attempting to understand others' meanings, students try to fit these understandings into their own knowledge structure (Cross, 1998). A learning community requires students to have an active role in the creation and negotiation of knowledge, which includes questioning, challenging, and interrogating.

The traditional Instruction-paradigm university has been adverse to the creation of learning communities. Students register for courses individually. They attend lectures, take down notes, study, and take exams individually. Collaboration in assignments and exams is even penalized with severe sanctions. To change this situation, in the last few years, several universities and colleges have adopted a learning community program. In many cases, this is limited to asking groups of students to register together in the same courses. In other cases, these students also live in the same residence. Other universities and colleges, such as La Guardia Community College in New York, Evergreen State College in the state of Washington, Georgia State, and Iowa State University, have long-established learning communities for their first-year students and in some cases for other students as well. A true learning community is formed when teachers and students participate in a learning community together and engage in a process of collective negotiation of meaning and construction of knowledge in an interdependent fashion. If students simply register together for the same courses, but the courses emphasize lectures and individual exams, there is no true learning community. Effective learning communities have three essential features: (i) shared knowledge, that is, learners construct a shared academic experience, usually around a theme rather than a discipline; (ii) shared knowing, that is, students develop socially and intellectually together; and (iii) shared responsibility, that is, students become responsible to each other in the learning experience (Tinto, 1994).

Learning communities help students succeed in their university and college studies. They reduce attrition and have proved to help students who have lower connections to their university settings, such as part-time students who do not live on campus (Tinto, 1995 and Tinto and Russo, 1994). Learning communities also help students achieve levels of deep learning that cannot usually be attained when students work in isolation (Tinto, 1995). The single most powerful influence on a student's cognitive and social development is other students (Tagg, 2003).

Learning communities at universities and colleges become more effective when they promote legitimate peripheral participation (Lave and Wenger, 1991). Learning communities enhance deep learning "when they give students more freedom to negotiate the rules and processes, when they maintain a balance between reification and participation in the process of negotiating meanings, and when they allow students to move developmentally toward more mature participation" (Tagg, 2003). This full participation takes place when we teachers join learning communities together with our peers to negotiate the meaning of teaching and learning and the

Collaborative Learning

resources we use in our practice, and we join learning communities with students to learn together by negotiating meanings interdependently.

The Experimental College, founded in the 1920s by Alexander Meiklejohn at the University of Wisconsin, and Berkeley's Experimental Program, created four decades later by Joseph Tussman, one of Meiklejohn's disciples, are examples of highly successful learning communities made up of teachers and students engaged in the learning process together. These initiatives aimed at analyzing big historical and contemporary questions through the discussion of classic works of literature. Meiklejohn's curriculum consisted of studying the Athens civilization during the first year and nineteenth century America during the second year. It was not a curriculum about civilizations. It was a flexible curriculum about problems, issues, and themes experienced in those civilizations. The goal was for students and teachers to become immersed in those civilizations as residents and not as foreign tourists who see only the landmark buildings and touristic sites. The curriculum aimed at encouraging students and teachers to discuss, solve, and deal with fundamental human problems.

The teachers were not content experts. They were drawn from a wide diversity of backgrounds. Alexander Meiklejohn was a philosopher focused on free speech. Tussman was a political scientist. Because they were not content experts, their role was not to transmit their expertise to their students, but rather to learn together with their students. And they did so by reading classical texts together, discussing the texts, embarking on broad projects, and, most important, by living together on campus.

5.9 CLASSROOM-LEVEL PEDAGOGICAL IMPLICATIONS

The nonfoundational approach to knowledge has significant consequences for our teaching practice at the classroom level. If knowledge is socially constructed, then we need to create opportunities in our classes so that our students can negotiate meanings collectively and construct knowledge interdependently. In his examination of current pedagogical approaches in the classroom, Bruffee (1999) distinguishes two types of teaching practices: lecture conventions and recitation conventions. In the lecture convention pedagogy, which includes traditional lectures, question-and-answer discussions, and some types of lab sessions, teachers are the center of the teaching practice. Teachers are seen as the knowledge authority; and students' questions and participation reinforce this role of the teacher as expert. Teachers control the classroom interactions. And teachers evaluate students' learning. The recitation convention includes seminars, tutorials, and writing seminars, where students present their work to the teacher, who still controls, evaluates, and performs. The nature and knowledge authority vested in the teacher and the classroom's hierarchical social structure remains unquestioned. Students, even when purportedly talking to other students or commenting on other students' work, are actually performing for the teacher. Their contributions are influenced by students' perceptions of the teacher's requirements. Furthermore, the teacher retains the prerogative to lecture at any time, even if he or she does it subtly while commenting on a student's paper, answering a question, or giving instructions.

True collaborative activities emphasize the collective negotiation of meanings among students as members of a community of knowledge or as candidates to join a new community of knowledge. This requires a radical shift in our role as teachers: from traditional evaluators to facilitators of student learning. In Bruffee (1995)'s terms, we can do this by "organizing students into transition communities for reacculturative conversation."

An effective way of implementing truly collaborative learning in the classroom is Donald Finkel's (1999) teaching-with-your-mouth shut approach, which we discussed earlier, where students learn by actively engaging in dialogs and conversations among themselves. Students discuss their readings, solve problems together, engage in discussions, and even write together. The teacher's participation consists of becoming a noncontrolling facilitator of this dialog or joining the community as another member in order to learn from this ongoing process of collective negotiation of meanings and social construction of knowledge.

5.10 STUDENTS' ATTITUDE TO COLLABORATIVE LEARNING

Richard Light (2001), a professor in the Graduate School of Education at Harvard University, conducted interviews with hundreds of students on their attitudes and opinions about their role at university. He was interested in understanding what those students who have a positive experience do and value during their university studies. Many of the ideas revealed in this study revolve around collaborative learning. Light has found that students value collaborative work. Students noted that working in small groups and study groups have a very positive impact in their university experience. They also appreciate close contact with faculty who act as mentors, whether in a mentored internship, small class, or research experience. Students also noted that participating in activities with teachers and other fellow students has a profound impact in their academic experiences. This is especially so when students and teachers work together on a specific academic project, such as a research endeavor.

Light's work does not mean that all students value collaborative learning. The Instruction paradigm disfavors collaboration and collective negotiation of meanings. Many students identify with the Instruction paradigm's emphasis on individualism. Many other students are at a developmental phase where they understand knowledge as an entity that is out there and subject to transmission rather than collective construction. This generally translates into student resistance, both passive and active. These students refuse to work in groups, or their contributions to the group are generally superficial (Weimer, 2002).

5.11 SUMMARY

Knowledge is a social construction, a negotiation among members of a community of knowledgeable peers. It is not an entity that exists in the world and that can be covered, transmitted, received, and reproduced in exams, papers, and presentations. Learning is both an individual and a collective process. It needs both individual and group instances of meaning negotiation and reflection. At the social level, learning implies either the reacculturation from one community of knowledgeable peers to another or a move from the periphery of a community to its center. This entails a significant change in the role of teachers. This new role requires us to give up control and to become facilitators of student learning. The teaching-with-your-mouth shut approach is a useful framework to implement this change.

108   Facilitating Deep Learning

Students' attitude toward collaborative experiences is generally favorable. But some express resistance, as they are influenced by the Instruction paradigm's excessive focus on individualism.

Learning communities in higher education institutions facilitate collaborative learning. The Experimental College at the University of Wisconsin and Berkeley's Experimental Program are interesting examples of successful learning communities where teachers and students learned together and negotiated meanings to construct knowledge.

The next two chapters explore academic reading and writing—two of the most fundamental competences needed to succeed in academic and professional fields.

PRACTICE CORNER

1. How can you help your students reacculturate from their community of knowledgeable peers to the community of knowledgeable peers in your discipline? What emotional implications may this have for your students, particularly for first-generation university students?

2. Bruffee (1999) argues that an important role of teachers is to adapt and translate the discourse of the community his or her students aspire to join. What does this mean in your own courses? Think of specific examples of this discourse adaptation and translation. What are some implications of this role?

3. As teachers, we participate in the community of knowledgeable peers in our base disciplines as well as in the community of teacher scholars or the academic community of our universities or colleges. Think of your own process in becoming a faculty member. Describe this process in terms of movement from the periphery of a community to its center. Can you think of other communities of knowledgeable peers that you belong to? Does your participation in one or some of these communities shape or affect your participation in others?

4. Remember or watch the film *The Weekend* (1999) directed by Brian Skeet. It offers a very clear example of situated learning. Can

Collaborative Learning

you identify the community of knowledgeable peers? Who are the members of this community? Can you identify the reacculturation process? Can you identify the movement from the periphery to the center of the community? Who experiences the deepest changes? What are examples of the linguistic and paralinguistic discourse shared by members of the community of knowledgeable peers in the film?

5. Remember or watch the film *12 Angry Men* (1957) directed by Sidney Lumet. This film also offers a clear example of situated learning. Can you identify the community of knowledgeable peers? Who are the members of this community? Can you identify the reacculturation process? Can you identify the movement from the periphery to the center of the community? Who experiences the deepest changes? What are examples of the linguistic and paralinguistic discourse shared by members of the community of knowledgeable peers in the film? Remember or watch the film *12* (2007) directed by Nikita Mikhalkov, a Russian remake of the original Sidney Lumet film. Do you see any differences in the movements between communities of knowledgeable peers or from the periphery to the center with respect to the original film?

6. Bruffee (1999) argues that "no one is a relativist locally. Locally, we are all foundationalists." What does he mean? Do you agree? Why or why not? Can you think of specific examples of Brufee's assertion from your own experience as a member of a community of knowledgeable peers?

7. It has been argued that the nonfoundational model of knowledge is closer to the way females approach knowledge. Do you agree? Why or why not? Do females approach knowledge differently than males? If so, how? What implications, if any, does this have in our classes?

8. The editor of a teaching and learning journal has asked you to contribute a one-paragraph analysis on the importance of collaborative learning in the promotion of deep learning for a section entitled "Collaborative Pedagogy." The editor would also like you to think of examples of classroom collaborative activities that foster deep learning. Write this paragraph and the examples.

110   Facilitating Deep Learning

9. The Instruction paradigm favors individualism. Consequently, many students resist working in groups with other students or work superficially without committing themselves to true collaborative learning. What can you do to overcome this resistance?

10. Bruffee (1999) argues that the nature of recitation conventions (e.g., seminars, tutorials, and writing seminars) is essentially the same as that of the lecture conventions. It can be inferred from this argument that recitation conventions also lead to surface learning. Do you agree with this argument? Why or why not? Can you think of a context for which recitation conventions might be conducive to deep learning?

KEYWORDS

- authority
- changes in or across communities of knowledge
- collaborative learning
- deep learning
- foundational knowledge
- knowledge and language
- learning communities
- nonfoundational knowledge
- situated learning
- social construction
- social interaction

REFERENCES

Ausubel, D. In defense of advance organizers: A reply to the critics. Review of Educational Research 1978, 48, 251.

Ausubel, D.; Novak, J.; Hanesian, H. Educational Psychology: A Cognitive View; Holt, Rinehart and Winston: New York, 1978.

Collaborative Learning

Bruffee, K. Collaborative Learning: Higher Education, Interdependence, and the Authority of Knowledge, 2nd ed.; The John Hopkins University Press: Baltimore and London, 1999.

Bruffee, K. Making the most of knowledgeable peers. Change, 1994, 26, 3.

Bruffee, K. Sharing our toys. Change, 1995, 27,1.

Bruner, J. The Process of Education; Harvard University Press: Cambridge, MA, 1977.

Chevallard, Y. La transposition didactique: Du savoir savant au savoir enseigné(Recherches en didactique des mathématiques); Pensée sauvage: Grenoble, 1985.

Cross, K. Why Learning Communities? Why Now? About Campus, 1998, 3, 4.

Filene, P. The Joy of Teaching. A Practical Guide for New College Instructors; University of North Carolina Press: Chapel Hill, 2005.

Finkel, D. Teaching With Your Mouth Shut; Boynton/Cook Publishers: Portsmouth, NH, 1999.

Hatano, G. Cognitive Consequences of Practice in Culture Specific Procedural Skills. Quarterly Newsletter of the Laboratory of Comparative Human Cognition, 1982, 4, 15–18.

Hatano, G.; Inagaki, K.Two Courses of Expertise. In Child Development and Education in Japan; Stevenson, H.; Azuma, H.; Hakuta, K., Eds.; Freeman: New York, 1986.

Kuhn, T. S. The Structure of Scientific Revolutions, 2nd ed.; Chicago: University of Chicago, 1970.

Lave, J.; Wenger, E.;Situated learning: Legitimate Peripheral Participation; Cambridge University Press: Cambridge, MA, 1991.

Light, R. Making the Most of College: Students Speak Their Minds; Harvard University Press: Cambridge, MA, 2001.

Mezirow, J. Transformative Dimensions of Adult Learning; Jossey-Bass: San Francisco, 1991.

Mezirow, J. Transformative Learning: Theory to Practice. New Directions for Adult and Continuing Education 1997, 74, 5.

Perry, W. Forms of Intellectual and Ethical Development in the College Years: A Scheme; Hold, Rinehart and Winston: Troy, Mo, 1970.

Piaget, J. *The Psychology of the Child; Basic Books: New York, 1972.*

Smith, F, Joining the Literacy Club. Further Essays into Education; Heinemann Educational Books: London, 1988.

Tagg, J. The Learning Paradigm College; Anker Publishing Company: Bolton, MA, 2003.

Tinto, V. Learning communities, collaborative learning, and the pedagogy of educational citizenship.American Association of Higher Education Bulletin, 1995, 47(7), 11–13.

Tinto, V.; Russo, P. Coordinated Studies Program: The Effect on Student Involvement in a Community College. Community College Review, 1994,22(2), 16–25.

Vygotsky, L. Mind in Society: The Development of Higher Psychological Processes; Harvard University Press: Cambridge, MA, 1978.

Weimer, M. Learner-Centered Teaching: Five Key Changes to Practice; Jossey-Bass: San Francisco, 2002.

PART II

ACADEMIC SKILLS AND DEEP LEARNING

CHAPTER 6

ACADEMIC READING AND DEEP LEARNING

We learn a lot from what we read; we learn a lot more from what we say to one another about what we read.

— KENNETH A. BRUFFEE

CONTENTS

6.1	Introduction	116
6.2	Surface and Deep Approaches to Reading	116
6.3	Reading Academic Texts Deeply	117
6.4	Motivating Problem and Cognitive Conflict	118
6.5	Higher-Order Competences: Individual and Collective Learning	120
6.6	Whole Game	122
6.7	Conceptual Change and Situated Learning	122
6.8	Evaluation	123
6.9	Categories of Analysis	123
6.10	Discipline-Specific Reading Styles	130
6.11	Specific Categories of Analysis: An Example from the Scholarship of Teaching and Learning	131
6.12	General Study Strategies	132
6.13	Constructive Alignment	133
6.14.	Summary	135
	Practice Corner	136
	Keywords	138
	References	139

6.1 INTRODUCTION

Reading is the key to the door that opens academic and professional communities of knowledge. It lets us see how members of these communities organize and express their thoughts. It also helps us understand how they negotiate meanings and construct knowledge. Despite the significant role that reading plays in academic and professional communities, university and college teachers generally take the teaching of reading skills for granted and seldom teach these skills, assuming that all students already learned how to read academic texts either as part of their high school studies or elsewhere at university or college (Erickson, Peters, and Strommer, 2006). Students, in turn, tend to resist those rare instances when teachers do attempt to help them learn to read academic texts, because they believe that they already know how to read. Students ignore that the reading skills that are required to read academic and professional texts greatly differ from the skills that they have been using to read other texts, such as books for pleasure, news, and texts assigned in high school. Consequently, most students employ nonuniversity strategies to read academic texts, which results in students taking a surface approach to reading.

This chapter begins with a discussion of the difference between a surface and a deep approach to reading, which parallels that of surface and deep learning. Then, I will explore the elements of the deep learning process as they apply to academic reading. I will also discuss the categories of analysis needed to read academic texts. Finally, I will look at some strategies and factors that contribute to an environment conducive to deep reading.

6.2 SURFACE AND DEEP APPROACHES TO READING

Since members of most academic disciplines and professional fields communicate their thoughts in writing, reading academic and professional texts is essential to learn the conventions, discourse, methods, and practices of communities of knowledge (Erickson, Peters and Strommer, 2006). Mastering these conventions and practices will help students become part of the knowledge community of the discipline they aspire to join and will

Academic Reading and Deep Learning

eventually allow them to move to the center of this community. But, this is only possible if students take a deep approach to reading. A deep approach to reading is an approach where the reader focuses on the author's message. Deep readers critically examine this message, challenge it, and recreate it by making connections to other texts, their existing knowledge, and disciplinary concepts and principles (Maleki and Heerman, 1992). In contrast, a surface approach to reading is the tacit acceptance of information explicitly mentioned in the text. Surface readers usually consider this information as isolated and do not make any connections between the new information and their own background. This leads to superficial retention of materials for examinations and does not promote deep understanding or the application of that information to new contexts and situations (Hermida, 2009). Simply put, surface readers focus on the sign, that is, the text itself, whereas deep readers focus on what is signified, that is, the meaning of the text (Bowden and Marton, 2000).

6.3 READING ACADEMIC TEXTS DEEPLY

Reading is a complex and sophisticated process of actively working with the text. This process is shaped partly by the text, partly by the reader's background, and partly by the situation the reading occurs in (Hunt, 2004). Reading a text deeply requires readers not to stop at the information explicitly contained in a text. "The explicit meanings of a piece are the tip of an iceberg of meaning; the larger part lies below the surface of the text and is composed of the reader's own relevant knowledge" (Hirsch, 1987).

The deep reading process is only possible if the reader uses a series of categories of analysis, some of which are common to most academic and professional communities of knowledge (general categories of analysis) and some of which are specific to each academic discipline or professional field (Carlino, 2005). The expert reader has incorporated these categories and applies them almost intuitively. But most students—particularly lower—year students ignore them. So, we need to teach both the general analytical tools and the discipline-specific values and strategies that facilitate disciplinary reading and learning (Bean, 1996). Additionally, deep reading requires acting on every aspect of the reading process. When we engage

118   Facilitating Deep Learning

students, foster students' connections with their knowledge background, and explicitly teach students these categories of analysis, students improve their reading effectiveness considerably (Hermida, 2009b; Munro, 2003).

Learning how to read academic texts deeply also necessitates the same steps and elements analyzed earlier for any deep learning endeavor. Like any other intellectual task, reading also presents specific issues that must be taken into consideration when creating an environment that helps students learn to read deeply. Let's have a look at the elements of the deep learning process as they apply to reading academic texts.

6.4 MOTIVATING PROBLEM AND COGNITIVE CONFLICT

After the initial evaluation of the students' academic reading abilities (which I will discuss in a later chapter devoted to evaluating to learn), the first step in a deep learning process is the creation of a problem, situation, or question that students will feel intrinsically motivated to solve or answer (Bain, 2004). This problem or question must create a cognitive conflict that students may only solve by reading academic texts deeply. So, for example just asking questions to check comprehension of the text or to answer teachers' interests or concerns will not encourage students to read and analyze a text in a profound way. We need to create a problem that students find motivating enough to resolve by reading academic texts. The best way to do so is by creating authentic performances that let students play the whole game of the discipline (Perkins, 2009). Reading in a discipline is just one aspect of the whole game. Students need to engage in all the activities that professionals and scholars in the discipline immerse in. Students will be motivated to read an academic text deeply when they actively participate in all aspects of the discipline. For example, a history student will be motivated to read a history text on the fall of the Soviet Union if he or she also does research on the historical causes that led to the decline and demise of the Soviet Union, presents in a conference on Eastern European history, teaches a class on this topic, and has to give advice to a museum curator preparing an exhibition on life and politics in the former Soviet Union. This student will approach the reading of academic texts on this topic with enthusiasm. He or she will feel the need to read the

Academic Reading and Deep Learning

texts deeply. This motivation will increase if the student can make—by himself or herself or with the teacher's help—connections between the readings and his or her personal life.

In my Introduction to Private Law course, I wanted students to learn to read law review articles deeply. For anyone not familiar with this genre, a law review article is a strange animal full of authority for every question of law and every matter of fact in the form of hundreds of footnotes with references to judicial cases and other law review articles, and with a writing style that is as dense as it is unique, even when compared to other legal publications. I chose some very arduous texts on the legal aspects of comparative advertising. I knew that if I simply asked students to read the articles they would not do so, or they would do so superficially. So, I asked them to create a comparative advertising campaign for small local companies (a sushi restaurant, a pizza store, and a bakery). They had to produce a magazine ad, a TV commercial, and an online ad. They had to meet with the store owners to discuss the characteristics of their businesses, to determine the competition, and to get as much information about their products as possible. After that, they had to work on the campaign, and then present it to their clients. During the initial interview, the owners not only provided students with the required information, but they also asked them lots of questions about the legal consequences of the comparative campaign. All groups had read the texts superficially or had not read them at all. So, they were not able to answer their clients' questions accurately. After these interviews, students felt the need to read the texts again. Also, while working on the comparative campaign, they had doubts about the legality of certain aspects of the campaign, such as when they could use a competitor's trademark, what tests they had to run before making comparative claims, and what disclaimers they needed to use. This task provided students with an interesting problem to solve, a cognitive conflict derived from social interaction; and the motivation to resort to texts to solve the problem.

Similarly, a colleague who teaches a cross-listed course on European history and politics wanted students to read Stéphane Hessel's (2011) *Time for Outrage* deeply. *Time for Outrage* is a political manifesto, which urges readers to rescue the French spirit of the WWII resistance to the Nazi Germany and apply it to fight capitalist power and to embrace democratic social values. The book inspired the *Indignados* movement in Spain, which, in turn, inspired other protests around the world, including the Occupy Wall Street movement. My colleague wanted to use this book as a stepping stone to other history and political science authors who are more difficult to understand and who write in a more detached and nonpassionate language. She asked students to adapt *Time for Outrage* to a theater play, which students had to perform on stage before a real audience. My colleague asked students to adapt Hessel's 40-page work into a fictional play, a love story, which had to respect the spirit of the book. In order to adapt it, students had to examine *Time for Outrage* very carefully and capture its philosophy and the spirit of resistance and fight. Students also had to consult the other texts to come up with a story that transpired Europe's contemporary political, economic, and social crisis. The play motivated students, most of whom knew very little about the crisis, to read the texts proposed by their teacher as well as to consult other academic texts on the topic.

6.5 HIGHER-ORDER COMPETENCES: INDIVIDUAL AND COLLECTIVE LEARNING

The second step in the deep reading process is students' use of higher-order cognitive and metacognitive competences while they make nonarbitrary and substantive connections between new knowledge and their cognitive structures both individually and collectively. This requires the use of general and discipline-specific categories of analysis on the individual and collective planes. We need to create situations where students will make connections to what they already know alone and together with other peers. For example, in the adaptation of *Time for Outrage*, students worked from what they knew about the Occupy Wall Street movement. This movement was in the news and in social media. Some students had even joined local groups of protesters. But they had not read the book, and they did not know what the situation was in Europe. My colleague had suggested that students read the book together on the stage and that they discuss ideas to adapt it. In these discussions, students talked about the spirit of the book, its meaning outside the specific context in which and for which it was written, and how this book could affect a young couple in

Europe. They chose to tell the story through the eyes of a twenty-six-year old Spanish male history graduate, who had been underemployed and unemployed since he graduated from university and through a twenty-five-year old Greek female political science graduate, who meet in the mythical *Puerta del Sol* during one of the protests. This forced students to make connections between what they knew about the employment and financial crisis in North America and the new information they were discovering about Europe. Students contacted recent graduates and other students in Spain, Greece, Italy, and other European countries through social media. They discussed the situation in Europe and how it affected them on a personal level. The connections they made between new knowledge and their existing notions of financial crises, resistance, and protest were possible, among other things, because the new knowledge was within their zone of proximal development. Another factor that facilitated these connections was the fact that my colleague introduced the notion of categories of analysis, which I will analyze in more detail in a later section, to help students read and discuss academic texts.

More conventional activities to help students resort to higher-order cognitive competences to make connections to the text include the use of double-entry journals and reading logs. Table 6.1 lists examples of teaching and learning activities that foster a deep approach to reading.

TABLE 6.1 Deep reading activities.

- **The Amazing Race.** Students in teams have to run from the classroom to the library, then to the computer lab, and then back to the classroom. In each of these stops, they have to analyze academic texts and answer some questions about those texts.
- **The Apprentice.** Teams have to read some articles and books in order to give a presentation on a given topic. Teams are given some reading guides that help them evaluate, judge, compare, and synthesize information from these texts. Students then have to make a presentation to the rest of the class. The worst teams are fired; and the best one is hired.
- **Twitter.** Students are given a text; and they have to tweet their reactions to the text. Or they can pretend that they are the author of the text or the subject whom the author discusses. They have to tweet their comments while they read the text. For example, if students have to read about a scientific experiment, they can pretend that they are that scientist and they tweet what that scientist thinks while conducting the experiment and making the discovery.
- **Facebook.** Students need to create a Facebook profile based on assigned readings and post information to their wall. For example, if students read about Lucrecia Martel's films, they have to choose a character and imagine that character's favorite songs, films, books, and friends not explicitly mentioned in the article or film. They also have to like pages and comments that the chosen character may be interested in. Or if students read about the theoretical models of criminal justice, they have to imagine a criminal justice agent that is enrolled in one of the theoretical models and build his or her Facebook profile.

TABLE 6.1   *(Continued)*

- **Treatment.** Students need to read an article on a topic discussed in class. Then, they need to write a treatment (script outline) for a documentary about the content of the article and pitch the idea for funding to executives from a film company.
- **Double-entry journal.** Students take down notes of their readings and enter them in a column. In a parallel column, students enter their reactions to their readings. These entries may include comments, questions, connections to their personal experiences, and relations to other issues discussed in class.
- **Concept mapping.** Students represent their understanding of a text by producing graphs that display the relationships between concepts and ideas. Students use concept maps to link concepts, develop interrelationships, create meaning schemes, connect their previous experiences, and construct knowledge.
- **Reading journals.** Students record their comments on the assigned readings in their journals. Students may react, question, argue, provide additional examples, or write about what the readings mean to them personally.

6.6   WHOLE GAME

In the previous examples, students' roles were not restricted to reading texts and answering questions from their teacher. Students played the whole game of experts. They immersed themselves in authentic performances; they relied on academic texts to achieve a task that they found highly motivating. They felt the need to read and understand the texts deeply in order to carry out the proposed task. By encouraging students to use the theater stage and by providing students with a real audience for the play, the teacher helped create an air of reality and authenticity, which increased students' motivation.

6.7   CONCEPTUAL CHANGE AND SITUATED LEARNING

As a result of their involvement in the adaptation and staging of the play, students changed their notions of the effects of the contemporary capitalist crisis and the meaning of resistance and protest. On the individual plane, their cognitive structures changed. They came to see the protest movements in a different way, and they had new theoretical lens to examine these movements. On the social plane, students became members of this movement. Some became more active than others. Students communicated with other members of these groups and joined them in different

Academic Reading and Deep Learning   123

respects. Students also joined the communities of individuals who read history and political science authors and who discuss these movements from theoretical and scholarly perspectives. Students could now engage in conversations with these authors by reading their articles and books.

6.8 EVALUATION

After the staging of the play, the group of students met again on the stage to reflect about their learning processes and how they had changed as a result of having gone through this process. My colleague facilitated these discussions and asked them to write personal reflections about their learning processes and their impact in their personal lives. For this purpose, she pretended to be a journalist who interviewed her students by email about their experiences in adapting the book and staging the play.

Another activity to foster evaluation and reflection of the learning process is the use of concept maps. Concept mapping is a technique where students represent their understanding of a text by producing graphs that display the relationships between concepts and ideas. Students use concept maps to link ideas, develop interrelationships, create meaning schemes, connect their previous experiences, and construct knowledge (Novak, 1984). Barbara Daley (2002) quotes a student who used concept mapping and explains her experience with this technique: "[it] is a way to take the idea, apply it, and get a deeper meaning out of it at the very end. It is not just a matter of learning a concept, learning about theory, defining a word and spitting back a definition. It is actually applying it to what you know so that it makes more sense in the actual world." Concept mapping helps students understand their own learning and fosters a learning-how-to-learn approach.

6.9 CATEGORIES OF ANALYSIS

Categories of analysis are tools that help readers think, discuss, and interact with academic texts. Some categories of analysis, known as general categories, apply to virtually any academic reading situation. Apart from

124   Facilitating Deep Learning

these general categories, each discipline has its own specific categories of analysis, which reflect the particular way experts in a discipline think and express thought.

General categories of analysis to interact with academic texts include the following: (i) purpose; (ii) connections to other texts and deconstruction of assumptions; (iii) context; (iv) author's thesis; (v) evaluation of the author's arguments; and (vi) consequences of the author's arguments.

6.9.1 PURPOSE

Expert readers approach an academic text with a specific purpose, for example, to explore learning theories to improve their teaching practice, to examine the effects of invasive species in a certain ecosystem, to understand the role of the clergy in medieval Europe, to analyze the formation of new synapses in the human brain, to understand the application of a theory, to analyze the use of swimming pool images in Lucrecia Martel's films, or to examine the characteristics of dysfunctional families in Alejandro Casavalle's theater productions. As novice readers in academic disciplines, when students—particularly lower-year students—read an academic text, they do not have a purpose of their own. They read because their teachers tell them to read. They read because the course syllabus contains a list of assigned readings. And they read because they will be tested on the assigned texts. So, we need to create problems, situations, or questions that students will feel motivated to solve or answer, and for which finding the solution or answer will create the need to read academic texts. In this case, students will approach a text in order to do something other than read the text to comply with external requirements.

Continuing with the previous examples, my students read the law review articles to learn about the legality of comparative advertising. They needed to know what may and may not be compared legally in order to design an advertising campaign. My colleague's students approached the reading of *Time for Outrage* to capture the spirit of resistance in the book and adapt it to a romantic play. In these cases, the texts are a means to achieve an end that students care about. In traditional Instruction-paradigm classes, reading academic texts is an end in itself in many cases.

Academic Reading and Deep Learning

A useful tool to help students understand the purpose of their reading is the elaboration of reading guides in the form of questions. The reading guides help students navigate through the texts and focus on their fundamental issues. They may also be helpful to preview the readings in class and explain their relevance and purpose. But reading guides are effective only if they are part of the deep learning process. If we simply assign texts for students to read and give them reading guides, students will still approach the reading of those texts superficially.

6.9.2 CONNECTIONS TO OTHER TEXTS AND DECONSTRUCTION OF ASSUMPTIONS

Academic texts are never written in isolation. They have implicit and explicit connections to other texts. The author refers to other articles or books in the literature review and elsewhere throughout the texts. Unlike authors of textbooks specifically designed for the college classroom, the author of an academic text makes reference to other theories, debates, and ideas that are part of the discipline without necessarily explaining them for nonexperts. The author of an academic text writes for other disciplinary expert readers, that is, peers in the community of knowledge. The expert reader is fully aware of these conversations and discourses. So, the author takes for granted that his or her readers know these debates and the works of other authors that he or she is referring to. Thus, the meaning of a text does not depend solely on the content of the text itself. It depends in large part on its relations with these other—prior, contemporary, and subsequent—discourses (del Rosal, 2009). But students, particularly those in the lower years who are novices in the discipline, ignore most of these disciplinary conversations. So, they need to become aware of the importance of identifying these connections and assumptions and learn how to deconstruct them. They need to be aware that if they ignore a theory, idea, or argument that the author is alluding to without explaining it, they need to consult other texts, such as textbooks, encyclopedias, reference books, other academic texts, or reliable web sites. This will help them uncover and understand those ideas and arguments. Similarly, if the author refers to a debate in the discipline or is responding to another article or book, they need to briefly read about these debates or articles in other publications. Table 6.2 defines the possible connections of a text with other texts and its environment. Although some of these connections are genre specific and may not be present in all academic texts, awareness of these possible connections which a text may have facilitates deep reading.

TABLE 6.2 Connections of a text.

Text	The information explicitly provided by the author.
Context	The historical, cultural, political, and social background of the text.
Subtext	The author's purpose, agenda, and voice.
Inter text	The connections between the text and other texts. • Horizontal inter text: the connections between the reader and the writer. • Vertical inter text: the connections between the text and other texts (prior, contemporary, and subsequent).
Hypertext	The links to other texts or to other parts of the text.
Pre-text	The ideological assumptions, that the reader brings to the text.
The repressed text	The texts that the author consciously or unconsciously fails to consider and incorporate in his or her text.

6.9.3   CONTEXT

Understanding the context helps students understand the background, environment, and circumstances in which the author wrote the text. In order to analyze the context of any given text, students need to be encouraged to do some research about the author. They need to understand whether the author's opinion usually reflects the mainstream school of thought in the discipline or whether the author writes from the margins of the discipline (Carlino, 2008). Students need to analyze the audience of the text as well as when and where the text was written. In order to truly appreciate the context, it is helpful to encourage students to read two or three articles written by the same author. For example, a colleague, who teaches Introduction to Contemporary Philosophy for majors and nonmajors, asked his students to read an article written by Noam Chomsky. Chomsky wrote

Academic Reading and Deep Learning

this article mainly for academic scholars. The article transpires a certain political agenda, which students find difficult to identify by reading only this text. My colleague's students found it useful to read a few articles that Chomsky wrote on Barack Obama and Mitt Romney for a general educated audience but not necessarily for experts. The themes of these articles were closer to the students' experiences and backgrounds. This helped them get a unique insight into Chomsky's ideas. When reading the assigned article, this familiarity with Chomsky's ideas became very helpful in understanding the assigned text. Another important factor in helping readers become immersed in the deep reading process is knowledge background. Hirsch refers to this knowledge background as cultural literacy, which he defines as "the network of information that all competent readers possess. It is the background information, stored in their minds, that enables them to pick up a newspaper and read it with an adequate level of comprehension, getting the point, grasping the implications, relating what they read to the unstated context, which alone gives meaning to what they read" (Hirsch, 1987).We need to know where students are and help them both activate and increase their knowledge background. The richer their knowledge background is, the deeper their understanding and recreation of the text are.

6.9.4 AUTHOR'S THESIS

Students also need to learn how to identify the author's thesis, main claims, and arguments dealing with the issues they are interested in. For this purpose, it is important to encourage students to try to understand what the author intends to do. They need to consider whether, for example, the author intends to challenge an existing position, he or she wants to examine a variable that previous researchers have missed, or intends to apply a theory or a concept in a new way. Students need to learn how to identify the different positions used by the author as well as the arguments and evidence used to support these positions.

Bean recommends an activity where students are asked to write what a paragraph says and what it does. This exercise helps students identify the purpose and function of academic texts (Bean, 1996).

128   Facilitating Deep Learning

6.9.5   EVALUATION OF THE AUTHOR'S ARGUMENTS

One of the most important aspects of reading academic texts is evaluating the strength or validity of the author's arguments. Many students, especially those who are in Perry's (1970) dualism stage of cognitive development or in Belenky's (1997) silence or received knowledge stages, tend to see academic texts as authoritative and defer to whatever ideas the texts express without ever questioning them. Thus, students need to recognize the importance of not taking the author's argument at face value; and they need to learn to challenge the author's arguments.

For this purpose, we need to help students learn to judge the argument's effectiveness in making its claims and considering the evidence the author offers in support of his or her claims. Students also need to assess the logical reasoning followed by the author and how to ponder possible counter-arguments. Furthermore, they need to assess any inconsistencies of thought and the relevance of examples and evidence.

One reading strategy that usually helps students evaluate the strength of the author's thesis and arguments is to focus on the text structure (Collins, 1994). Knowledge of the text structure permits readers to identify the organization of the text. This, in turn, helps readers see how the author develops his or her arguments, how he or she makes connections between arguments, and the hierarchy of these arguments. For example, in many academic texts—particularly those reporting research studies—topics, main ideas, and details are organized hierarchically into superordinate, co-ordinate, and subordinate ideas (Caverly, 1997). Prediction and inference of the content of the text are also helpful. The reader may anticipate the content by looking at the title, organization, abstract, and any visual information, such as charts, tables, and appendixes. This permits the reader to look for additional information in other texts and skip the parts of the texts that are not relevant for the reader's purpose. It also allows readers to anticipate any gaps in their knowledge, which may lead to comprehension failures. Solving comprehension failures involves recognizing that as readers we do not always know everything about a text and that we need to come up with solutions to deal with these deficiencies. Collins (1994) identifies the following techniques that readers use to remedy comprehension failures: "forming a mental image, rereading, adjusting the rate

Academic Reading and Deep Learning

of reading, searching the text to identify unknown words, and predicting meaning that lies ahead."

Another factor that helps students evaluate the author's arguments consists of identifying the hidden or repressed texts. In most academic and professional texts, the author consciously or unconsciously ignores or fails to consider other texts such as books, articles, theses, conference presentations, and papers that directly or indirectly deal with the author's arguments. These other texts may offer a different perspective to the author's arguments. They may elaborate upon opposing views. In some cases, these repressed texts may point to flaws in the arguments under analysis. In other cases, they may even contradict the author's arguments. So, uncovering these repressed texts helps students better assess the author's arguments by considering the full spectrum of ideas, theories, and concepts that surround the arguments the author is trying to make.

6.9.6 CONSEQUENCES OF THE AUTHOR'S ARGUMENTS

Finally, it is important to help students consider the nonimmediate consequences of the arguments used by the author. This includes helping students reflect about the implications and applications of the author's thesis. As for the other categories, it is also necessary to help students make connections to other texts, to relate the arguments to other topics learned in class, and to relate the author's arguments to their own experience. For example, a colleague who teaches a course on terrorism in a political science program asks students to read an article on terrorism in the aviation industry where the author proposes a series of measures to prevent terrorist acts. Although these measures may undoubtedly deter new terrorist attacks, a careful look at the author's proposal leads to the—unstated—conclusion that if this proposal were adopted, very few people would qualify to fly. So, students usually argue that measures that will exclude the majority of passengers from flying are not a very sensible way of controlling terrorism.

Atwell (2007) cautions that the teaching of these categories of analysis should not be done at the expense of removing students from what she refers to as the "reading zone," a state when readers are captivated by the

130   Facilitating Deep Learning

text. Atwell's concern is allayed when reading is done in a context of a motivating problem or question, authentic performances, and the discipline's whole game.

6.10 DISCIPLINE-SPECIFIC READING STYLES

Each discipline—or to be more precise each community of knowledgeable peers organized around a discipline or some aspects of a discipline, or around a discipline in one particular context, such as geographic—has its own specific way of reading texts. For example, when reading a medical text describing a patient's symptoms, the community of knowledgeable peers of American physicians tends to figure out the causes of those symptoms by the ease with which relevant examples come to mind (Groopman, 2007). A community of Islamic scholars tends not to question academic texts, particularly when those are somehow derived from sacred texts. Method actors, who follow Strasberg's teachings and Stalisnavsky's ideas, have a very distinct way of approaching a text, which differs from the way actors from other communities of knowledge read texts. Method actors approach a text by immersing themselves in an intellectual process of analysis of the character's motives and goals. They read a text in order to figure out each character's—unstated—history, motivation, relation to other characters, and his or her objective in each scene (Stanislavsky, 1936). For communities of knowledge formed by nonmethod actors, such as those that follow Harold Guskin's teachings, the process of deep reading is a process of letting words activates the unconscious repertoire of images, ideas, and thoughts.

> [First,]"the actor looks down at the phrase and breathes in and out while he (sic) reads the words to himself, giving himself time to let the phrase into his head. Then he looks up from the page and says the line, no longer reading but speaking. Taking [...] time to breath in and out while [...] looking down at the page to read the phrase for [oneself] allows [the reader/actor] to access whatever unconscious thoughts or images it evokes" (Guskin, 2003).

Brooke Shields (1987) compares the reading process of scripts with the making of suits. She argues that actors and directors need to be prepared

Academic Reading and Deep Learning   131

to modify the text if the actor does not feel comfortable with it. Shields (1987) asserts that "when you put [the text/suit] on an actor you have to adjust it because it doesn't necessarily fit." Guskin (2003) uses a different metaphor to exemplify the same idea. He equates this reading method with Freud's notion of word association.

When reading an academic text, it is important to help students identify and embrace the reading style of the community of knowledgeable peers they are trying to join.

6.11 SPECIFIC CATEGORIES OF ANALYSIS: AN EXAMPLE FROM THE SCHOLARSHIP OF TEACHING AND LEARNING

In order to analyze texts within a certain community of knowledgeable peers, it is also necessary to employ some categories of analysis that reflect the way in which members of that community read texts, think, and express thoughts. A disciplinary category of analysis is a framework to evaluate those thoughts and the discourse from within the discipline. As with general categories of analysis, a disciplinary expert reader has incorporated these categories. He or she analyzes an academic text by unconsciously sifting through the text with a colander of categories of analysis.

In order to understand how specific categories of analysis work, let's look at an example from the scholarship of teaching and learning. When reading about pedagogical practices, we can employ categories that can help us assess the effectiveness of the teaching method, initiative, or practice analyzed in the text. These categories, which are specific to communities of knowledgeable peers involved in teaching in higher education, can include the following categories formulated as questions:
- Does the practice foster a deep approach to learning?
- Does the teaching practice take into account students'existing cognitive structures?
- Does the teaching practice create an adequate cognitive conflict?
- Does the teaching practice help students use higher-order cognitive skills?
- Does the practice promote metacognition?
- Does the teaching practice intrinsically motivate students?

132   Facilitating Deep Learning

- Does the teaching practice help students discover knowledge by themselves?
- Does the teaching practice help students make connections to a larger framework?

Shulman's (2004) signature pedagogy dimensions are also helpful for this purpose, even if the teaching practice under analysis is not considered signature. These categories include the analysis of the teaching practice's (i) surface structure, that is, the observable behavioral features of the teaching practice; (ii) deep structure, that is, the underlying intentions, rationale, or theory that the practice models; (iii) tacit structure, that is, the values and dispositions that the practice implicitly models; and (v) shadow structure, that is, the absent aspects of the practice.

These categories of analysis help the reader examine an academic text on teaching and learning profoundly. In the example, the categories of analysis help us assess the effectiveness of a teaching method described in a text. These categories are not to be understood as rigid. For other texts in the scholarship of teaching and learning, one can think of variations of these categories and even different categories. Ideally, as students become more expert readers they should learn to formulate their own specific questions and to reformulate and adapt these categories of analysis to their specific purposes.

6.12 GENERAL STUDY STRATEGIES

The use of general study techniques also helps students read texts deeply, provided they are taught within a deep reading context and not merely as isolated tools. Effective readers employ a myriad of useful general study techniques when reading. These include: underlying, highlighting, making notes on the text, drawing, taking notes, producing outlines, transcribing main ideas, and crossing out irrelevant information. Like the categories of academic text reading, these general strategies need to be taught and practiced in the university and college classroom. A popular method that helps practice some—but not all—of these strategies is known as SQ3R. First, students learn to survey a text; that is, they have a quick glance at the title, summary, and conclusion in order to have a general idea of the

Academic Reading and Deep Learning

content of the text. Then they formulate questions about the main aspects of the text. After that, students read the text—or a part of it—to look for the answers to these questions. Finally, they recite the answers to these questions, that is, they paraphrase the answers, write them down, and think of the implications and consequences of those answers. A variation of this method includes the addition of other steps, such as relating, or, making connections, reviewing the answers to those questions, and writing about these answers. Research studies show that although this method may be effective, students achieve deeper reading levels when all strategies are taught simultaneously and several methods are combined (Hermida, 2009; 1997; Munro, 2003).

6.13 CONSTRUCTIVE ALIGNMENT

Another factor that helps promote a deep reading environment is constructive alignment. As discussed before, John Biggs proposes aligned teaching to foster a deep approach to reading and learning. In aligned teaching, "the objectives define what we should be teaching, how we should be teaching it; and how we could know how well students have learned it" (Biggs and Tang, 2007). So, in order to promote a deep approach to reading, we need to design a course where the main goals should be to encourage students to take a deep approach to reading, to use higher-order cognitive and meta-cognitive skills to understand and process academic texts, and to negotiate meanings with the author of academic texts. It is important to make those goals explicit to students, as most students tend to see only information as the sole content of courses (Herteis, 2007). Similarly, as students tend to value what happens in class over what takes place outside class, we should give time for students to read in class. Otherwise, students may perceive that reading academic texts is a marginal activity done only in isolation.

In order to promote students to take a deep approach to reading, the teaching and learning activities have to be designed in consonance with the proposed goals. If, for example, we lecture from the textbooks, students will probably not read the texts, as they will rely solely on our oral explanations and the notes they take from these lectures (Hermida, 2009). The evaluation has to measure whether students use higher-order cognitive skills to read assigned materials, whether they can effectively negotiate meanings with the author, whether they can evaluate the strength of the author's arguments, whether they can deconstruct hidden assumptions in the texts, and whether they can see the nonimmediate implications and applications of the author's arguments (Carlino, 1999).

However, as discussed earlier, aligned teaching should not become an inflexible and rigid tool. We should make room in our classes for oblique, indirect, and incidental learning through reading. We should also allow students ample opportunities to freely formulate their own reading and learning goals.

TABLE 6.3 Media literacy: Learning to produce and interpret media texts.

Media texts

The revolution in media and global communications in the last few decades has transformed the way we apprehend reality, the way we express thought, and the way we communicate. It has also shaken the structure of societies globally. In addition, it has radically altered the dissemination and production of information and knowledge.

Media texts are pervasive in the professions and academic disciplines. At a general level, media texts influence and even define key concepts of the disciplines and professions. For example, media texts contribute to define the public notion of health. There is a perceived expectation among both the general public and health professionals that the ideal healthy body must conform to images routinely shown in Hollywood films, American television shows, and fashion magazines. At a more specific level, members of the knowledgeable communities use social media, online articles, blogs, documentaries, and TV news programs to construct knowledge and negotiate meanings.

Media Literacy

Media literacy places audiovisual and other media languages at the forefront of classroom teaching and not as mere supplements to traditional classroom and print-based education. Media literacy is "the process of critically analyzing and learning to create one's own messages – in print, audio, video, and multimedia, with emphasis on the learning and teaching of these skills through using mass media texts" (Hobbs, 1998). It also includes the cognitive and affective processes involved in viewing and producing audiovisual materials. Media literacy recognizes the unique advantages that audiovisual media have as powerful transforming tools. When used as a tool in the classroom, the power of audiovisual media enables a level of interactivity and critical thinking not seen in traditional schooling (Goldfarb, 2002).

Media Literacy and Media Texts at the Margins of University and College Education

The Instruction-paradigm universities and colleges were laid in an era of nearly total print dominance. The central educational concepts articulated were print-centered, where the main objective has been to transmit knowledge contained in books and articles in the form of lectures for students to reproduce in print form through exams and essays.

Although there is a history of media education in Europe and North America that dates back to the end of the Second World War, media education has been at the margins of formal university and college teaching. Media literacy was developed in primary and secondary schools, as well as

Academic Reading and Deep Learning

TABLE 6.3 *(Continued)*

in vocational schools. In the last two decades, pedagogical authors have been advocating for the development of media literacy across the university and college curricula (Goldfarb, 2002; Hobbs, 1998). However, at the university setting, media literacy was relegated to some communications or film studies programs. It has not yet entered the curriculum in the majority of disciplines. Very few teachers regularly help students learn the conventions of media language in their disciplines.

The Importance of Teaching Media within the Disciplines

Members of knowledgeable communities are involved in the production and analysis of media texts in a wide array of academic disciplines and professional fields. These texts have both a general common language and a specific language that is unique to each discipline and field.

Because of the importance that media has in these fields, the university and college curricula should include the teaching of media literacy. Teaching the conventions of media language, alongside the analysis of substantive disciplinary contents, gives students the necessary tools to both "read" and produce media texts. From a pedagogical point of view, a focus on media texts motivates students, who are immersed in a visually and-technologically oriented culture. At the same time, this helps students acquire the skills, competences, and practices that are necessary to become fully fledged members of the communities of knowledgeable peers that they aspire to join.

6.14. SUMMARY

Learning how to read academic texts deeply requires the same actions needed to learn any other task in a profound way. The deep reading process begins with a careful evaluation of the learner's cognitive structure. Then, it needs the creation of an interesting and motivating problem, situation, or question that produces a cognitive conflict in the students. This cognitive conflict, which derives from interaction with peers, must lead students to feel that they need to interact with academic texts in a profound way by discussing texts together with their peers and by making nonarbitrary and substantive connections between new knowledge and their existing cognitive structures. These connections must activate students' higher-order cognitive and metacognitive competences, which requires the use of general and discipline-specific categories of analysis on the individual and collective planes.

Categories of analysis are tools that help readers analyze an academic text. General categories of analysis apply to any academic reading situation. These include: (i) purpose; (ii) connections to other texts and deconstruction of assumptions; (iii) context; (iv) author's thesis; (v) evaluation of the author's arguments; and (vi) consequences of the author's arguments. Apart from these general categories, each discipline has its own specific categories of analysis, which reflect the way experts in those disciplines think and read.

The deep reading process is possible only if students are intrinsically motivated to engage in this process. Helping students play the whole game of disciplinary experts facilitates their intrinsic motivation. Engagement in this process leads to conceptual change and a move from one community of knowledgeable peers to another one or from the periphery of a community to its center. For the change to be meaningful, it requires a careful evaluation of the whole process.

When we design an aligned course that places academic reading at the forefront of the course and encourage students' interaction with academic texts through categories of analysis and general study strategies in a deep learning environment, students tend to take a deep approach to reading.

The next chapter will deal with writing. It will examine both how to write in order to learn deeply and how to learn to write deeply.

PRACTICE CORNER

1. Think of a course you are teaching or one that you have recently taught. What specific changes could you introduce to promote a deep approach to reading? How can you motivate students to take a deep approach to reading?

2. Each community of knowledgeable peers has a particular way of reading academic texts. For example, social workers read texts differently than physicians. Engineers read texts differently than linguists. How do members of your discipline read an academic text? Think of your own approach to an academic text in your discipline or specialized field. Try to identify what you do and what you think when reading a text. What are the specific categories of analysis in your discipline or area? Can you formulate these categories in the form of questions?

3. As suggested in Table 6.3, apart from reading books and articles, one can also read films and other media texts. Are there any films or other media texts in your discipline or about your discipline that have a discipline-specific language or categories of analysis? How

Academic Reading and Deep Learning 137

can you help students develop media literacy in your academic discipline or professional field?

4. Soccer players and coaches "read" a soccer match. They can "read" what their opponents are doing, the players' tasks and functions, changes in ball possession, and what strategies the opposing team is following to attack and defend, among many other issues. Think of your favorite sport (or another sport if soccer is your favorite one). Watch a game and discuss how to "read" the game. What specific categories of analysis can you come up with in order to "read" the game? How can you use the analogy of "reading" a sports game in the college or university classroom?

5. Think of international students with limited fluency in English taking a course in your discipline together with native speakers of English. What strategies can you adopt so as to encourage the non-native speakers to read academic texts deeply in English?

6. Learning is both an individual and a collective enterprise. Design collaborative reading activities so that students can read together and negotiate meanings collectively in your discipline.

7. In *The Actor Speaks*, Patsy Rodenburg (2000) describes the meaning of "owning words" as a process of knowing words "on three different levels: in the head, in the heart and then in the whole body." As part of this process, an actor knows words deeply and thoroughly and can feel words coming to him or her from different places. How can you know words (and a text) on these three levels? Is it possible to own words while reading an academic text outside the realm of theater and literature? What does owning words mean in your discipline or in your specific area of specialization? Is owning words part of the deep learning process?

8. How can you incorporate social media to help students read academic texts deeply? Think of an article or a series of articles you want your students to read and a corresponding activity involving social media.

9. Evaluating the author's arguments is an essential aspect of deep reading. Suppose you teach an introductory course in your discipline for first-year students. All of these students are in Perry's (1970) dualism stage and in Belenky's (1997) silence stage. How

138 Facilitating Deep Learning

can you help these students challenge an author's arguments in an academic text in your discipline? What can you do so that students will approach the text in a deep fashion?

10. In the Los Angeles version of the play *Leap of Faith*, written by Janus Cercone and Glenn Slater and directed by Rob Ashford, Marla McGowan, signs the song *I Can Read You like an Open Book*. What do you think the song means? Can you "read" a person? If so, how? What role, if any, plays System 1 thinking in "reading" people? What role, if any, plays System 2 thinking in "reading" people? What signals can you look for in order to "read" people? Should universities and colleges teach students how to "read" people? Should you teach how to "read" people in your discipline? If so, how can you teach students to "read" people deeply?

KEYWORDS

- academic reading
- academic skills
- academic texts
- categories of analysis
- constructive alignment
- deep learning
- deep reading
- deep reading activities
- discipline-specific categories of analysis
- general categories of analysis
- general study strategies
- media literacy
- reading styles
- surface reading

REFERENCES

Bain, K. What the Best College Students Do; The Belknap Press of Harvard University Press: Cambridge, MA, 2012.

Bain, K. What the Best College Teachers Do; Harvard University Press: Cambridge, MA, 2004.

Bain, K.; Zimmerman, J. Understanding Great Teaching. Peer Review 2009, 11, 9.

Bean, J. Engaging Ideas: The Professor's Guide to Integrating Writing, Critical Thinking, and Active Learning in the Classroom; Jossey Bass: San Francisco, 1996.

Belenky, M.; Clinchy, B.; Goldberger, N.; Tarule, J. Women's ways of knowing: The development of self, mind, and voice; Basic Books: New York, 1997.

Biggs, J. What the Student Does: teaching for enhanced learning. Higher Education Research and Development, 1999, 18. 1.

Biggs, J.; Tang, C. Teaching for Quality Learning at University; Open University Press: Maidenhead, 2007.

Bowden, J. and Marton, F. (2000) University of Learning. London: Routledge.

Carlino, F. Evaluación Educacional: Historia, Problemas. Aique: Buenos Aires, 1999.

Carlino, P. Do we write only to teach how to write? Tools to write in foreign language courses. Textos. Didáctica de la lengua y de la literatura, 2008, 49.

Carlino, P. Escribir, Leer y Aprender en la Universidad. Una Introducción a la Alfabetización Académica; Fondo de Cultura Económica: Buenos Aires, 2005.

Caverly, D. Teaching Reading in a Learning Assistance Center, Proceedings of the 17th and 18th Annual Institutes for Learning Assistance Professionals, Tucson, AZ, 1996–1997, 27–42, University of Arizona: University Learning Center, 1997.

Erickson, B. L., Peters, C. B.; Strommer, D. W. Teaching First-Year College Students; Jossey-Bass: San Francisco, 2006.

Gabriel, K. Teaching Unprepared Students: Strategies for Promoting Success and Retention in Higher Education; Stylus Publishing: Sterling, VA, 2008.

Gibbs, G. Improving the quality of student learning; Technical and Educational Services: Bristol, 1992.

Groopman, J. How Doctors Think; Houghton Mifflin Company:New York, 2007.

Guskin, H. How to Stop Acting; Faber and Faber: New York, 2003.

Hermida, J. Strategies to Promote a Deep Approach to Reading. Tomorrow's Professor Digest, 2009, 31, 3 (b).

Hermida, J. The Importance of Teaching Academic Reading Skills in First-Year University Courses.Proceedings of the Association of Atlantic Universities Teaching Showcase, 2009.

Herteis, E. Content Conundrums. PAIDEIA: Teaching and Learning at Mount Allison University, 2007, 3,1.

Hessel, S. Time for Outrage; Twelve: New York, 2011.

Hirsch, E. D. Cultural literacy: What every American needs to know; Houghton Mifflin: Boston: 1987.

Hunt, R. A. Reading and Writing for Real: Why it Matters for Learning. Atlantic Universities' Teaching Showcase, 2004, 137–146.

Light, R. Making the Most of College: Students Speak Their Minds; Harvard University Press: Cambridge, MA, 2001.

Marton, F.; Säljö, R. On Qualitative Differences in Learning — 1: Outcome and Process."British Journal of Educational Psychology 1976, 46, 4.

Millis, B.J. Using Classroom Assessment Techniques (CATs) to Promote Student Learning, Oklahoma Higher Education Teaching and Learning Conference, Oklahoma, April 9–11, 2008.

Munro, J. What Learning Means. International Journal of Learning, 2003, 10.

Novak, J.; Gowin, B. Learning How to Learn; Cambridge University Press: Cambridge, MA, 1984.

Perkins, D. Making Learning Whole. How Seven Principles of Teaching can Transform Education; Jossey-Bass: San Francisco, 2009.

Perry, W. Forms of Intellectual and Ethical Development in the College Years: A Scheme; Hold, Rinehart and Winston: Troy, Mo, 1970.

Rodenburg, P. The Actor Speaks; Palgrave MacMillan: New York, 2000.

Shields, B. The Initiation. From Innocence to Experience: The Pre-Adolescent/Adolescent Journey in the Films of Louis Malle, Pretty Baby and Lacombe Lucien,B.A. Thesis, Princeton University, Princeton, NJ, 1987.

Stanislavski, C. An Actor Prepares; Theatre Arts: New York, 1936.

Tagg, J. The Learning Paradigm College; Anker Publishing Company: Bolton, MA, 2003.

Wendling, B. Why is there Always Time for Their Facebook but not my Textbook?, Oklahoma Higher Education Teaching and Learning Conference, Oklahoma, April 9–11, 2008.

CHAPTER 7

DEEP WRITING

If it sounds like writing, I rewrite it.

— ELMORE LEONARD

CONTENTS

7.1 Introduction 142
7.2 Connection between Writing and Learning 142
7.3 Writing to Learn Deeply 145
7.4 Students' Attitude about Writing 146
7.5 Teaching Students How to Write Academic Texts 147
7.6 The Problem or Situation 149
7.7 Reasons for not Engaging in a Process of Changing Writing
     Styles 149
7.8 Higher-Order Cognitive Processes, Skills, and Competences:
     Encouraging Revision 151
7.9 Playing the Whole Game of Expert Writers: Real Readers 154
7.10 Absence of Grades 156
7.11 Fighting with Your Neighbors 156
7.12 Collaborative Learning 158
7.13 Teacher Feedback and Metacognition 158
7.14 Problems with Teachers' Comments 159
7.15 Summary 161
Practice Corner 162
Keywords 164
References 165

7.1 INTRODUCTION

Until the 1970s, writing had traditionally been relegated to the margins of university and college instruction. Academic writing was a pervasive activity, but teachers did not pay any attention to the writing process in their classes. They simply requested students to write essays for exams and assignments and to write for occasional projects without actually teaching students how to write. Teaching writing was the responsibility of college composition and English classes for first-year students.

With the writing across the curriculum movement in the 1970s and 1980s in the United States, the United Kingdom, and other countries, writing became the focus of much attention in higher education. Today, many teachers usually refer to writing as an essential skill that students need to master. Few, however, actually teach writing in a way that helps students learn deeply how to write. Still fewer teachers effectively teach students how to write in order to learn deeply.

In this chapter, I will first analyze the connection between writing and deep learning. I will then discuss what we can do to help students write to learn deeply in our disciplines. Finally, I will explore strategies to help students learn deeply how to write academic texts in the disciplines.

7.2 CONNECTION BETWEEN WRITING AND LEARNING

There is a heated debate about whether or not writing produces learning and whether deep learning necessitates an instance of writing, that is, whether writing texts leads to deep learning and whether students can learn deeply without writing. Janet Emig (1977) argues that writing constitutes a unique mode of learning. She claims that "writing serves learning uniquely because writing as a process-and product possesses a cluster of attributes that correspond uniquely to certain powerful learning strategies. Higher cognitive functions, such as analysis and synthesis, seem to develop most fully only with the support system of verbal language—particularly, it seems, written language." Emig's claims gave rise to a movement known as Writing to Learn. Its main tenet is that writing enhances learning (Durst and Newell, 1989). Although this proposition is quite attractive,

Deep Writing   143

empirical research has not demonstrated the validity of its claim (Ackerman, 1993; Newell, 1998). There are some studies that show that in certain specific circumstances writing can help improve the learning process. However, there are other studies—sometimes even conducted by the same researchers—that show contradictory results (Klein, 1999).

There are four models that try to explain the connection between writing and learning (Klein, 1999). Two of the following four models appear to help writers learn deeply, at least under some circumstances:

- **Point-of-utterance model**: writers spontaneously generate knowledge without planning and revision. In the point of utterance model, the writer simply writes whatever was already on his or her mind, almost as if he or she were speaking. This model coincides with Bereiter and Scardamalia's (1987) knowledge-telling approach. The basic steps include the mental representation of the writing task, the generation of topic identifiers, and the use of these topic identifiers as cues to retrieve information through a process of "spreading activation." The writer tends to retrieve and write down all the ideas he or she has, until the use of the cues is exhausted. At the same time, the writer draws on appropriate identifiers of discourse knowledge to match the task (e.g., opinion essay). The knowledge-telling model, although appropriate for routine writing tasks, does not foster the generation of new knowledge, because it relies on already established connections between content elements and readily available discourse knowledge. From a biological perspective, it does not generate new neuronal connections in the brain. The point-of-utterance model does not promote learning and does not result in any conceptual change (Gonyea and Anderson, 2009).
- **Forward-search model**: writers externalize ideas in text, reread the text, and then make new inferences based on the text. This model does not lead to deep learning, either. In this model, the writer polishes the coherence and consistency of the text, but there is no fundamental change in the writer's cognitive structure.
- **Genre model**: writers use genre structures to organize relationships among discursive elements of the text and connect elements of knowledge. "A genre is distinguished by a rhetorical intention, expressed through discourse elements that form particular relationships with one another" (Klein, 1999). Each discipline implements genre in its own distinctive way, with different norms about discursive

elements. Klein (1999) himself recognizes that not all genres force writers to engage in a deep learning process. Even within those genres that promote deeper understandings, students have to adopt the goal of composing a text in that specific genre, and they have to implement a strategy involving higher-order cognitive skills to realize this goal in order to produce new knowledge. Similarly, Gonyea and Anderson (2009) find that the genre-based model emphasizes the reorganization of existing knowledge rather than the production of a conceptual change in the students' cognitive structures.

- **Backwards-search model**: writers set rhetorical goals. They derive content subgoals from rhetorical goals and problem-solving goals from content goals.The backward-search model explains the creation of rhetorically good writing and may lead to deep learning in certain circumstances. This model is similar to Bereiter and Scardamalia's (1987) knowledge-transforming model. When writers engage in the knowledge-transforming model of writing, they increase their knowledge acquisition through content-processing and discourse-processing interaction. In the content space, the problems of knowledge and beliefs are considered, whereas in the discourse space, the problems of how to express the content are considered. The output from each space serves as input for the other, so that questions concerning language and syntax choice reshape the meaning of the content, and efforts to express the content direct the ongoing composition. It is this interaction between the problem spaces that provides the stimulus for reflection in writing. The dynamic relationship between the content space and the rhetorical space in the knowledge-transforming model may lead to instances of deep learning.

These models show that when writing is articulated as a cognitive strategy, such as in some types of the genre model and in the backward-search model, students may profit from writing in order to learn deeply (Klein, 1999). Similarly, Bereiter and Scardamalia's (1987) knowledge-transformation model may contribute to deep learning. Bazerman (2009) argues that "it is not simply the act of writing that leads to learning. [...] Learning takes place because of the practices that are engaged as one produces the text. The produced text itself is not that relevant." So, although it may not be affirmed that all writing leads to learning or that there may be no deep learning without an instance of production in writing, these arguments

Deep Writing 145

show that when writing is embedded in a deep learning process, it may enhance the quality of learning. It is not the amount of writing that matters when it comes to achieving the higher-order learning goals. Instead, it is the amount of writing that promotes deep learning that actually matters.

The inconclusiveness of research on the relation between writing and learning also shows that writing in itself is not an essential aspect of the discovery and construction of knowledge. In other words, someone can learn a discipline deeply without routinely engaging in writing. This conclusion is supported by those studies that found deep learning where there was not an instance of production of knowledge in writing (Marton and Saljo, 1976).

7.3 WRITING TO LEARN DEEPLY

What can we do in the classroom to use writing to enhance the learning process? There are various writing formats and types of texts that have shown to enhance learning. Learning can profit from writing if writing takes place within the deep learning context and process that I have discussed throughout the book. This implies that in order to be effective, students must be presented with a problem, situation, or question that generates a cognitive conflict (that arises from interaction with peers) between the new knowledge embedded in the situation, problem, or question and the students' cognitive structure, which the learner is motivated to solve. In order to resolve that conflict, the learner must make—nonarbitrary and substantive—connections between the new knowledge (which must be within the learner's zone of proximal development) and the learner's prior cognitive structure. While doing so, the learner must employ higher-order cognitive and metacognitive skills, processes, and competences both at the individual and collective levels.

To illustrate this point, I will refer to my own experience in using writing to solve a problem. A few years ago, I was invited to lead a full-week educational development workshop abroad for full-time faculty in the sciences. I mentioned the importance of including an instance of writing production in our sessions so that participants could learn deeply about an aspect of teaching and learning. Kaitlyn, who had invited me to lead this workshop, was hesitant about this and did not want me to ask participants to do a writing project. Kaitlyn showed me some research results reported in the literature indicating that writing does not lead to learning (those that I cited earlier, but which at that time I ignored). I mentioned to Kaitlyn that there were other studies showing the opposite results. But I must admit that I was intrigued about Kaitlyn's argument and the line of research she referred to. So, I promised her that I would look into the articles she told me about and that I would report the results of my research back to her and the workshop participants before asking them to do a writing project. So, I had a problem that I was very motivated to solve: whether writing always leads to deep learning or not. I carefully read the articles that Kaitlyn had given me. While reading them, I made notes. My notes were not verbatim. I wrote the gist of each article; I also made connections to the articles I had read and my own experience as a teacher and educational developer. While making these connections, I critically evaluated the research findings, I challenged the authors' claims, I compared the research findings, I formulated some hypotheses, and I came up with some preliminary theories. I wanted to report back my analysis of the research findings and my theories to the workshop participants. So, I wrote workshop notes, following a style that I find interesting to communicate to teachers in educational development events. While writing my analysis and conclusions, I went back to the articles. After I finished the notes, I reread them. I noticed some inconsistencies. I called Kaitlyn, and we had a lengthy discussion. I also had conversations with other colleagues. Then, I felt that I needed to read some research studies that Kaitlyn had not given me. I revised the text again and incorporated the ideas I had while discussing and reading the new material. I finally came up with a text that I could share with Kaitlyn and the workshop participants about my new understanding of the problem, that is, that writing does not always enhance learning, but it may do so if writing is embedded in the deep learning process.

7.4 STUDENTS' ATTITUDE ABOUT WRITING

In a study of the attitudes and activities of Harvard University students, Richard Light (2001) argues that students value good writing and suggestions

Deep Writing   147

to improve it. They particularly appreciate courses that emphasize writing. However, this conclusion is not found in other studies focusing on non-elite universities and colleges. For most students—and faculty—writing is painful. They tend to avoid writing and postpone it until the deadline. Most experience writer's block and feel frustrated when writing (Boice, 2000).

These feelings are exacerbated when students read teachers' comments on their papers. Teachers tend to read students' papers as if they were final products for publication. Teachers respond to most writing as if it were a final draft, thus reinforcing an extremely constricted notion of composing. As I will develop later in this chapter, these comments often reflect the application of a single ideal standard rather than criteria that take into account how composing constraints can affect writing performance. Furthermore, teachers' marks and comments usually take the form of abstract and vague prescriptions and directives that students find difficult to interpret. These comments rarely seem to expect students to revise the text beyond the surface level. These responses to texts give students a very limited and limiting notion of writing, for they fail to provide students with the understanding that writing involves producing a text that evolves over time. For these reasons, many students dread writing papers for university and college.

7.5   TEACHING STUDENTS HOW TO WRITE ACADEMIC TEXTS

In this section, I will discuss the process of how to help our students learn to write in the disciplines we teach. Here, the writing is the specific target, not the discipline's content.

Students learn how to write in the same way they learn other competences, skills, and practices. But, writing—like many other complex processes—presents also some specific issues that need to be taken into account.

In order to learn how to master disciplinary writing deeply, students need to be faced with a problem or situation, that their current disciplinary literacy level is not sufficient to solve or to effectively deal with the situation faced, that is, students' writing is the problem and the new knowledge arising from the problem or situation is about a different writing style (or a higher level of writing) that students have not yet mastered. Additionally, students need to be motivated to do something about this conflict. The challenge—in this case learning to write at the new disciplinary level—must be within the students' zone of proximal development. While working to solve this conflict, students need to make—nonarbitrary and substantive—connections between the new writing genre and style and their current writing style. This process must encourage students to use higher-order cognitive and metacognitive skills, processes, practices, and competences. Students also need to negotiate meanings collectively with their peers. They also need to reflect about the process of the construction of their new disciplinary literacy and the resulting conceptual changes. For example, a colleague of mine teaches a Communications Systems course in an electrical and computer engineering undergraduate program. His students were motivated to discuss the possible changes to energy efficiency standards for information and communications technology equipment that the International Telecommunication Union (ITU) was considering. The ITU in Geneva launched an invitation to stakeholders from across industry and civil society to provide input about the changes in energy-efficiency standards. My colleague's students were particularly interested in providing input about the energy-efficiency metrics and measurement methods for small networking equipment used in homes and small enterprises. So, my colleague encouraged them to make a written presentation to the ITU. The students worked hard on the content and submitted their report to the ITU. An ITU officer contacted the students. He told them that he was impressed with their work, but he had to reject their presentation, because it did not comply with many—discursive—formalities. Their teacher explained to the students that their writing style did not coincide with the style usually used in industry communications with international intergovernmental organizations. So, students decided to resubmit their presentation. They asked their teacher for presentations to standardization processes. Students deconstructed, analyzed, and discussed the language style of these presentations. Students compared them with the format and style of their original presentation. They made changes. They read them several times. They made revisions and discussed their changes. Then, they gave a new draft to their teacher. Students expressly asked the teacher

Deep Writing 149

to comment on the language of the presentation. The teacher gave them feedback, which students incorporated. Then, students submitted the new version of their proposal, which was accepted. Finally, the teacher helped students reflect about their learning process. Students reconstructed every step they took until they submitted the new version of the proposal. They even reflected about the conventions of presentations related to standardization matters.

Now let's break down the process of helping our students write in a number of steps; as well, let's analyze each of these steps, as we did earlier with the deep learning process.

7.6 THE PROBLEM OR SITUATION

Expert academic writers generally engage in writing in order to find a solution to a problem (Bean, 1996). Designing a problem for our students to solve is one of the most important elements of teaching writing. The problem has to attract students' attention. Students need to care enough to want to resolve the problem. The problem has to lead students to recognize that their existing literacy skills and knowledge are not sufficient to solve the problem or face the situation.

7.7 REASONS FOR NOT ENGAGING IN A PROCESS OF CHANGING WRITING STYLES

When faced with a problem or situation that requires students to change the way they write, students may or may not engage in a process of learning to write differently. In other words, they may or may not adopt the goal of composing a text in a new genre (Klein, 1999). There are several reasons for this phenomenon, which are worth exploring.

First, the problem or situation that we create to help students change their writing styles may not deal with a situation that leads students to realize that they need to change the way they write. This happens when, for example, a teacher assigns students a situation where they have to resolve a problem or express their opinions, or even research a theory. These are all issues that may lead to student learning if appropriately embedded in the deep learning process, but students will not necessarily change the way they write to solve a problem, express their opinion, or research a theory if the task in question does not help them see that they need to modify their writing. Students tend to believe that they can already write clearly and effectively. After all, they have been writing since they were in grade school. So, the problem or situation must lead them to discover that the way they write is in fact ineffective to accomplish the task.

Second, the problem may not be motivating enough for students to want to engage in a process of changing their writing. Recall that Ken Bain (2004) argues that students will embark on a deep learning process only if they face a problem, question, or situation that they find significant, intriguing or beautiful. Students need to come to understand for themselves the importance of changing their writing. One of the most powerful motivating factors is when students feel the need to become part of the community of knowledgeable peers or, as Smith (1988) puts it, to join the club. For example, when I taught twelfth-grade English as a foreign language in South America in an all boys' high school, I designed an activity where students were matched with pen pals from the United States. Those boys who were matched with girls found that their writing was not enough to impress these girls, which all wanted to do. So, they worked hard at improving the way they wrote in English.

Third, the new level of writing may be outside the students' zone of proximal development. For example, in a first-year college course, students who still write as high school students may not all of a sudden write like experienced disciplinary experts. This literacy level is completely outside their zone of proximal development. We need to carefully evaluate the writings level of our students and take them gradually to higher levels within their zones of proximal development.

Fourth, the cognitive conflict does not arise from social interaction. Students need to come to the realization that their writing capabilities are not effective to deal with the situation or problem through interaction with their peers. When the conflict is perceived as purely individual or exclusively as something induced by the teacher, it will not produce the desired effect of encouraging students to embark on a deep learning process to change their approach to writing.

Deep Writing   151

Fifth, the problem or situation is not clear for students, or it gives so many instructions that it restricts students' freedom to engage in meaningful writing. We need to define boundaries clearly. "Good assignments clearly define the boundaries within which students are free to write. Writers must have some freedom to take positions, develop ideas, and choose language that communicates what they have to say. Freedom becomes meaningful and constructive only within boundaries, and unclear boundaries tend to restrict freedom by making every move seem potentially a wrong move" (Gottschalk and Hjortshoj, 2003). Gottschalk and Hjortshoj (2003) caution us about the inclusion of counterproductive clarifications in writing assignments. They argue that "teachers often obscure the boundaries of an assignment by offering suggestions, hints, examples, and clarifications that imply a hidden agenda and thus qualify the freedom that they have previously defined. Students should know where your role as the teacher ends and where their roles, choices, and responsibilities as writers begin."

Finally—and this applies to every single step of the teaching writing process—deep learning will not occur if the teacher does not create a stress-free, safe, and enjoyable climate. An encouraging and trusting environment is essential for any learning endeavor. If teachers do not care about their students, if they do not trust that they can achieve the fullest potential, and if they do not hold very high expectations of their students, then students will probably not embark on the challenging deep learning process.

7.8 HIGHER-ORDER COGNITIVE PROCESSES, SKILLS, AND COMPETENCES: ENCOURAGING REVISION

Expert writers engage in several cognitive activities while writing. After having identified a problem, expert writers obtain data from other sources, interview people, talk to colleagues, make notes, write several drafts, reread their drafts, revise, take some time off to think about their ideas, and make new revisions (Bean, 1996). These activities usually imply that writers employ higher-order cognitive skills, such as reading critically, analyzing, applying, evaluating, and theorizing. Expert writers also edit their drafts, but they generally do so when they consider that their drafts

152   Facilitating Deep Learning

are ready to be published. Editing for spelling, punctuation, grammar, and even sentence structure does not require the use of higher-order cognitive skills and competences.

We need to encourage students to engage in the process of critically analyzing the problem, finding a solution, writing, rereading, revising, and reformulating their ideas in writing, because this is the process that expert writers follow to write effectively. Students need to learn how to embrace this process in order to be able to write as experts.

The problem with many students is that they tend not to engage in this process. Students tend to consider that their first draft is the last one and that this draft is ready to be handed in to the teacher, who, after all, will know what it means. So, students' first and only drafts usually look like the first drafts of expert writers, that is, there is no clear solution to the problem, thoughts are disconnected, the organization is poor, and there are many editing problems. The main difference is that the first drafts of expert writers are drafts that only the writers read; these drafts will undergo several layers of revisions in ideas, focus, structure, organization, and even spelling and grammar. Table 7.1 shows the very first draft of this chapter. As you can see, it is full of mistakes, inconsistencies, unfinished ideas, and structural problems.

So, it is very important to help students understand the importance of rereading and making extensive revisions. How can we do this? First, we need to bear in mind that there are two kinds of revisions: (i) personal revisions, where the expert writers revise their drafts before submission to an editor for publication, and (ii) editor-or reviewer-mandated revisions, where the expert writer must incorporate the suggestions and make the changes indicated by the editors and reviewers. "Most experienced writers revise their work extensively as a malleable substance before they submit a complete draft" (Sommers, 1982). Once expert writers feel that their work is ready for the readers to read, they submit it for publication. In academia, most publications need to be peer reviewed. And in commercial literature, most publications have to be approved by several editors. Peer reviewers and editors usually offer many suggestions for changes. After all, it is their job to do so. Many expert writers are reluctant to introduce these changes. Not because they are nonsensical—although anyone who has submitted a manuscript to a journal or publisher knows that in many

Deep Writing

cases they are—but because the expert writer feels that he or she has already decided that the text is done. The writer had finished the text before, when he or she sent it for publication. Nancy Sommers (1982) refers to this moment as the point in which the text solidifies. At this point, the text is no longer malleable. It is solid. Except for a few typos here and there, expert writers refuse to revise the text. Most still do, of course, as otherwise their texts will not be published. But, they do so reluctantly without much effort and, in many cases, without employing those higher-order cognitive and metacognitive processes that they did employ while revising their texts before they solidified. "Student writing, by contrast, solidifies at the moment it hits the page. The student has never lingered in the first stage of writing during which revision usually takes place for experienced writers" (Sommers, 1982). This problem is compounded by the type of suggestions we usually offer our students for revision. Nancy Sommers (1982) vividly exemplifies this process: "when we simply give students the opportunity to revise their papers without little guidance, they tend to make only cosmetic changes. When we offer detailed suggestions, students confine their revisions to the changes we recommend, leaving us in the awkward position of evaluating the fruits of our own labor. Peer reviews from other students often yield superficial revisions." So, Sommers proposes delaying that sense of completion of the student submission. Again, how can we do this? How can we delay this feeling that the text is prematurely finished?

Finkel (1999) suggests creating a dialog on paper between the student and the teacher and among students themselves (Finkel, 1999). John Tagg (2003), who was an English teacher at Palomar Community College, separates the grade from the comments on his students' papers. He believes that if he gives students a grade accompanied by comments on their papers, students will look at the grades and not the comments; or they will read the comments superficially without acting upon them, particularly if the grade corresponds to their expectations. Katherine Gottschalk and Keith Hjortshoj (2003) recommend that we need to tell our students how well their papers worked and offer suggestions that might be useful in further revisions.

These are all very interesting but partial solutions to the problem of teaching writing. We have all tried them in one way or another in our own classes. Still, students do not always seem to engage in further revisions.

The key to this problem is to fully understand the whole process of expert writers and not to focus only on revisions and suggestions for revisions. The whole game includes real readers, absence of grades, and a myriad of academic and nonacademic activities.

7.9 PLAYING THE WHOLE GAME OF EXPERT WRITERS: REAL READERS

The most substantial difference between expert writers and students is that expert writers write to communicate with real readers. In contrast, students write, at best, to communicate with their teachers, and, at worst, to get a grade in a course. Even when we ask the other students in the class to act as peer reviewers, the student writer feels this is still a very artificial process. So, we cannot ask students to engage in the process of revisions and reformulations that expert writers follow when we deprive our students of the most important aspect of this process: real readers.

Giving students the possibility of having a real audience is an essential aspect of what David Perkins (2009) refers to as playing the whole game. You can't play soccer without a ball. You can't write like expert writers without real readers. Perkins suggests that if you cannot let your students play the whole game, you need to create for them at least a junior version of the whole game. For example, if you want your students to learn how to play soccer, instead of playing 11 on 11 in an 80-by-120-yard (73.15-by-109.72-meter) field with a professional No. 5 ball in two halftimes of 45 min each, you mayplay 8 on 8 in a smaller field with a No. 4 ball. But students will still be playing soccer. They can still play soccer if they play for 30 min periods instead of 45. They can even play without the offside rule, as I did when I was a child growing up in a soccer-intensive culture. But no one can play soccer without a ball. It would not be soccer. Likewise, no writer can play the game of expert writers without real readers. We need to provide authentic opportunities for our students to reach their own readers.

My colleague Jane teaches a fourth-year undergraduate course for majors in any discipline who plan to apply to graduate programs. She asked her students to write an admissions essay to their program of choice. She

Deep Writing

told her students that she would give them plenty of advice on their writing, and if they wanted they could submit that essay as part of the admissions application. She made it clear to her students that she would give them the kind of advice that is appropriate in the circumstances and that she would not suggest ideas or even correct spelling mistakes as this might be incompatible with the admissions process. The results were extraordinary. Students engaged in a writing process resembling that of expert writers. She simply created the problem, which was connected to their lives. She helped them realize that they needed to improve their writing to be accepted into graduate school. In addition, she encouraged their revision without becoming any of the types of graders that Katherine Gottschalk and Keith Hjortshoj (2003) refer to, that is, grading machines, who read papers only to determine the grade; instructive graders, who want to be helpful by providing comments, corrections, and questions in the text while they read, along with more general summary comments and suggestions at the end; or copy editors, who mark and correct everything that conflicts with their personal literary taste. My colleague's role was to be there for her students to read their drafts and to answer students' questions. Most of her students wanted to know if their papers made sense and if their style coincided with the expected style. Some asked her for extra sources on writing admissions essays in their disciplines. A few asked her for her opinion on the quality of the essays. Students were eager to act upon their teacher's feedback and make changes to their essays. They cared about their work. They wanted their essays to be powerful and effective. They revised their essays several times, as they wanted to impress their readers: the graduate admissions officers.

Similarly, in a fourth-year undergraduate course, I asked my students to send their essays for publication to an academic publishing company. My role was to be that of a supportive coach who is there to help students with the questions they have during their writing process rather than to give grades and lots of comments that students are unable to process. The essays were accepted for publication, subject to substantive revisions suggested by the reviewers. Students worked hard at improving their writing, because they wanted readers to learn about the causes they were researching and writing about. The essays were finally published in a book.

156   Facilitating Deep Learning

If asking your students to send their essays to an academic journal or publishing company is not feasible, then encourage them to play in a smaller field. Maybe they can present their papers in an academic or professional conference, or even in a student conference. Or they can post their texts in a blog. The essential aspect is to seek real readers outside the university or college.

7.10 ABSENCE OF GRADES

Another essential element of playing the whole game of expert writers is to bear in mind that readers do not grade their writers. So, as John Tagg (2003) suggests, the writing process should be divorced from summative evaluation and grades. We should not assign a grade to students' texts. This does not mean that we should refrain from commenting on the quality of students' work. But we can do so in a way that is responsive to students' needs and in a way that helps them improve. Real readers do judge the quality of expert writers, too. They buy books from some authors and refuse to buy books from others. They may write reviews online. Some readers may recommend their friends and family to buy some books and not buy others. But no reader ever gives a grade to the writer.

7.11 FIGHTING WITH YOUR NEIGHBORS

Playing the whole game also means engaging in a variety of activities that are usually not fostered in the classroom. Expert writers in academia are not simply writers—they are mathematicians, sociologists, historians, legal scholars, anthropologists, biologists, engineers, architects, or psychologists, for example. These scholars play a game where writing is only one aspect. It is not the whole game. I write a lot about teaching and learning issues. I also write a lot about law. So far, I have around 80 publications, including several books. I consider myself quite productive. But I am not writing all the time. Writing is one—important—aspect of what I do. As a teacher and educational developer, I spend a lot of time in the classroom and the Teaching and Learning Center. I teach students; give workshops to

Deep Writing

faculty; supervise theses; present in conferences; talk to colleagues; attend workshops and seminars; give consulting services for universities and colleges about their educational development programs; organize conferences; review articles for journals; produce educational videos; conduct empirical research; buy books for the Teaching and Learning Center; read books, articles, and newsletters; invite colleagues to speak at our Teaching Forum; deal with budgetary issues; and even get to give input on the building renovations of our Teaching and Learning Center. Many of these activities require that I travel extensively. Except for dealing with budgets, I love all that I do. I learn from these activities. I find problems that feed my research and writing. For me, the whole game of teaching and learning and educational development is very attractive. I feel the same passion when I work in legal issues. I engage in lots of different activities, such as going to court, talking to lawyers and clients, and participating in arbitration and contract negotiations—to name but a few. Even those professional writers whose jobs consist of writing play a game that is broader than just writing. Lucrecia Martel—a world renowned and acclaimed screenwriter—says that in order to write good scripts, she needs to be actively involved in everyday life. In her own words, "I have to go to the supermarket, take the bus, and fight with my neighbors. Otherwise, I cannot write. I cannot write if I am isolated" (Sarmiento Hinojosa, 2010).

Because of institutional constraints, we usually deprive our students of all, or most of, these other activities. We simply ask them to read and write. This makes the game less attractive for students. But it also makes it quite artificial. Students lack the learning experience that comes from engaging in the full spectrum of activities that constitute the academic profession. Our role as teachers is to re-create all of these aspects of the game not only to make it worth playing (Perkins, 2009) but also to give students the full experience, so that they can engage in the same kinds of activities that create cognitive conflicts and create opportunities to negotiate meanings collectively and to reflect about their learning process. The confines of the classroom walls do not help re-create the wide array of diversely rich experiences of expert writers. So, we need to be as creative as possible in order to help students engage in these experiences within the existing institutional and financial constraints.

7.12 COLLABORATIVE LEARNING

Writing requires an instance of collaborative learning. Assigning an essay topic to students for them to work on individually, receive comments from us, and then revise their drafts to hand them in is a recipe for failure. Learning to write requires extensive negotiation of meaning with members of the community of knowledgeable peers and other people interested in the topics we write about. Professional writers engage in conversations with a diverse array of people. They need to fight with their neighbors. So, we need to provide our students with plenty of opportunities to engage in a multitude of conversations. Donald Finkel (1999) suggests the creation of a community of writers to foster a dialog on paper, where the teacher assumes the role of an experienced peer, and students exchange drafts and review drafts. Many teachers use peer review of drafts with their students, where students read, comment, and incorporate feedback they receive into their texts. Although this certainly helps students with their learning process, student peer review is a rather limited—albeit valuable—conversation. We need to open up these conversations so that students can talk to a wider community. Florencia Carlino matched Spanish language students from Sault College (Sault Ste. Marie, Canada) with Spanish language students from Dalhousie University (Halifax, Canada). Students conversed about different topics, many of which they later included in their writing performances. Students also discussed the obstacles they found in their writing processes. Florencia Carlino also connects her students with Spanish native speakers in Sault Ste. Marie. Her students meet with them to talk about different issues. These conversations also find their way into the students' writing projects. Occasionally, students may ask a native speaker about a grammar rule or how a phrase sounds to them. This extended conversation re-creates the collective negotiation of meanings that is necessary for any learning process. It also emulates the fighting-with-your-neighbors experience that professional writers continually engage in.

7.13 TEACHER FEEDBACK AND METACOGNITION

Feedback is an essential aspect of the writing process, just like it is of any aspect of the learning process. The characteristics and elements of effec-

Deep Writing 159

tive feedback discussed later in the book apply to feedback about writing. In order to be effective, we need to evaluate students' initial knowledge, attitudes, and conceptions about the particular genre and style we want them to develop. We also need to observe their composing process. And we need to reflect about the learning-to-write process and the resulting conceptual changes. More important, we also need to provide our students with the necessary metacognitive skills so that they can monitor their own writing. And we need to do this in an encouraging climate while letting our students play the whole game.

7.14 PROBLEMS WITH TEACHERS' COMMENTS

As mentioned while discussing the writing-to-learn approach, teachers' prevailing way of providing feedback about student writing is through comments made onto student papers. Studies about teacher's comments have proved that teachers' comments do not enhance student writing. These studies also show that in some circumstances comments may even be harmful (Sommers, 1982). The most important characteristic of prevailing teacher comments is that they do not encourage revision. They tend to treat students' drafts as final. They do not offer clear and motivating text-specific reasons for students to profoundly revise their drafts. They do not create cognitive conflicts that will force students to reaccommodate their conceptions about writing (Sommers, 1982). Teachers' comments identify grammar, spelling, and organization errors, which students feel compelled to fix. This is because some of us do not always know how to help students embark on a learning process that will take them from novice writers to expert writers. So, for many of us, it is easier to concentrate on surface errors. Joseph Williams (1981), an English language professor, writer, and grammarian, wrote a famous article where he argues that teachers find lots of errors in students' papers because they are looking for errors. He claims that when those teachers read articles from scholars they do not find errors. To prove this point, Williams has identified errors in the text of well-reputed writers who wrote texts on grammar and style. At the end of the article, Williams reveals that he has sprinkled his text with 100 errors. He imagines that readers have not identified so many errors because they were not expecting to find them. Readers probably engaged with the message rather than with surface-structure errors. Furthermore, for Williams many of the errors that teachers find in student papers have to do with style choices and preferences rather than with actual violations of grammar rules.

Teachers' comments sometimes offer contradictory messages to students. We may ask students to develop ideas and fix surface structure errors at the same time. If students need to develop these ideas, they will probably delete entire sentences and paragraphs in later drafts. So, correcting grammar and organization errors may contradict the message that students need to revise, that is, read, reread, delete, reorganize, write, and rewrite.

In some cases, those surface-level errors may even be a sign of learning progress. Learning to write is a process where learners experience ups and downs. They make progress, and then they retrocede. This is particularly evident when students begin to write in a new discipline or about a new topic or when they try to resolve a more complex problem. For example, studies show that when law school students—who were proficient writers during their undergraduate years—start to write about Law in Law School, their writing suffers from grammar, spelling, and organization errors that were not present in those students' texts in their last years of undergraduate university studies. So, these errors are actually a sign of learning progress. If we penalize those errors, what we might be doing is actually hindering our students' natural learning process toward becoming effective writers. If we do so, students will probably focus on sentence-level errors instead of grappling with the new challenges offered by a new discipline or problem. This approach will lead to less effective texts in the long run (Gottschalk and Hjortshoj, 2003). Another example is that of students who learn to write well in an English writing course that they take in their first year of higher education but who cannot write a good essay when they take second-year courses in their disciplines (Prosser and Trigwell, 1999).

Another aspect that is common to many teachers' comments is that these comments tend to deprive students of the ownership of their own texts. The teacher pushes students in directions that he or she would like to see instead of trying to understand and respect each student's path (Sommers, 1982). We should try to see the logic behind students' papers rather

Deep Writing

161

than dismiss them for lack of clear logic; particularly because, in many cases, we do this simply because the students' logic differs from our own (Lindemann, 1995).

Finally, in some cases, teachers write their comments to justify the grade they assign to the students' texts rather than as mechanisms to help students learn how to write effectively. This emphasis on grades and excessive comments may produce student reactance. Expert writers do not receive written comments—let alone a grade—while they compose their texts. They receive feedback in many different ways. Some writers may give their drafts to colleagues they trust to look for accuracy in an aspect of the discipline. Others may give some parts of their manuscripts to a spouse or friends to look for clarity. Expert writers also rely on metacognition strategies. Classroom feedback should emulate this process. Students should receive feedback and comments from a wide variety of sources—not just their teachers and classmates.

7.15 SUMMARY

There are four models that attempt to explain the connection between writing and learning: point-of-utterance model, forward-search model, genre model, and backward-search model. These models show that writing in itself does not necessarily lead to deep learning. Only when writing is articulated as a cognitive strategy, such as in some types of the genre model and in the backward-search model, may it help students learn deeply. In other words, writing leads to deep learning only when student writers engage in the—individual and collective—cognitive processes associated with deep learning. The key is to re-create the writing process in the classroom and make it as authentic as possible.

When learning to write as expert writers, students need to play the whole game, that is, they need to be engaged in the full spectrum of activities that expert writers do, which goes beyond reading and writing. In Martel's words, they need to fight with their neighbors. Students also need real readers; they also need to be encouraged to revise their drafts as experts do before their texts solidify.

162 Facilitating Deep Learning

Excessive teachers' comments, grades, and lack of authentic experiences associated with writing do not contribute to this process. We need to develop more appropriate responses for commenting on student writing. We need to facilitate revision by responding to writing as a work in progress rather than judging it as a finished product. We also need to bear in mind that writing is a nonlinear process, where students experience progress and regression. In many cases, errors in writing may reflect signs of learning.

The next chapter will analyze the connection between diversity and deep learning. It will focus on the need to create deep learning environments to help all students achieve deeper levels of learning.

PRACTICE CORNER

1. You want your students to write a relatively short paper. You want them to revise and rewrite their drafts several times. You know that you need to help students rewrite their texts before they solidify. But how can you do this? What specific actions can you take so that students will rewrite their texts several times?

2. You assign a term paper to your students. You know that students need real readers for their drafts. You do not want to ask other students in the class to read the papers, because students will probably try to be nice to their classmates and will offer only cosmetic suggestions. What can you do to provide students with real readers to critique their papers and offer meaningful recommendations to improve them?

3. You want your students in your introduction to your discipline course for nonmajors to play the whole game of the experts in your discipline and write an academic or professional paper. What can you do to help your students play the whole game of disciplinary experts?

4. In *Girls Talk*, a play written and directed by Roger Kumble, Lori is a screenwriter and stay-at-home mom whose everyday, simple tasks do not let her write. Think of the multiple constrains that

Deep Writing   163

your students may face that may prevent them from writing deeply. What can we do to help them overcome these constraints?

5. It has been argued that the framework of assigning an essay topic to students for them to work on individually, receiving comments from us, and then revising their drafts to hand in is a recipe for failure. Do you agree with this assertion? Why or why not? Why do you think this practice is so widespread at universities today? What changes can we make to this widespread practice?

6. The chair of the department wants all students to improve their writing skills in the discipline. He does not know what to do. He comes to you for suggestions to come up with a department-wide plan to help students deeply learn how to write in the discipline. What can you suggest? What will the plan consist of?

7. In a scene in Theresa Rebeck's (2012) play *Seminar,* Leonard, an accomplished novelist who is paid $5,000 by five aspiring writers to teach a private seminar, tells one of his students to get himself kidnapped in an African country before writing a novel. What do you think he means by this? Do you agree? Why or why not? Would you tell something similar to your students before having them write papers for your class? How can you create a meaningful experience in your course so that students can immerse themselves in your discipline before writing a paper?

8. A former undergraduate student of yours emailed you to tell you that he had just started a master's program in a cognate discipline. He had to write a paper for one of his first-semester classes. He was asked to rewrite his paper because he had made too many grammatical and organizational errors. The student was very surprised, as he had always got very high marks on papers and other written assignments while he was an undergraduate in your program. What happened to your for mer student? How can you explain his problem in terms of the deep learning process? What can you tell him? What advice can you give him?

9. A colleague of yours is very disappointed with the quality of her students' papers. She comes to see you for advice. She tells you that in her third-year undergraduate course, every week she assigned a journal article for students to discuss in small groups. Toward the

164 Facilitating Deep Learning

end of the class, each group reported on the discussion. Your colleague occasionally lectured on the context of each reading. At the end of the term, she assigned a 20-page paper on one of the discussed readings. While most students had very good ideas, according to your colleague, their writing was very poor. What happened? Why? What advice can you give to your colleague?

10. The dean sends you an email that reads as follows: "The issue of academic integrity is one that is becoming increasingly important to faculty given the easy access of online sources, paper mills, and essay-writing services available to students. I would like to know if your department is interested in acquiring a plagiarism detection software tool. As many of you know, these tools compare submitted essays against a database of millions of previously submitted papers and perform a thorough search of Internet resources." Is there a connection between writing and plagiarism in the Instruction-paradigm University? Why or why not? Why do some students resort to plagiarism? Why are some teachers vehemently opposed to plagiarism? What is the biological explanation for plagiarism? How would you answer the dean?

KEYWORDS

- **academic skills**
- **deep learning**
- **deep writing**
- **learning to write deeply**
- **students' attitude**
- **teacher feedback**
- **teaching writing**
- **writing to learn**

REFERENCES

Bain, K. What the Best College Teachers Do; Harvard University Press: Cambridge, MA, 2004.

Bazerman, C. Genre and Cognitive Development: Beyond Writing to Learn. Pratiques, 2009, 143–144.

Bean, J. Engaging Ideas: The Professor's Guide to Integrating Writing, Critical Thinking, and Active Learning in the Classroom; Jossey Bass: San Francisco, 1996.

Bereiter, C.; Scardamalia, M. The Psychology of Written Composition; Erlbaum: Hillsdale, NJ, 1987.

Boice, R. Advice for New Faculty Members. Nihil Nimus; Allyn and Bacon: Needham Heights, 2000.

Carlino, P. Escribir, Leer y Aprender en la Universidad. Una Introducción a la Alfabetización Académica; Fondo de Cultura Económica: Buenos Aires, 2005.

Durst, R. K.; Newell, G. E. Monitoring Processes in Analytic and Summary Writing. Written Communication, 1989, 6, 340–363.

Emig, J. Writing as a Mode of Learning. College Composition and Communication, 1977, 28, 2, 122–128.

Finkel, D. Teaching With Your Mouth Shut; Boynton/Cook Publishers: Portsmouth, NH, 1999.

Gonyea, R.; Anderson, P. Writing, Engagement and Successful Learning Outcomes, Annual Meeting of the American Educational Research Association, San Diego, CA, April 14, 2009, http://writing.byu.edu/static/documents/org/1144.pdf (accessed Aug. 12, 2013).

Gottschalk, K.; Hjortshoj, K. The Elements of Teaching Writing; Bedford/St. Martin's: Boston, 2003.

Klein, P.D. Reopening Inquiry into Cognitive Processes in Writing-To-Learn. Educational Psychology Review, 1999, 11, 3, 203–270.

Light, R. Making the Most of College: Students Speak Their Minds; Harvard University Press: Cambridge, MA, 2001.

Lindemann, E.A Rhetoric for Writing Teachers, 3rd ed.; Oxford University Press: Oxford, 1995.

Marton, F.; Säljö, R. On Qualitative Differences in Learning 1: Outcome and Process." British Journal of Educational Psychology 1976, 46, 4.

Meiers, M. Writing to learn. Research Digest, 2007, 1. http://www.vit.vic.edu.au (accessed Aug. 12, 2013).

Perkins, D. Making Learning Whole. How Seven Principles of Teaching can Transform Education; Jossey-Bass: San Francisco, 2009.

Prosser, M.; Trigwell, K. Understanding Learning and Teaching: The experience in higher education; Open University Press: Buckingham, 1999.

Rebeck, T. Seminar; Samuel French: New York, 2012.

Sarmiento-Hinojosa, J. Lucrecia Martel: Interviewed. http://www.youtube.com/watch?v=QFITzNaygkE (accessed Aug. 12, 2013).

Smith, F, Joining the Literacy Club. Further Essays into Education; Heinemann Educational Books: London, 1988.

Sommers, N. Responding to Student Writing.College Composition and Communication, 1982, 33, 2, 148–56.

Tagg, J. The Learning Paradigm College; Anker Publishing Company: Bolton, MA, 2003.

Williams, J. The Phenomenology of Error.College Composition and Communication, 1981, 32, 152–68.

PART III
DEEP LEARNING AND DIVERSITY

CHAPTER 8

INCLUSIVE DEEP LEARNING ENVIRONMENTS AND KNOWLEDGE MODES

We make the assumption that everyone sees life the way we do.

— MIGUEL RUIZ

CONTENTS

8.1 Introduction 170
8.2 Connection between Diversity and Deep Learning 171
8.3 Knowledge Modes 173
8.4 North American Knowledge Mode and Academic Skills 174
8.5 Non-Western Knowledge Modes and Academic Skills 174
8.6 Crossing Over Knowledge Modes 175
8.7 Strategies for Creating an Inclusive Deep Learning Environment 177
8.8 Summary 179
Practice Corner 180
Keywords 182
References 83

8.1 INTRODUCTION

Students achieve the highest degree of deep learning when they interact with peers from diverse backgrounds, and when teachers incorporate these backgrounds into the class to help students explore answers to questions and solutions to problems from diverse perspectives.

This depth in student learning does not occur spontaneously, even in those classes made up of a large percentage of students from different backgrounds and from different parts of the world. It requires the creation of inclusive deep learning environments that take into account and privilege students' diverse knowledge modes. A knowledge mode is the frame of reference through which we see the world around us. It helps us construct, understand, and interpret reality. It also affects the way we create, organize, and express thought. Non-traditional students, particularly students from non-Western societies, have a way of seeing the world around them that greatly differs from the mainstream North American academic knowledge mode.

In an inclusive deep learning environment, these different knowledge modes are incorporated into the classes, and students learn from diverse worldviews, perspectives, and languages, including their own.

This approach contrasts with the predominant practice in the Instruction paradigm, which teaches from a single knowledge mode and pushes all—traditional and nontraditional—students to learn from a mainstream disciplinary perspective and to adopt mainstream academic skills. In the Instruction-paradigm institutions, when mainstream North American teachers judge nontraditional students' work, they tend to perceive it as inferior, without realizing that this work simply reflects a different knowledge mode and worldview perspective.

I begin this chapter with an analysis of the connection between diversity and deep learning. This first part of the chapter will answer the question "How does diversity enhance the deep learning process?" Second, I will explore knowledge modes from the perspective of both mainstream and nontraditional students as well as the perceptions that teachers and students have when they cross over knowledge modes. Finally, I will examine some strategies to create inclusive deep learning environments. This discussion will be complemented in Chapter 9 with the examination

Inclusive Deep Learning Environments and Knowledge Modes 171

of other components of the deep learning inclusive environment that also enrich the deep learning process, that is, an international and plurilingual education.

8.2 CONNECTION BETWEEN DIVERSITY AND DEEP LEARNING

There is a strong—albeit not necessarily evident at first glance—connection between diversity and deep learning. As discussed throughout the book, the deep learning process requires a cognitive conflict. This cognitive conflict is generated through social interaction with peers (Vygotsky, 1978) who are at different developmental stages (Magolda, 2002; Perry, 1970). The cognitive conflict is produced because the learner interacts with peers who offer ideas, examples, perspectives, angles, concepts, topics, or methods that the learner has not thought of or has not fully explored individually. When the learner interacts with peers who have very different backgrounds, the exploration of the problem or question that the learner is trying to solve or answer will be richer than if he or she only interacts with peers who come from the same cultural background.

Let me illustrate this point with a personal example. When I was writing this book, I gave the first draft to a very close friend. We grew up together. We went to the same high school. Then, we also went to law school together. We both went into teaching after completing graduate studies. We both delved into the scholarship of teaching and learning at similar times in our teaching careers. My friend gave me useful advice on how to improve the manuscript. I learned deeply about some ideas and concepts that my friend and I discussed. But I did not radically change the approach to this book. Nothing my friend told me led me to fundamentally transform the way I see the world of teaching and learning. Then, I gave the draft to three other colleagues. Like my friend, all of them are seasoned higher education teachers and educational developers. But, they have very different backgrounds. One is a neuroscientist by training, the other one is a cultural communication expert, and the third one is a writing specialist. One of them is from Eastern Europe, the other one is from India, and the third one is from China. Their native languages are very different from mine. And their teaching experiences in other disciplines and countries also differ from mine. Like my friend, they all made comments to my draft. Because these comments reflected their cultures, trajectories, and backgrounds, they made me look at most of the concepts in the original draft of this book from angles that I had never thought of. These colleagues are not smarter than my friend. They do not know more than my friend. But they have a background that is very different from mine and my friend's. The interaction with these three colleagues resulted in a fundamental change in the way I see the discipline of teaching and learning. In Vygotsky's (1978) terms, they made me change my cognitive structure in a way that was not possible when my conversations included only my friend who grew up seeing and interpreting the world as I did.

Similarly, another colleague teaches script writing in a film studies program at an American university. In the fall and spring terms, she teaches regular classes attended mostly by American students and only a handful of international students. During the summer, this program brings students from all over the world to an intensive 12-week seminar. For one of the activities, she asked her students in the summer course to discuss the notion of "child" and to write a script for a film about childhood. My colleague seemed genuinely interested in learning about students' diverse cultures and encouraged them to share the conceptions of child and childhood from their own cultures. She had students with very different backgrounds. Students came from China, South America, Mexico, India, Europe, the United States, Saudi Arabia, Nigeria, and Kenya, among many other countries. Some of these students were religious. They represented virtually every major religion. My colleague also had nonreligious students. Some of the students were mature, whereas others were fresh from high school. They spoke different languages as their native tongues. And they grew up in very different cultures. During the discussions, each offered radically different notions of child and childhood. The discussions—at times quite heated—forced every student to think very deeply about what a child is and what childhood means. It forced students to look at these notions from angles that they would not have considered if the discussions had been among students from the very same culture. The scripts they wrote were quite sophisticated and reflected these rich discussions. She tried the same activity in her fall and spring courses where most of the students were from the United States. Students were highly motivated. The discussions were also

Inclusive Deep Learning Environments and Knowledge Modes 173

heated, and the resulting scripts reflected instances of deep learning. But the discussions and the scripts were not as rich, complex, and nuanced as the ones in the summer course.

So diversity plays a very important role in the deep learning process. But this role is only possible if teachers actively and explicitly recognize and incorporate diverse worldview perspectives into the classroom. If, on the contrary, even when there is a diverse group of students, teachers repress students' backgrounds, experiences, and cultures, they insist on teaching from a single cultural perspective, and they reject diverse ways of generating and expressing thought, then the cognitive conflict and the resulting conceptual change will be significantly poorer.

Additionally, as I will discuss in the next chapter, helping students examine problems, questions, and situations in several languages and from a global or international perspective—both within and outside the classroom—also enriches the connections that students make in the process that leads to a change in their cognitive structures.

8.3 KNOWLEDGE MODES

People have different ways of seeing and understanding the world around them. And they do so through a frame of reference that shapes their understanding of what they see (Ruiz, 2009). This frame, referred to as knowledge mode, permits people to see, interpret, and understand the world (Haigh, 2009). It shapes behavior by judging everybody and everything we do. It also influences the way people speak, write, listen, think, and interact with others.

Every culture has its own knowledge mode. The knowledge mode in one culture may be similar to the knowledge mode in other cultures, such as the predominant knowledge modes in North America and Western Europe. Other knowledge modes, such non-Western ones, may be radically different when compared to others, for example, the North American knowledge mode.

8.4 NORTH AMERICAN KNOWLEDGE MODE AND ACADEMIC SKILLS

Most teachers in North American higher education institutions approach the teaching of disciplinary content, academic skills, and thought processes from traditionally Western and North American perspectives or knowledge modes. For example, the predominant knowledge mode in North America is external, socially mitigated, and objectively measurable (Haigh, 2009). So, subjective, relational, and nonmeasurable approaches are considered unworthy of the mainstream university classroom. Critical thinking, which is conceived of as a self-directed, self-disciplined, self-monitored, and self-corrective thinking mode in which the thinker analyzes, assesses, and reconstructs evidence (Bok, 2006), displaced other forms of thinking, such as creative and integrative (Boyer, 1990; Clark, 2009). Teaching writing has been reduced to teaching disciplinary thesis-based writing, where students learn how to develop a thesis, pose questions, gather and weigh evidence, and construct arguments as members of a certain discipline (Bean, 1996).

The North American knowledge mode is a very particular—even elitist—way of interpreting the world around us. It is by no means universal. It does not coincide with ways of producing and expressing thought in other cultures. Furthermore, it has been criticized within North American academic circles for being patriarchal and for distorting the way of knowing (Bean, 1996).

8.5 NON-WESTERN KNOWLEDGE MODES AND ACADEMIC SKILLS

Non-traditional students have a way of seeing themselves and understanding the world that derives from their own cultures and traditions. These differ from the perspectives that predominate in North American universities. Like for their mainstream colleagues, this different ways of seeing the world have repercussions in most academic areas. They influence the way students think, express themselves, interact in the classroom, and think in the disciplines. For example, many nontraditional students tend

Inclusive Deep Learning Environments and Knowledge Modes 175

to see things in a subjective, inward-looking fashion (Haigh, 2009). Other students from non-Western societies are holistic in their thoughts. They tend to emphasize and value how things are interconnected. They tend to give contextual and emotional information. Some even show a tendency to digress when writing.What is important in their written works is "seeing, feeling, and being situated in the web of relations that surround the subject" rather than developing a thesis (Fox, 1994). In an analysis of the way highly educated Sri Lankan and other non-Western scholars write academic research papers, Canagarajah (2002) notices that introductions are generally brief, and citations are used only to provide definitions of key terms and to endorse the writer's own positions. Prior works are usually mentioned but not discussed in length. Similarly, the methodology is only briefly alluded to in the final lines of the introduction but not fully explained in the paper. The discussion is generally "a linear exposition or narration of the key issues surrounding the subject in a very personal voice by the author" (Canagarajah, 2002). Along the same lines, Arabic-speaking scholars tend to express the same idea in more than one way, usually with a colorful vocabulary (Leki, 1992). Latin American students and scholars show a tendency to digress, to give colorful contexts, to repeat ideas, and to argue in circles.

8.6 CROSSING OVER KNOWLEDGE MODES

When a student or teacher from a certain tradition, who lacks experience and education in appreciating knowledge diversity, crosses knowledge modes, he or she tends to judge different knowledge modes in a very negative way (Haigh, 2009). Thus, nontraditional students tend to perceive North American academic writing as inferior, arbitrary, and disrespectful of the audience. For example, according to a Chilean student reported in Helen Fox's (1994) book, when he "reads something written by an American it sounds so childish." Other non-Western students consider that North American writers belittle their audience by making explicit their arguments and by making explicit connections between different arguments. Students from highly contextual societies interpret the North American linear discursive style as simple and arrogant: "simple because it lacks the richness of detail necessary to establish context, and arrogant because the speaker is deciding what particular points you should hear and then what point you should draw from them" (Bennett, 1998). Another example quoted by Fox shows that for non-North American students it should be the responsibility of the audience —not the writer—"to do the analysis, to draw meaning from the context. [The writer does] not [even have the] responsibility to make sense" (Fox, 1994). For Sri Lankan scholars, papers written by American authors

> lack the esthetic and emotional appeal that comes from a more relaxed development of the thesis [...] that simply annihilating the views of others doesn't necessarily mean that [the American authors'] view is superior [...] that papers displayed an aggressive individualism that bordered on unseemly pride, attention-grabbing, and self-congratulation, and that the need to pit one's own research against that of others leads to unnecessary, hair-splitting arguments that end up confusing and baffling the audience (Canagarajah, 2002).

In most cases, nontraditional students, particularly non-Western, feel that following North American conventions is against "what everything inside you is telling you to do" (Fox, 1994).

At the same time, mainstream North American teachers—and those minority teachers educated in mainstream Western higher education institutions—perceive nonmainstream student writing and other academic skills as signs of unpreparedness for university studies (Côté and Allahar, 2007; Gabriel, 2008). For example, when nontraditional students write an essay where they do not cite a few sentences they borrowed from an author, or when they digress instead of supporting the thesis with arguments and evidence, most teachers do not understand that these students are responding to the way in which they have been brought up to see and understand the world. Teachers tend to believe that these are signs of low-quality learning and lack of academic preparation for higher education.

When students and teachers came to university from the same privileged and homogeneous social backgrounds, they shared similar values and principles (Bowden and Marton, 2004). So, there was no difference of perspective between teachers and students and among students, which resulted in poorer social interactions and less profound learning experiences.

8.7 STRATEGIES FOR CREATING AN INCLUSIVE DEEP LEARNING ENVIRONMENT

The deepest degree of learning takes place when university and college teachers encourage, include, and value the cultures of both minority and mainstream students and incorporate them into their classes. "By becoming aware of other people's ways of seeing various phenomena one's understanding is enriched and therefore becomes more powerful; one can see one's own way of seeing exactly as a way of seeing (rather than 'seeing what something is like')" (Bowden and Marton, 2004).

In practice, this entails encouraging students to interact, exchange, and share their perspectives with their peers while dealing with problems, questions, and situations so that everyone can explore answers and solutions from a wide array of diverse perspectives.

In an inclusive deep learning environment, all students engage in conversations that promote rich connections between new and existing knowledge, which results in a profound change in their cognitive structures at a level that cannot be achieved when the social interaction takes place between peers that have the same cultural background or when the teacher consciously or unconsciously represses the knowledge modes of nontraditional students, or when he or she approaches the teaching process from a single worldview paradigm.

Table 8.1 contains inclusive teaching strategies to create an inclusive deep learning environment in our classes.

TABLE 8.1 Inclusive teaching strategies.

- Place student learning of diverse knowledge modes and ways of generating, organizing, and expressing thought at the forefront of the curriculum. Include these within the course intended learning goals. Make explicit to your students that they must learn to approach the discipline and to generate, organize, and express thought from multiple traditions.
- Align your course so that the evaluation and teaching and learning activities match your intended learning goals. Make sure you also give ample room for oblique and incidental learning to maximize opportunities to learn from diverse world perspectives.
- Change the preconception that non-Western ideas are exotic. Introduce non-Western knowledge modes, academic skills, and disciplinary content as something normal.
- Help your students see the intrinsic value of acquiring diverse, nontraditional ways of seeing the world. Include a wide array of non-Western and nontraditional worldviews and values, even if you do not have students from a certain culture. For example, even if you do not have aboriginal students, teach your students how to transmit knowledge through stories as is done in aboriginal communities.

TABLE 8.1 *(Continued)*

- Show your students how useful it is to be prepared to live and work in different cultures.
- Teach multiple ways of writing instead of restricting writing to North American academic styles. For example, teach your students how to organize thoughts and express ideas as is done in Chinese culture. Ask a Chinese graduate student who completed his or her undergraduate education in China to show you how Chinese scholars write academic papers, or invite that student to your class to talk to your students. Then, ask your students to write a short paper in English following an academic Chinese structure and organization.
- Vary pedagogical methods, that is, teach as is taught in other cultures and traditions. For example, use story-telling, organize circles, potlucks in—or ideally outside—the classroom to acknowledge aboriginal traditions. Or base part of your pedagogy on notions of Dharma, which emphasizes personal introspection, self-awareness, self-realization, and self-improvement (Haigh, 2009).
- Include texts in foreign languages that some of your students speak as alternative or supplementary to texts in English. Even if you do not read in a foreign language, as disciplinary expert, you are probably familiar with the text and the author, or you probably read an English translation. Most foreign language journals bring an abstract in English. So, it is not very difficult to know the content of an article in your discipline, even if you do not speak that language. Invite the students that read those articles to comment them in class. Unilingual speakers will see the value of reading the discipline in other languages.
- Invite guests from nonmainstream traditions, such as an aboriginal elder, a visible minority professional, or a foreign religious leader. They can discuss topics related to your course, and your students can gain insight into their worldviews.
- Organize student presentations where students discuss a problem from their own tradition. A variation of this activity is to ask students to present a topic from a tradition that is different from their own.
- Discuss disciplinary content that interests diverse groups of students. For example, recent immigrant students want to see issues related to immigration, assimilation, and heritage discussed in class. If you teach American literature, you can include Chicano authors' short stories dealing with problems faced by Latino immigrant families, such as stories by Francisco Jimenez. If you teach contracts, you can include the notion and formation of contracts found in legal traditions outside North America.
- Assess whether students can generate, organize, and express thought in a multitude of diverse ways. Assessment is the component in the aligned teaching system that most greatly influences the approach students take to learning (Gibbs, 1999). So, if your assessment actually evaluates whether and how well students have mastered a wide array of knowledge modes, diverse academic skills, and nontraditional disciplinary perspectives, students will probably achieve your intended learning goals (Biggs and Tang, 2007).
- Design assessment tasks that are representative of different cultures and traditions. Do not restrict your assessment tasks to exams, multiple-choice tests, research papers, and group presentations. Adopt assessment tools used in other cultures, such as informal dialogs, holistic evaluation of student performance throughout the course, or self-evaluation. Another alternative is to ask your students to gather evidence that is customary in their traditions to show how well they have achieved the intended learning goals.

8.8 SUMMARY

The deep learning process is closely connected to and necessitates diversity of worldview perspectives, cultural approaches, and a plurality of languages. Diversity enriches the social interaction of learners with their peers and helps them grapple with problems and questions from a wide array of angles that cannot be considered when teaching from one single worldview, cultural approach, and language.

The demographic of today's classroom has changed drastically in the last decades. Today, significant numbers of nontraditional students have gained access to higher education. This increase in participation has not translated into deep student learning, as teachers insist on teaching from one single perspective. Furthermore, teachers tend to perceive nontraditional students as academically underprepared. Students' preparation reflects their own cultures, traditions, and beliefs. Non-traditional students have been prepared to see the world and express thought in ways that differ from those of North American mainstream teachers and students. In the Instruction paradigm, the predominant approach to dealing with a diverse student population has been to ignore or repress nonmainstream backgrounds, cultures, and voices.

The inclusive deep learning environment recognizes and incorporates diverse knowledge modes, thought processes, and expressive styles into the classroom, as they enrich the social interaction that leads to more complex and sophisticated cognitive conflicts and the resulting conceptual changes. Additionally, an inclusive deep learning environment prepares both mainstream and minority students to succeed as interculturally knowledgeable citizens in today's globalized world.

The next two chapters delve into other essential aspects of the inclusive deep learning environment. Chapter 9 focuses on international and plurilingual education. Chapter 10 explores one of the most important challenges of the creation of inclusive deep learning environments: teaching nonnative speaking students and helping them achieve academic proficiency in the disciplines in their second or foreign language.

PRACTICE CORNER

1. It has been argued that the deepest degree of learning takes place when teachers include the values and cultures of both minority and mainstream students in their classes. Do you agree with this statement? Why or why not? Can you think of examples from your teaching practice where you saw a connection between diversity and deep learning? How can the argument that diversity enhances the deep learning process be reconciled with Bruffee's notion of movement from one community of knowledgeable peers to another?

2. Think of a course you are currently teaching or a course you have recently taught. What specific changes could you implement to incorporate diverse worldviews and academic cultures in your course? How can you deal with resistance from traditional students?

3. What institutional changes, if any, are required to create inclusive deep learning environments and to promote diversity in your university or college? How would you implement these changes? Can you anticipate resistance from colleagues and administrators? If so, how could you deal with resistance?

4. Miguel Ruiz (1997), a Mexican aboriginal healer and educator, argues that every society has a dream, which includes all of society's rules, beliefs, laws, religions, and cultural norms. Individuals, in turn, also have a personal dream, which is the internalization of society's dream through a process of socialization. According to Ruiz, children do not have the possibility to choose their beliefs. They have to agree with the system that is transmitted to them by their parents, teachers, priests, and other adult members of society. Can Ruiz's arguments be used to explain diversity in university and college classrooms? Why or why not? If so, what negotiations can we make between individual and collective dreams? Is it legitimate for higher education teachers to change individual and societal dreams?

5. A colleague, who teaches business and marketing courses, has several Mexican students. He has heard about inclusive deep learning

Inclusive Deep Learning Environments and Knowledge Modes 181

environments, but he is reluctant to let the Mexican students write business reports following the digressive and high-context style of native Spanish speakers. He says to you: "I am not going to encourage them, or anyone else, in my class to follow this writing style. I talked to these Mexican students; and they all want to be professionals in Canada or the United States. So, they really need to write in English as we all do. What's the use for Mexican students to practice this digressive writing, anyway? And for my English speaking students? They will never learn to write properly if I let them experiment with other styles." Do you agree with your colleague? Why or why not? What would you do in this case? What can you tell your colleague?

6. A student from Pakistan, who completed his undergraduate degree in Karachi and is studying in North America seeking a second degree, approaches you and says: "I know how you want me to write, but when I sit down in front of my laptop, I just can't. I feel I am betraying myself. I cannot write as you want." What would you say to this student? Why do you think he feels this way? What can you do so as to prevent his sense of betrayal?

7. Watch or remember the film *Sahara* (1983), directed by Andrew McLaglen, about a young American female who participates in a car race in Africa and is abducted by a Muslim sheik. Can you identify instances of cultural miscommunication in the film? What role do cultural and gender stereotypes play in intercultural communication in the film? Are there any instances of remedial teaching? Can you identify any instances of deep learning?

8. What specific actions can you take to create an inclusive deep learning environment in your classes? Which of the strategies suggested in Table 8.1 can you include in your courses? How would you implement them? Which of those strategies would you not include? Why?

9. A colleague of yours teaches history. He is a First Nations aboriginal professor. In his classes, he introduces Aboriginal issues and teaches from an aboriginal perspective. He had his students sit in a circle to discuss their thoughts on the history of Canadian immigration. He brought an eagle feather to class and each student would

pass it along after speaking his or her thoughts on this topic. Before this activity started, he proceeded to talk to the class about the menstrual cycle. He explained that this is a special time in the month and under no circumstances can menstruating women touch the eagle feather because of the sacred and special time in a woman's life. So students who happened to be at that time of the month had to put the feather down. Most of the female students were very embarrassed and felt left out when they had to put the feather down. You are the department chair. These students come to complain to you. What can you do? What can you say to the students?

10. Juhua is a third-year exchange student from China. She wrote a paper for a history course. The ideas in the paper were her own, but she used words and expressions from the textbook because she felt that her English was not good enough and the author's words sounded better than hers. Her professor accused Juhua of plagiarism. You are a member of the Disciplinary Committee who receives the plagiarism complaint. Why do you think this happened? What role, if any, did Juhua's knowledge mode play in this incident? What would you tell your colleague? What would you say to the student? What decision would you make in this case?

KEYWORDS

- academic skills
- deep learning
- diversity
- inclusive deep learning environment
- inclusive teaching
- inclusive teaching strategies
- knowledge modes
- non-Western knowledge modes
- North American knowledge mode

REFERENCES

Arkoudis, S. Teaching International Students. Strategies to Enhance Learning; Centre for the Study of Higher Education, University of Melbourne. http://www.cshe.unimelb.edu.au/pdfs/international.pdf (accessed Aug. 12, 2013).

Bean, J. Engaging Ideas: The Professor's Guide to Integrating Writing, Critical Thinking, and Active Learning in the Classroom; Jossey Bass: San Francisco, 1996.

Bennett, M. J. Intercultural Communication: A Current Perspective. In Basic Concepts of Intercultural Communication: Selected Readings; Bennett, M. J., Ed.;Intercultural Press: Yarmouth, ME: 1998.

Biggs, J.; Tang, C.Teaching for Quality Learning at University; Open University Press: Maidenhead, 2007.

Bok, D. Our Underachieving Colleges; Princeton University Press: Princeton, NJ, 2006.

Bowden, J. and Marton, F. (2004) University of Learning. London: Routledge.

Boyer, E. Scholarship Reconsidered. Priorities of the Professoriate; Jossey Bass: San Francisco, 1990.

Bruffee, K. Collaborative Learning: Higher Education, Interdependence, and the Authority of Knowledge, 2nd ed.; The John Hopkins University Press: Baltimore and London, 1999.

Canagarajah, A. S. *A Geopolitics of Academic Writing*; University of Pittsburgh Press: Pittsburgh, 2002.

Clark, M. Beyond Critical Thinking.Pedagogy, 2009, 325.

Côté, J.; Allahar, A.Ivory Tower Blues: A University System in Crisis; University of Toronto Press: Toronto, 2007.

Crockett, D. S. Advising Skills, Techniques, and Resources; ACT National Center for the Advancement of Educational Practice: Iowa City, Iowa, 1984.

Cummins, J. Cognitive/academic language proficiency, linguistic interdependence, the optimum age question and some other matters. Working Papers on Bilingualism, 1979, 19, 121–129.

Fox, H. Listening to the World: Cultural Issues in Academic Writing; NCTE: Urbana, IL, 1994.

Gabriel, K. Teaching Unprepared Students: Strategies for Promoting Success and Retention in Higher Education; Stylus Publishing: Sterling, VA, 2008.

Gibbs, G.Improving the quality of student learning; Technical and Educational Services: Bristol, 1992.

Haigh, M. Fostering Cross-Cultural Empathy with Non-Western Curricular Structures. Journal of Studies in International Education, 2009, 13, 2. 271.

Krashen, S. D.Second Language Acquisition and Second Language Learning; Prentice-Hall International: New York, 1988.

Krashen, S. D.The Input Hypothesis and its Rivals. In Implicit and Explicit Learning of Languages; Ellis, N., Ed.; Academic Press: London,*1994.*

Krashen, S. D.; Brown, C. L. What is Academic Language Proficiency? Singapore Tertiary English Teachers Society Language and Communication Review, 2007, 6, 1.

Leki, I. Understanding ESL Writers. A Guide for Teachers; Boynton/Cook Publishers: Portsmouth, NH, 1992.

Magolda, M. In Epistemological reflection: The evolution of epistemological assumptions from age 18 to 30; Hofer, B., Pintrich, P., Eds.; Personal epistemology: The psychology of beliefs about knowledge and knowing; Erlbaum: Mahwah, NJ, 2002.

Perry, W. Forms of Intellectual and Ethical Development in the College Years: A Scheme; Hold, Rinehart and Winston: Troy, Mo, 1970.

Ruiz, M. The Four Agreements: A Practical Guide to Personal Freedom; Amber-Allen Publishing: San Rafael, CA, 1997.

Seidman, A. The community college: A challenge for change. Community College Journal of Research and Practice, 1995, 19(3), 247–254.

Slocum, S. ESL Strategies. Facilitating Learning for Students Who Speak English as a Second Language; Alverno College: Milwaukee, 2003.

Tinto, V. Learning better together: The impact of learning communities on student success in higher education. Journal of Institutional Research.2000, 9(1), 48–53.

Tinto, V. Leaving College: Rethinking the Causes and Cures of Student Attrition; University Of Chicago Press: Chicago, 1994.

Tinto, V. Moving Beyond Access: College Success for Low-Income, First Generation Students; The Pell Institute for the Study of Opportunity in Higher Education: Washington DC, 2008.

Vygotsky, L. Mind in Society: The Development of Higher Psychological Processes; Harvard University Press: Cambridge, MA, 1978.

Weimer, M. Learner-Centered Teaching: Five Key Changes to Practice; Jossey-Bass: San Francisco, 2002.

Zeegers, P.; Martin, L.A learning to learn program in a first-year chemistry class. Higher Education Research and Development. 2001, 20(1), 36–52.

CHAPTER 9

INTERNATIONALIZATION AND DEEP LEARNING

The world is a book and those who do not travel read only one page.

— SAINT AGUSTINE

CONTENTS

9.1 Introduction 186
9.2 Brief Historical Overview of Internationalization of
Universities and Colleges 186
9.3 Need to Change 188
9.4 Summary 198
Practice Corner 199
Keywords 200
References 201

9.1 INTRODUCTION

The examination of problems, questions, and situations from diverse knowledge modes creates the possibility of richer interactions that enhance the deep learning process. This process is also enriched when we help our students examine these problems, questions, and situations from global and international perspectives and in a plurality of languages. Thus, an international and a plurilingual education constitutes an essential aspect of the inclusive deep learning environment.

This chapter focuses on international and plurilingual initiatives that help students maximize learning. It begins with a brief historical overview of internationalization efforts of universities and colleges. I will then focus on four key aspects that promote an international and plurilingual education: internationalization of the curriculum, integration of study abroad programs, cultural preparation of students, and plurilingual teaching.

9.2 BRIEF HISTORICAL OVERVIEW OF INTERNATIONALIZATION OF UNIVERSITIES AND COLLEGES

International education is a crucial element of any postsecondary educational endeavor. An international perspective helps students achieve deep learning, as it stretches them to see the world from a different and global viewpoint (Bowden and Marton, 2004). It also helps students become internationally knowledgeable citizens who are capable of succeeding in a globalized world (AUCC, 2008). International education is "that learning which enhances the individual's ability to understand his or her condition in the community and the world and improves the ability to make effective judgments" (Hanvey, 2004).

Internationalization is not a new phenomenon in higher education. It was an essential aspect of the universities when they were created in Europe over a millennium ago. Academics and students traveled from all over Europe to participate in medieval universities (Stier, 2002). These universities constructed knowledge that was essentially international. For centuries, universities showed an interest in ideas, theories, and problems that had a clear international focus.

Internationalization and Deep Learning

Most used Latin as a common language of instruction to attract students from all over Europe. During medieval times, it was customary for university graduates to travel to other European universities to complete their education. These trips were known as cavalier journeys. At the beginning, they had an explicit educational component. For example, these journeys included meetings and discussions with university professors and other students, as well as visits to the library. Later, these journeys dropped the formal educational component, as it was understood that simply visiting other countries and experiencing diverse cultures were sufficient educational experiences. John Amos Comenius, one of the most influential educators of the seventeenth century, argued that university education has to be complemented by travel. "In this country, there is not a nobleman, who has not seen, at least Holland, France, and Italy; and really they have to travel because education, which they receive, is not exactly the best" (Charles-Louis, 1734).

With the emergence and consolidation of the modern national state, universities retreated from an international focus to a more national approach. During this time, universities began to teach in local languages (e.g., French in France and Spanish in Spain). The content itself also became more local. As a way of illustration, faculties of law began to teach the law governing the jurisdiction where the university was located (e.g., French law in France and Spanish law in Spain) instead of Roman law or cannon law, which were considered more universal.

With the advent of globalization, universities and colleges have been looking to embrace an international perspective again. European and North American higher education institutions have been implementing internationalization plans. Europe leads the way with long-standing ERASMUS and SOCRATES programs and with the recent creation of the European Higher Education Area. International mobility, exchanges, foreign languages, and European ideas are integral components of university education in Europe. Internationalization constitutes part of a large-scale political process of European integration (Stier, 1998).

North American universities and colleges have been designing and implementing internationalization initiatives in part to compete with their European counterparts. In North America, most of these initiatives revolve around the adoption of student exchange programs and the adoption of some courses or programs with international content. "The piecemeal approach—a language requirement here, some study abroad there, and an internationally focused course or two—has not succeeded in deeply internationalizing higher education institutions or student learning" (Greene, 2002). Study abroad programs tend to fail when students do not speak the language of the country, spend too much time with their fellow students from their home university or college, and when they participate in field trips that resemble tourist excursions rather than exploration activities (Brewer and Cunningham, 2009).

9.3 NEED TO CHANGE

The internationalization of universities and colleges needs a radical cultural change in higher education institutions, particularly in North America. It needs a commitment from the administration to foster an international ethos across campus and the necessary funding to support international initiatives. It also requires teachers to foster an international perspective in their own courses and programs (AUCC, 2008). "It is not easy to attain cross-cultural awareness or understanding of the kind that puts you into the head of a person from an utterly different culture. Contact alone will not do it. Even sustained contact will not do it" (Hanvey, 2004). The solution lies in a 180-degree change in the way students, teachers, and administrators approach international and intercultural issues. "There must be a readiness to respect and accept, and a capacity to participate.[…] And the participation must be sustained over long periods of time.[…][O]ne may assume that some plasticity in the individual, the ability to learn and change, is crucial" (Hanvey, 2004).

Apart from the creation of inclusive deep learning scenarios as discussed earlier, this change toward full internationalization requires the internationalization of the curriculum, the integration of study abroad programs with an internationalized home-campus curriculum, a thorough cultural preparation of students before they travel abroad, and a plurilingual education across campus. Let's examine each of these key factors.

Internationalization and Deep Learning

9.3.1 INTERNATIONALIZATION OF THE CURRICULUM

A significant aspect of internationalization of universities and colleges is the internationalization of the curriculum. An international curriculum is "a curriculum with an international orientation in content, aimed at preparing students for performing (professionally and socially) in an international and multicultural context and designed for domestic students and/or foreign students" (Stronkhorst, 2005).

The content must reflect the questions, problems, situations, and theories that transcend the boundaries of the region the university or college is situated in. That content must be approached from an ethnorelative perspective, that is, it must be addressed as people in other regions and countries deal with those problems, questions, and situations. For example, the typical undergraduate criminology curriculum in the United States and Canada focuses on North American criminal problems. Crime in Latin America or in Africa is different from crime committed in North America. The typical curriculum simply ignores criminal phenomena in the developing world. The theories that tend to explain criminality in North America fail to explain criminal events in other parts of the world, even if they claim otherwise; and the curriculum generally ignores the vast and rich theories generated outside North America, Europe, and other mainstream regions. In science, the typical medical schools' curriculum in North America and Europe is dominated by a pharmaceutical and allopathic conception of medicine. Chinese, Indian, and aboriginal notions of medicine are either ignored or treated as marginal.

This international content needs to be accompanied by readings from authors from other countries, including authors from non-Western parts of the world. Authors who do not write in English usually offer a perspective that reflects ideas generated in their cultures that are not tainted by Western thought. If you don't read foreign languages, you can ask international students and international colleagues (even from other disciplines) to help you identify and translate (if necessary) key readings. For example, a colleague of mine who teaches nutrition at the graduate level wanted to incorporate nutritional approaches from different parts of the world, particularly those that are not well known in North America and Western Europe. She traveled throughout South East Asia, South America, and

Central America and incorporated nutritional habits from those regions in her curriculum. She used Internet translation websites to translate stories, recipes, and texts from those cultures. Then, she edited those translations and asked members of the community who were born in those regions to check for accuracy. Her students also helped her with nutritional perspectives from their families and their own travels. She has been doing this for years; her courses benefit from a fairly extensive collection of nutritional trends from all over the world.

9.3.2 INTEGRATED STUDY ABROAD PROGRAMS

In Europe and North America, most higher education institutions have study abroad components. However, in North America, few universities and colleges include study abroad programs as part of their required curricula. In most cases, study abroad is disconnected from the campus curricula. In some other cases, students even find it hard to have credits earned abroad be recognized as part of their majors. This is because the Instruction-paradigm university revolves around credits and courses that are considered unique—and essentially nontransferrable.

The most successful study abroad programs are those, which integrate the home campus curriculum, as it is the home curriculum that is the most influential in shaping students' educational experience. In these integrated curricula, students learn to recognize and value international approaches to the disciplines they learn in their home institutions.

Integration between the home program and the study abroad program requires the coordination and articulation of both programs. Ideally, both should be seen as two aspects of the same program. At the institutional level, this requires negotiation of a common curriculum between the home and the foreign programs. This should be accompanied by a cultural change cutting across the entire campus—from the president to the cafeteria employees and including teachers, students, educational developers, and staff. This cultural change must be expressed in institutional values, policies, funding, support, recognition of learning, and other inclusive practices throughout the university or college (AUCC, 2008).

Internationalization and Deep Learning

At the classroom level, we can coordinate with the department or teachers receiving our students the kind of learning experiences that our students need in order to make the most of the study abroad program.

As with most other aspects of the learning process, teachers play a fundamental role in students' international education. When we are interested in international projects and incorporate them in our classes, students are more likely to want to complete their studies abroad. Teachers' interest usually increases when we had an international education as students or when we go abroad to do research, teach a course, or participate in a workshop.

Another essential aspect of the integration of the home curriculum with the study abroad program is the adoption of measures to incorporate in our classes the experiences of students while they are studying abroad and when they return (Brewer and Cunningham, 2009). For example, I usually ask students studying abroad to Skype® into my classes so that they discuss their experiences with the students taking my courses. I sometimes ask them to prepare a short talk on something they are learning. I also ask my students to interview the students who are studying abroad. This generally encourages students to want to do a study abroad program. At the same time, the students already studying abroad feel connected to their home institution and feel that what they are doing is valued at home.

It is also important to give continuity to what the students learned abroad. One way of doing this is to offer a seminar or workshop where returning students can continue exploring the topics or issues that they learned abroad. Another way to give continuity is to offer a course in the language in which students studied abroad. For example, if chemistry students went to Russia to do part of their program there, the department could offer a chemistry course in Russian so that students can keep using Russian and will not forget it.

The other side of the coin in integrated study abroad programs is the accommodation of the curriculum of the host institution that receives international students. This, too, requires a permanent open dialog with the sending university or college. This dialog has to make sure that the hosting university understands the learning goals and academic needs of the international students it receives. For this purpose, it is essential to get to know the students as well as possible. Clinical interviews, one-on-one conversations, placement tests, observations, and the range of initial evaluation strategies suggested later in the book constitute effective methods to attain this objective. These methods can help the host institution plan the learning experiences for the students coming for their study abroad programs. These experiences can include courses, dedicated workshops, advising, and out-of-class performances.

9.3.3 STUDENT PREPARATION AT THEIR HOME INSTITUTIONS

If students see study abroad programs as life-changing experiences, the home curriculum must adequately prepare them for this transformation and, especially, must acknowledge and value this transformation upon their return (Brewer and Cunningham, 2009).

A successful study abroad program requires students to be developmentally ready to embark on educational experiences abroad and to be fully prepared to make the most of these experiences (Brewer and Cunningham, 2009). Like with Perry's (1970) cognitive developmental process, there are also developmental stages in cultural adaptation. When interacting with other cultures, we usually go through the following stages:

(i) denial: we are unable to perceive significant cultural differences;
(ii) defense: we assign negative characteristics to cultural differences;
(iii) minimization: we perceive cultural differences, but we minimize them by thinking that they are not significant, that essentially we are all the same and we all want the same things;
(iv) acceptance: we accept existence of cultural differences even when we do not like them;
(v) adaptation: we internalize a different cultural frame of reference and become bicultural or multicultural;
(vi) integration: we reconcile the internalized conflicting frames of reference and become intercultural mediators; we become interculturalists and multiculturalists (Bennett, 1998).

The first three stages are considered ethnocentric; the last three are ethnorelative. Students have to be in one of the ethnorelative stages of intercultural development in order to profit from the study abroad experience.

Internationalization and Deep Learning 193

The move from ethnocentric to ethnorelative stages of cultural adaptation requires preparation by the home university. Adequate preparation entails embracing the creation of inclusive deep learning environments as discussed earlier. It also requires helping students develop ethnographic and participant observation skills (Edwards, 2000) and helping them understand the history, culture, arts, and politics of the country that they will study in (Pusch and Merrill, 2008). An adequate level of acquisition of the language of the foreign country is also essential, as is the students' ability to learn experientially (Brewer and Cunningham, 2009).

Students also need to have the intercultural resources to be able to understand "the nature of intercultural dynamics and the cognitive, behavioral, and affective dimensions of the experience" (Brewer and Cunningham, 2009). These resources include cognitive aspects, that is, place-specific knowledge, knowledge about oneself, and knowledge about intercultural theory. Place-specific knowledge can be developed through projects, readings, case studies, and other student performances focused on the country and culture that the students will visit. Knowledge about oneself can be developed through reflective journals, scenarios, role-playing, and other activities focused on exploring oneself and how one relates to situations involving people from different cultures. Intercultural theory helps students understand other human beings when they do not share a common cultural experience by focusing on identifying and analyzing the factors that influence our experience of other cultures and cultural phenomena (Bennett, 1998). These factors include stereotyping and generalization processes, such as deductive and inductive stereotyping, intercultural communication processes, perceptual reality, verbal and nonverbal behavior, communication styles, values, and assumptions (Bennett, 1998).

Students also need to be equipped with ethnorelative attitudinal resources such as the ability to suspend judgment, tolerance of ambiguity, curiosity, and confidence (Brewer and Cunningham, 2009). In addition, adequate preparation needs to focus on the skills and competences that students need to develop in order to be prepared to make the most of their study abroad experiences. These include the abilities to listen, observe, describe, interpret, and reflect from ethnorelative perspectives (Brewer and Cunningham, 2009). When these resources and knowledge are embedded throughout the home curriculum, students will be able to apply them easily and in a natural way in their study abroad experiences.

9.3.4 PLURILINGUAL EDUCATION

Learning the academic disciplines or professional fields in a plurality of languages is another essential aspect of both a rich deep learning process and the inclusive deep learning environment. It permits learners to examine them from angles that cannot be considered when analyzing problems or questions from a single language. This is so because language is a system of representation for perception and thinking (Bennett, 1998). Thus, learning a discipline in a second language enables learners to achieve a degree of depth that cannot be achieved when teaching and learning in only one language.

Knowledge of more than one language is also crucial to compete with graduates from universities in Europe and other countries that have extensive foreign and second language policy programs. For example, the Council of Europe adopted policy that recommends its member states to adopt a plurilingual approach to education at all levels. Within this framework, authorities have to ensure that language instruction is fully integrated within the core of the educational aims of universities and to consider and treat each language not in isolation but as part of a coherent plurilingual education for all students across the entire curriculum (Council of Europe, 2008). A plurilingual education also fosters an increased awareness of and sensitivity for multicultural issues (Haigh, 2009).

From a biological point of view, exploring academic issues in a plurality of languages increases the neuronal networks in the prefrontal cortex of the brain (Kaushanskaya and Marian, 2007). Additionally, research has shown that being plurilingual, or even bilingual, can have positive effects on the brain, improving cognitive abilities beyond language and protecting against brain diseases in old age. These benefits apply not only to those who acquire a language during childhood but also to adults who learn a second language (Bhattacharjee, 2012).

With notable exceptions, most of North American undergraduate education is unilingual. Unlike in European higher education institutions, plurilingual education, that is, the acquisition and development of several second languages, is not a priority in North American universities and colleges. In 1991, 35 percent of Canadian universities required a second language for undergraduate graduation. This percentage plummeted to 9 percent in 2006 (AUCC, 2008). A similar situation takes place in the United States, where

Internationalization and Deep Learning

foreign language education at the postsecondary level has been considered scandalous (Panetta, 1999). Although the United States and Canada are multicultural societies (and Canada is also a bilingual country) with a plurality of languages and immigrant minorities, instruction in North American colleges and universities is essentially unilingual. This has resulted in two interrelated phenomena. First, unilingual students do not acquire a second language. In Canada, most students graduate without even speaking the other official language. Second, students who are already bilingual —mostly first—and, to a lesser extent, second-generation immigrants—do not become fully literate in their first language, because higher education institutions do not give them the possibility to pursue part of their education in their first language.

In the United States and Canada, we have relegated the teaching of second languages essentially to literature or modern languages departments. Although these play a very important role in higher education, their efforts do not guarantee a plurilingual education for all students. The result has been that languages are treated as subjects like any other discipline "in terms of time allocation, organization of curriculum time, and assessment and certification, as if languages were objects of study like other subjects. Languages therefore compete with other subjects for curriculum time and learners' attention" (Council of Europe, 2008). This parallels the development of writing in U.S. and Canadian universities (Kearns and Turner, 2008). When teaching writing was confined exclusively to English departments, students did not achieve writing literacy in the disciplines. Disciplinary departments had to assume the role of teaching students how to write in their fields. And some still do so reluctantly. Learning a second language necessitates similarly coordinated and massive efforts across the curriculum. In the meantime, we teachers in the disciplines need to assume responsibility for helping our students acquire a second language. We need to help our students obtain an education that will fully prepare them to succeed in today's interconnected world.

Those of us who teach in nonlanguage disciplines may think that we are not prepared to help our students learn a second language. Those who are unilingual may find this even ludicrously unattainable. I suggest that we can help our students develop a second language in the long-term, even if we do not speak it fluently, by making small but constant changes aimed at introducing and fostering the development of a second language in our courses, while maintaining the core of instruction in English. Table 9.1 includes some practical suggestions to adopt plurilingual teaching in our classrooms.

TABLE 9.1   Plurilingual teaching strategies.

- Choose a second language (L2) and connect it to your course.
  - o Choose the language that you want your students to develop according to your and your students' preferences and the resources available in your community. Then, connect your substantive course to the target L2. Make it a natural path for students to learn that L2. For example, if you teach nutrition and there is a food laboratory whose holding company is in France, include discussions on French and European food policy into your course.
- Start small and introduce changes gradually.
  - o The first time you teach a course, you cannot expect unilingual students to become fully proficient in the L2. This will never happen in one single course. But you may aim at instilling in students an awareness of the importance to learn a second language throughout their university studies. You can be more ambitious in future courses. Additionally, try to see the big picture. Most of us have the same students in different courses throughout their university years. So, maybe we can try to help students develop a very basic notion of a second language in the introduction to our discipline course and progressively aim at slightly higher levels in subsequent courses.
- Educate yourself about theories of second language acquisition.
  - o Become familiar with the theories of second language acquisition and the predominant methods for teaching second languages. If you are already familiar with learning theories and effective teaching methods, you will have strong foundations to understand second language theories easily.
- Provide input in the L2
  - o Learners acquire a second language when they receive input in the second language that is within their zone of proximal development (Vigotsky, 1978), which is known as input + 1 (Krashen, 1988). Give students plenty of appropriate input in the L2.
  - o For example, introduce yourself in the L2, write the agenda for the class in the L2 on the board, and give students a short and simple text about your discipline in the L2, preferably one with photographs, graphics, charts, figures, and other nonlinguistic information. Ask them to infer the content based on linguistic and paralinguistic clues. If one or two students already speak the L2, ask them to present a topic in the L2 at a simple level for other students to follow.
  - o If you don't speak the language, look for alternative sources of input, for example, a short video, or invite a student who speaks the L2 in your class to do so.

Internationalization and Deep Learning

TABLE 9.1 *(Continued)*

- Encourage your students to use the L2 in class.
    - o After the initial silent period (Krashen, 1988), you should encourage your students to start using the L2 in class. For example, if they have to give an oral presentation in English, ask them to introduce themselves and the presentation in the L2 or encourage them to ask a simple question in the L2 during a lecture.
- Help students experiment with the L2.
    - o Devote a few minutes every class to discuss specific aspects of the language. Help students deduce a grammatical aspect of the L2. For example, if students are trying to express opinions in the L2, show some examples of how people do so in the L2 and ask them to discuss and deduce the grammatical forms in small groups. Then, you can write students' conclusions on the board. Let students experiment with these forms. If you don't speak the L2 ask a student or a friend who does to help you. Remember it is the students who need to negotiate meaning and construct knowledge in the L2.
- Take them out to the field.
    - o Show your students the importance of speaking the L2 in the real world. Plan field trips to visit companies, organizations, and people that speak the L2. For example, if you teach accounting arrange a visit to a company whose head office is in a country where people speak your target language. Meet with a manager in the accounting department who speaks the L2, Ask your students to talk to him or her in English and, if possible, in the L2. Ask the manager to show a balance sheet or other accounting documents written in the L2. Even if your students have a rudimentary knowledge of the L2, they will be familiar with a balance sheet and will be able to deduce the information written in the L2. Encourage the manager to explain accounting terms in the L2. It is by making connections between new knowledge (L2) and their existing knowledge (accounting) that students will learn the L2.
- Hook them up with other L2 learners and native speakers of the L2.
    - o Learning is a collective enterprise. It implies an acculturation in communities of knowledgeable peers (Bruffee, 1999). So, encourage students to connect to other speakers of the L2. You can match them with learners of the L2 from other universities so that they can exchange emails about general issues related to your discipline. You can ask your students to tweet in the L2 and to follow a native speaker, who tweets about your discipline in the L2

TABLE 9.1 *(Continued)*

- Deal proactively with natural resistance.
  - o You will meet resistance from the administration, colleagues, and students. The best way to do deal with resistance from your colleagues and administrators is by engaging in action-research projects to collect data about the success of your courses. Share the results in presentations at your institution or publish them (Weimer, 2002). Research shows that students are more enthusiastic about unconventional teaching. If you communicate your goals clearly, you are passionate about the learning enterprise, and treat them fairly, students will soon embark with your linguistic goals.
- Take risks and have fun!
  - o If we do not take these risks, our students in unilingual universities will not have the possibility of a plurilingual education that may help them fully prepare to work and live in an increasingly globalized world.

9.4 SUMMARY

An international and plurilingual education is an essential aspect of the inclusive deep learning environment and contributes to enhance the connections that learners make while engaged in the process of construction of knowledge, which leads to a richer and more profound learning experience. The Instruction-paradigm universities and colleges, particularly in North America, have failed to develop an international and plurilingual education. At the classroom level, the implementation of an international and plurilingual education requires the internationalization of the curriculum, the integration of study abroad programs with an internationalized home-campus curriculum, cultural preparation to help students move from ethnocentric to ethnorelative stages, and the development of, at least, more than one language.

In the next chapter, I will address a related issue: how to help students who speak English as a foreign language who come to North American universities and colleges to study in English.

Internationalization and Deep Learning 199

PRACTICE CORNER

1. Think of a course you are teaching or one that you have recently taught. What changes can you make to include a more international perspective? What changes can you make to integrate your course with study abroad programs? What pedagogical adjustments, if any, would you have to make to accommodate these changes?
2. What specific actions can you take to encourage more students to participate in study abroad experiences? How can you promote study abroad programs in your classes?
3. How can you help returning study abroad students continue with their learning experiences initiated abroad? What can you do to help them maintain a foreign language learned abroad? How can you help them reintegrate back to your courses and program? What can you do in your courses so that returning study abroad students can share their experiences with other students?
4. It has been argued that students need to move from ethnocentric to ethnorelative stages to make the most of their experiences abroad. What specific actions and initiatives can you think of to help students in the defense stage move to acceptance or adaptation stages?
5. What can you do in your program to internationalize the curriculum? What institutional factors can help in this effort? What institutional factors can hinder this effort?
6. Suppose you want to review your program to introduce international components in the curriculum. A colleague with no international experience vehemently opposes this idea and is trying to convince untenured faculty to oppose it, too. What can you do to deal with this opposition and resistance?
7. Remember or watch *Endless Love* (1981) directed by Franco Zeffirelli. David refers to Jade as an international student who has just come from the People's Republic of China to study capital investments in the United States. Suppose that you teach this class and that Jade is in fact a foreign exchange student from China. What can you do to maximize her experience in your course? What can you do to learn about her learning goals and curricular needs?

What can you do so that your local students will learn from this and other visiting and foreign exchange students in your courses?

8. What specific actions can you take to promote a plurilingual education in your program? Which of the teaching strategies suggested in Table 9.1 can you include in your courses? How would you implement them? Which of those strategies would you not include? Why?

9. It has been argued that the main factors that contribute to a global education are: internationalization of the curriculum, integration of study abroad programs, cultural preparation of students, and plurilingual teaching. Can you think of other factors that may also contribute to a global and international education? What classroom and institutional actions are needed in relation to those factors? What kind of support is needed?

10. An essential aspect of cultural preparation for international experiences is the development of ethnorelative attitudinal competences and skills, such as the ability to suspend judgment and tolerance of ambiguity. How can you include the teaching of these skills into your courses? How can you help students develop these skills?

KEYWORDS

- **deep learning**
- **integration**
- **internationalization**
- **internationalization of the curriculum**
- **plurilingual education**
- **student preparation**
- **study abroad programs**
- **teaching strategies**

REFERENCES

AUCC (2008). *Internationalization of the curriculum: A practical guide to support Canadian universities' efforts.*http://www.aucc.ca/_pdf/english/publications/curriculum-primer_e.pdf (accessed Aug. 12, 2013).

Bennett, M. J. Intercultural Communication: A Current Perspective. In Basic Concepts of Intercultural Communication: Selected Readings; Bennett, M. J., Ed.;Intercultural Press: Yarmouth, ME: 1998.

Bhattacharjee, Y. Why Bilinguals are Smarter. New York Times, March 17, 2012.

Bowden, J. and Marton, F. University of Learning. London: Routledge, 2004.

Brewer, E.; Cunningham, K.*Integrating study abroad into the curriculum: Theory and practice across the disciplines;* Stylus Press: Sterling, VA, 2009.

Bruffee, K. Collaborative Learning: Higher Education, Interdependence, and the Authority of Knowledge, 2nd ed.; The John Hopkins University Press: Baltimore and London, 1999.

Council of Europe (2008). Recommendation CM/Rec(2008)7 of the Committee of Ministers to member states on the use of the Council of Europe's Common European Framework of Reference for Languages (CEFR) and the promotion of plurilingualism.

Edwards, J. The "other Eden": Thoughts on American study abroad in Britain. Frontiers: The Interdisciplinary Journal of Study Abroad, *2000,* 6, 83–98.

Green, M. F. Internationalizing undergraduate education: Challenges and lessons of success; American Council on Education: Washington, DC, 2002.

Haigh, M. Fostering Cross-Cultural Empathy with Non-Western Curricular Structures. Journal of Studies in International Education, 2009, 13, 2, 271.

Hanvey, R. G. An Attainable Global Perspective.The American Forum for Global Education, 2004.http://www.globaled.org/an_att_glob_persp_04_11_29.pdf(accessed Aug. 12, 2013).

Kaushanskaya, M.; Marian, V. Age-of-acquisition effects in the development of a bilingual advantage for word learning. Proceedings of the 32nd Annual Boston University Conference on Language Development. Cascadilla Press; Somerville, MA, 2007.

Kearns, J.; Turner, B. The Historical Roots of Writing Instruction in Anglo-Canadian Universities.European Journal of Writing. 2008, 1–8.

Krashen, S. D. Second Language Acquisition and Second Language Learning; Prentice-Hall International: New York, 1988.

Panetta, L. Foreign Language Education: If 'Scandalous' in the twentieth century, What Will It Be in the twenty-first century? Foreign language study in American universities at the end of the twentieth century, Stanford University conference, June 2, 1999. https://www.stanford.edu/dept/lc/language/about/conferencepapers/panettapaper.pdf (accessed Aug 12, 2013).

Perry, W. Forms of Intellectual and Ethical Development in the College Years: A Scheme; Hold, Rinehart and Winston: Troy, Mo, 1970.

Pusch, M.; Merrill, M. Reflection, reciprocity, responsibility, and committed relativism: Intercultural development through international service learning. In Developing intercultural competence and transformation: Theory, research, and application in international education; Savicki, V., Ed.; Stylus: Sterling, VA, 2008.

Stier, J. Dimensions and Experiences of Human Identity: An Analytical Toolkit andIllustration. Monograph 69, Department of Sociology, Goteborg University, Goteborg. 1998.

Stier, J. Internationalization in higher education: unexplored possibilities and unavoidable challenges, European Conference on Educational Research, University of Lisbon, Lisbon, 11–14 September, 2002.

Stronkhorst, R. Learning outcomes of international mobility at two Dutch institutions of Higher Education.Journal of Studies in International Education, 2005, 9(4), 292–315.

Vygotsky, L. Mind in Society: The Development of Higher Psychological Processes; Harvard University Press: Cambridge, MA, 1978.

Weimer, M. Learner-Centered Teaching: Five Key Changes to Practice; Jossey-Bass: San Francisco, 2002.

CHAPTER 10

INTERNATIONAL STUDENTS AND ACADEMIC PROFICIENCY

Language is not a genetic gift, it is a social gift. Learning a new language is becoming a member of the club—the community of speakers of that language.

— FRANK SMITH

CONTENTS

10.1 Introduction 204
10.2 Demographics 204
10.3 Challenges and Concerns 205
10.4 Academic Proficiency 206
10.5 Language Acquisition Process 207
10.6 Strategies to Help ESL Students 210
10.7 Obstacles to Academic Proficiency in a Second Language 213
10.8 Summary 215
Practice Corner 216
Keywords 221
References 221

10.1 INTRODUCTION

A related issue to inclusive deep learning environments and an international and plurilingual education is teaching students whose native language does not coincide with the language of instruction of the university or college. Although the ideas of inclusive deep learning environments such as respect and recognition of diverse cultures, traditions, and worldviews apply here and are the main factors to help nonnative-speaking students succeed in the classroom, I will further address some specific aspects of this phenomenon.

The chapter begins with a brief examination of nonnative student demographics in North America to contextualize this phenomenon. Then, I describe the challenges and concerns arising from teaching nonnative speaking students, particularly those from the non-Western world. Then, I explore the concept of academic proficiency and some relevant aspects of second language acquisition theories. Finally, I will delve into strategies to help nonnative-speaking students achieve academic proficiency in the disciplines as well as common practices that hinder the attainment of academic proficiency.

I will focus the discussion on nonnative-speaking students studying in universities and colleges where the language of instruction is English. However, all of the challenges, theories, and strategies in this chapter also apply to nonnative-speaking students studying in any second or foreign language. As in the previous chapters dealing with diversity and learning, the goal is to explore opportunities to maximize student deep learning.

10.2 DEMOGRAPHICS

First of all, it is important to bear in mind that nonnative speakers of English constitute a large percentage of the student population in North American higher education institutions. This group is made up of diverse students with varied skills, backgrounds, and levels of language proficiency. Nonnative English speakers include: (i) international students who come to do an entire academic program for two, three, or four years, some of whom may settle down in North America, whereas others return to their home

International Students and Academic Proficiency

countries; (ii) foreign exchange students, who come for one or two semesters and then return to their home institutions; (iii) recent immigrants who have been living in an English speaking country for a few years; (iv) citizens of the country who normally speak a language other than English at home and have been educated in that language or mainly in that language rather than English during their primary and secondary schooling, such as Francophone Quebeckers in Canada and some aboriginal students who speak their native language in the United States or Canada; and (v) some students who speak an English dialect that is not considered standard for mainstream North American academics are often included in this category, even if technically they are native speakers. These include certain Asian and African variations of English.

10.3 CHALLENGES AND CONCERNS

Two years ago, a small, undergraduate university—located in a relatively isolated and predominantly unilingual, homogeneous, and white town in northern Canada—received hundreds of students from the Middle East. This massive influx of students dramatically changed the demographics of the campus and even the city.

These students met all the admissions requirements. They had good TOEFL scores, comparable to scores that would give them access to virtually any university in North America, including some elite institutions. They also had very good grade-point averages (GPAs) from their high schools. Although some teachers, particularly those with an international background, welcomed these students, most faculty members reacted very negatively. They claimed that Middle East students were not prepared to study in North America. They argued that they could not speak English correctly, that they did not have the critical thinking skills to analyze complex materials, and that they could not write essays in English (as if local students could in first year). Some even claimed that the TOEFL test and other similar standardized tests were ineffective to measure English language proficiency. Others came up with stories that they claimed to have read online that getting a decent grade in high school in the Middle East is simply a matter of giving expensive presents to the teachers. Others vociferated that they felt intimidated by groups of Middle

East male students speaking in Arabic in the hallways. Some of these faculty members informally and formally raised some of the strangest proposals in various academic organs. These proposals ranged from stopping admitting international students (except for students coming from England, the United States, and Australia) to segregating Middle East students into courses with no local students.

Even in larger universities and colleges, many teachers frequently complain that it is difficult to teach their disciplines to students who do not understand English and who cannot communicate in English. Although this may seem to be a legitimate concern, I believe it is not the case. Most English as a second language (ESL) students have a basic knowledge of English. They have passed standardized English language tests, have lived in the country for a few years, or have received some education in English. What they often lack is academic proficiency in the disciplines in English. Incidentally, most domestic students also lack academic proficiency in the disciplines even if they are native speakers of English.

10.4 ACADEMIC PROFICIENCY

Academic proficiency, a concept first proposed by Cummins (1979), means having the capacity to use language efficiently in academic settings. For example, you can use language to formulate a hypothesis, to discuss the literature in an academic discipline, to write a thesis, to engage in a debate about opposing theories, or to present at a conference. This is in contrast to basic interpersonal communication skills, which deal with language use in everyday situations such as ordering coffee, talking about the weather with a neighbor, or commenting about a sports game. Most ESL students have basic interpersonal communications skills, albeit at different levels of competence.

Academic proficiency consists of three aspects: (i) knowledge of academic language, that is, the discourse of the academic disciplines or professions; (ii) knowledge of specialized subject matter, that is, the content of the discipline or profession; and (iii) strategies, that is, a series of actions that contribute toward the acquisition and development of both academic language and subject matter content (Krashen and Brown, 2007).

International Students and Academic Proficiency 207

As mentioned before, it takes nonnative speakers of English longer to become academically proficient than their native counterparts. ESL students who are already academically proficient in their first language need a period of five to seven years to become academically proficient in English (Slocum, 2003). So, this means that ESL undergraduate students will probably not become academically proficient until, and if, they go to graduate school. This period is even longer for those ESL students who are not academically proficient in their first language, such as international students who come fresh from high school to study a discipline that they have not studied in their home countries (Slocum, 2003).

10.5 LANGUAGE ACQUISITION PROCESS

It is important to understand the process of second language acquisition in order to best help our ESL students achieve academic proficiency in our disciplines.

Succinctly, we acquire a second language in the same way we have acquired our first language. This implies a process of communicating and interacting in the target language. Krashen (1981), a specialist in second language teaching and learning, has developed five hypotheses about the second language acquisition process. These five hypotheses are described next (Krashen, 1988).

10.5.1 THE ACQUISITION-LEARNING DISTINCTION

The process of acquiring a second language is similar to the process by which we learn our first language as children. We learn the language in a subconscious way while we are engaged in multiple natural activities. Language learning is a formal, conscious process that focuses on the language itself—its rules, vocabulary, and pronunciation. Formal language learning does not result in the development of a second language. So, for example, focusing on correction of grammatical errors does not help ESL students improve their English competence.

10.5.2 THE NATURAL ORDER HYPOTHESIS

Learners acquire language structures in a progressive order, that is, there is a natural order in the acquisition of different aspects of the language, such as grammatical structures. This implies that there is no point in forcing students to use certain grammatical structures when they are not yet developmentally ready.

10.5.3 THE MONITOR HYPOTHESIS

Acquired language leads to fluency; and learned language produces correctness. Learned language acts as a monitor or editor and corrects spontaneous use of language. Some students over use the monitor and find themselves correcting themselves all the time or simply not speaking so as to avoid using language incorrectly. Other students underuse the monitor and hand in written assignments full of mistakes that they could have easily corrected.

10.5.4 THE INPUT HYPOTHESIS

Learners acquire a second language when they receive comprehensible and meaningful input in the second language that is within their zone of proximal development (Vygotsky, 1978), which Krashen (1987) refers to as input+1. Understanding language that uses grammatical structures that are beyond the students' language level is possible when students can make use of the context, nonlinguistic information, and outside knowledge to understand the message, that is, the input. When ESL students are forced to produce in English at a level beyond their knowledge, their production is regarded as incorrect and inappropriate by native English professors. Moreover, this hinders students' progress in the process of learning the language.

The input hypothesis contradicts the skill-building hypothesis, which is an approach that still persists in the Instruction paradigm. The skill-building approach focuses on helping students "to consciously learn their 'skills'(grammar, vocabulary, spelling). […] Only after skills are mastered

International Students and Academic Proficiency

can [students] actually use these skills in real situations" (Krashen, 2004). This approach to language learning is not conducive to language acquisition and hinders the process toward academic proficiency.

10.5.5   THE AFFECTIVE FILTER HYPOTHESIS

Learners can only acquire a second language if they find themselves in a motivating and low anxiety environment. A stressful and high anxiety environment hinders the language acquisition process. For example, an environment that is perceived by students to be too demanding or that does not give students freedom to express will prevent students from receiving the input, which will in turn hinder acquisition. Although we may do our best to create a friendly and relaxing atmosphere, we need to be aware that the context in which some ESL students find themselves may create a high affective filter. For example, in *The Girl Who Wouldn't Sing*, Kit Yuen Quan (1990), a Chinese immigrant who emigrated to the United States at the age of seven, recounts her experience with the English language.

It was really hard deciding how to talk about language because I had to go through my blocks with language. I stumble upon these blocks whenever I have to write, speak in public or voice my opinions in a group of native English speakers with academic backgrounds. All of a sudden as I scramble for words, I freeze and am unable to think clearly. Minutes pass as I struggle to retrieve my thoughts until I finally manage to say something. But it never comes close to expressing what I mean. I think it's because I'm afraid to show who I really am. I cannot bear the thought of the humiliation and ridicule. And I dread having to use a language that has often betrayed my meaning. Saying what I need to say using my own words usually threatens the status quo (Quan, 1990).

So according to Krashen (1981), "the best methods [for helping students acquire and develop a second language] are therefore those that supply 'comprehensible input' in low-anxiety situations, containing messages that students really want to hear. These methods do not force early production in the second language, but allow students to produce when they are 'ready', recognizing that improvement comes from supplying communicative and comprehensible input, and not from forcing and correcting production" (Krashen, 1981).

10.6 STRATEGIES TO HELP ESL STUDENTS

The fact that ESL students need long periods of time to become academically proficient does not mean that we have to sit down and do nothing for five years. Neither does it mean that we have to punish our students for being quiet in class or for not writing in English correctly. What we do need to do in order to support ESL students in their process toward becoming academically proficient in English is to employ some teaching strategies founded upon the principles of second language acquisition. Equally important, we also need to refrain from adopting practices that hinder second language development.

All college or university teachers can help their ESL students acquire high levels of academic proficiency in their disciplines. Most of the actions needed to help ESL students reach academic proficiency are the same as the ones analyzed earlier to help non-ESL students. The main difference is that ESL students come from different communities of knowledgeable peers than students who are native English speakers. So, we need to be aware of the needs, backgrounds, knowledge, and discourse abilities of members of these communities of knowledge. And we need to help them acculturate in the community of knowledge of our discipline by providing them with appropriate input in a low-anxiety environment so that they can gradually develop their English language skills and eventually become academically proficient in our disciplines. Table 10.1 discusses some specific classroom strategies to help ESL students in this process.

TABLE 10.1 Strategies to help ESL students.

- Provide opportunities for students to receive input+1.
  - o Students need to receive appropriate comprehensible input in English about our disciplines. For this purpose, we need to identify students' current levels of competence and provide them with input that they can understand with the help of extralinguistic clues, such as visual aids, or with the help of peers. As students progress in their language abilities, input needs to become more challenging.
  - o Krashen (2007) suggests a strategy that he refers to as narrow reading, where students focus on reading a series of texts by one author or a series of texts about the same topic. This helps students receive comprehensible input. At the same time, it

International Students and Academic Proficiency

TABLE 10.1 *(Continued)*

provides students with enough background knowledge to make that input more comprehensible. Krashen (2007) argues that experts follow the narrow reading approach to become competent in their fields. Additionally, narrow reading motivates readers to focus on the message and results in deep reading. After a considerable time focused on one area, ESL students can gradually move to a closely related area and transfer the acquired knowledge, structures, and vocabulary to the new area (Krashen, 2000).

- Create a nonthreatening environment.

  o The creation of a learning environment where students feel comfortable and safe to communicate in English is essential for their progress toward academic proficiency.

  o Speaking, writing, and thinking in English cause emotional stress to speakers of other languages. It is important to acknowledge the feelings and emotions that ESL students experience while expressing in English.

  o It is also important to recognize the perceptions that foreign students have of North Americans. For example, for Indians, North Americans are selfish and self-centered and do not speak English properly (Ramisetty-Mikler, 1993). For Chinese students, Americans are arrogant and aggressive, and the United States is regarded as hegemonic (Johnston and Stockman, 2005). South Korean students perceive Americans as unfriendly (Won, 2005). Other cultures regard North Americans as frivolous, naïve, and even false (Louis, 2002). Studies show that achievement of academic proficiency in a second language is dependent on the student's favorable attitude toward native speakers of that language (Clément, Gardner and Smythe, 1977).

  o In order to soften the negative effects on the development of academic proficiency in English, Louis recommends employing performative pedagogy (Louis, 2002). Performative pedagogy "combines performance methods and theory with critical pedagogy in an effort to carry out the dual project of social critique and transformation. Performance offers an efficacious means of completing this project by privileging students historicized bodies, by implementing contingent classroom dialog, and by exposing students to the value embedded in performance risk" (Louis, 2002). For Elyze Pineau, performance pedagogy is more than a teaching method, "it is a location, a way of situating one's self in relation to students, to colleagues, and to the institutional policies and traditions under which we all labor. Performance Studies scholars and practitioners locate themselves as embodied researchers: listening, observing, reflecting, theorizing, interpreting, and representing human Communication through the medium of their own and others' experiencing bodies" (Pineau, 1998).

TABLE 10.1 *(Continued)*

- o Performative pedagogy may be used to encourage ESL students, particularly those coming from societies, which feel oppressed by North American governments and corporations, to create performance spaces to voice their oppressions and rehearse solutions to remove obstacles hindering their English language acquisition (Louis, 2002).
- Give students time.
    - o Because it takes years for students to achieve academic proficiency in a second language, in a Learning Paradigm university or college, ESL students should be given ample periods of time to reach academic proficiency that exceed the traditional semester or academic year. These periods of time should extend to several years in order to respect the natural order hypothesis (Krashen, 1988). During these extended periods of time, teachers should not force production in English beyond ESL students' zone of proximal development and should suspend judgment until ESL students reach a sufficiently high level of language proficiency.
    - o In the current Instruction Paradigm, the traditional scheduling formats do not permit teachers to suspend ESL students' grading. In many cases, this translates into a forced acceleration of ESL students' natural development, which hinders the process of language acquisition and promotes language learning and does not facilitate the achievement of academic proficiency.
- We should help students become optimal monitor users.
    - o We should help students acquire and develop metacognitive strategies that are specific and appropriate for second language learners.
    - o We should also teach our students to use these monitoring strategies when using them is contextually appropriate and, most important, when this fosters language acquisition.
    - o The effective use of communication strategies can also help students improve their academic proficiency (Faerch and Kasper, 1980). Communication strategies are classified as (i) reduction strategies, such as topic avoidance, message abandonment, and meaning replacement; (ii) achievement strategies, for example, cooperative strategies such as circumlocution, approximation, and appeals for assistance; and (iii) uncooperative strategies, for example mime, restructuring, language switch, borrowing, literal translation, exemplification, and word coinage (Ting and Phan, 2008). Faucette (2001) argues that the recommended strategies that teachers should encourage ESL students to master are those that help the learner to communicate the intended goal and facilitate language acquisition. These include approximation, circumlocution, and word coinage, together with appeal for assistance if verbal and in English. The non-recommended strategies are the reduction and the uncooperative strategies (Faucette, 2001).

10.7 OBSTACLES TO ACADEMIC PROFICIENCY IN A SECOND LANGUAGE

Apart from the strategies aimed at supporting ESL students' acquisition of the English language and development of academic proficiency in English, we need to refrain from taking actions that hinder their process toward academic proficiency in English. One of these obstacles is the overcorrection of mistakes. This may take place in the form of express comments to grammatical, vocabulary, and spelling mistakes on papers and other written assignments or in more subtle ways, as when teachers paraphrase a question or comment made in class by an ESL student when they never do so for statements made by native English speakers. Correction of mistakes does not lead to any improvement in ESL students' language progress. Language acquisition is a natural process that requires comprehensible input in a nonthreatening environment for long periods of time. Many teachers believe that they help ESL students when they identify their mistakes, when in actuality this practice has the opposite effect, as it produces an overuse of and overdependence on their language monitors (Krashen, 1988). Similar consequences arise when we refer ESL students to writing labs or writing centers so that writing tutors will help students correct their mistakes and hand in error-free papers. These effects are exacerbated when teachers punish ESL students for these mistakes, such as when they give lower grades for papers or exams that have language mistakes.

Forcing output, whether in written or oral form, also hinders the process toward academic proficiency. Research has long demonstrated that learners do not develop a second language by producing outcomes. Learners will be able to produce in their second language when they are developmentally ready to do so after having received sufficient, appropriate, and comprehensible input (Krashen, 1998). Written output such as the production of essays and the writing of exams "do[es] not contribute directly to language acquisition" Krashen (2007). Furthermore, according to a wide array of research studies, "we can develop extremely high levels of language and literacy without any language production at all" (Krashen, 2007). Moreover, forcing premature output can give rise to anxiety and can create a negative environment, which also impedes language acquisition and academic proficiency (Krashen, 1994).

Another practice that also hinders the academic proficiency process is isolating ESL students in courses that only ESL students take instead of integrating them into mainstream courses. Some universities and colleges offer these courses as a sort of transition before allowing ESL students to take regular courses with local students.

Remedial courses also produce negative effects. These courses tend to focus almost exclusively on language learning as opposed to language acquisition and tend to encourage the acceleration of the natural order in language acquisition, which is not conducive to academic proficiency in a second language.

Additionally, it is important to bear in mind that learning in general is not linear. Some of the errors that ESL students make while producing in English, whether in writing or orally, are actually signs of progress. Repressing these errors hinders ESL students' process toward becoming academically proficient. Error analysis is a field that views errors as an integral part of language acquisition. It deals with the differences in the way second language learners and native speakers speak (Richards, 1971). Understanding ESL errors gives us a unique insight on where our ESL students are in their academic proficiency process. Jack Richards (1971) has compiled a taxonomy of errors committed by ESL learners that helps us identify ESL students' stage in this process. According to Richards (1971), errors can be attributed to one of the following factors:

> (1) interference, the use of aspects of another language at a variety of levels; (2) strategies of learning such as over overgeneralization and analogy by means of which the learner tests out his (sic) hypotheses about the structure of the language; (3) strategies of assimilation, in which the learner makes his (sic) learning task easier; and (4) strategies of communication, whereby the learner adapts what he (sic) knows into an efficient communication model, producing an optimal utility grammar from what he (sic) knows of the language (Richards, 1971).

Apart from these errors, it is important to distinguish between performance and competence errors. Performance errors are "occasional and haphazard and are related to such factors as fatigue and memory limitations. [Competence errors] are systematic and may represent either a transitional stage in the development of a grammatical rule or the final

International Students and Academic Proficiency   215

stage of the speaker's knowledge" (Richards, 1971). In order to understand ESL students' stage in the process toward academic proficiency in English, we should focus the error analysis solely on competence errors. When conducting error analysis, it is important to bear in mind that for some aspects of English language acquisition such as some function words (words that have little lexical meaning and whose purpose is to signal grammatical relations in a sentence) the order of acquisition is substantially the same across ESL learners, despite their first language backgrounds (Bailey, Madden and Krashen, 1974). Furthermore, research studies show that "second language errors are not, by nature, different from those made by children learning English as a mother tongue, hence they should not be of undue concern" (Richards, 1971).

10.8 SUMMARY

Many students in our university and college classrooms speak English as a second or foreign language. These students need longer time periods to become academically proficient than native speakers of English. Being academically proficient means having the capacity to use language effectively in academic environments. Academic proficiency encompasses three aspects: (i) knowledge of academic language, (ii) knowledge of specialized subject matter, and (iii) strategies to develop both academic language and subject-matter content.

Knowledge of the process of second language acquisition becomes an important tool to help ESL students attain academic proficiency in the disciplines. Concisely, one learns a second language in the same way as one acquired the first language, that is, by receiving comprehensible input in the target language.

Strategies that respect the natural order in the process of acquisition of language tend to facilitate ESL students' acculturation in disciplinary communities of knowledgeable peers. Forcing ESL students to produce output in English and overcorrecting errors tend to hinder the process toward academic proficiency.

216 Facilitating Deep Learning

The next two chapters focus on evaluation. They deal with the evaluation of student performances and the evaluation of teaching effectiveness from a deep learning perspective.

PRACTICE CORNER

1. Think of a course you are currently teaching or a course you have recently taught. What teaching strategies can you implement to help ESL students in their path toward academic proficiency in your discipline? What specific teaching practices do you think may hinder ESL students' academic proficiency? What changes, if any, would you make to this course next time you teach it?

2. Why do you think that the admission of Middle East students to the small, undergraduate university recounted earlier in this chapter caused so much resistance? Read the measures that the university took that are described in Table 10.2 at the end of this chapter. What do you think of these measures? Do you agree? Why or why not? What, if anything, would you have done differently? What do you think of the placement test? Does it reflect an inclusive or an exclusive pedagogical perspective? Why? What changes could you make to the test? What other method would you adopt to know your international students better? What institutional changes, if any, are required to help ESL students become academically proficient in the disciplines in English at your university or college? How would you implement these changes? Can you anticipate resistance from colleagues and administrators? If so, how could you deal with resistance?

3. It has been argued that correction of mistakes does not lead to any improvement in ESL students' language acquisition process. What does this argument mean in practice? Do you agree? Why or why not? If so, what implications does this argument have in our classes?

4. Watch or remember the film *Our Italian Husband* (2004) directed by Ilaria Borrelli. Focus on the scene when Maria, a recent Italian immigrant, and her children first meet Charlene in New York. What strategies do they use to communicate? Which of these strategies

International Students and Academic Proficiency 217

foster communication? Which strategies, if any, may hinder communication? What other factors foster/hinder communication? If Maria and her children were students in your class, what would you do to help them become academically proficient in English?

5. One of your colleagues has problems with a Korean student whose command of English is very limited. Your colleague says to you: "I agree with inclusive teaching goals and with trying to respect everybody's background. But this student does not speak English. What can I do? Shouldn't she go to a remedial ESL class and then come back to take my course when her English is better?" Do you agree with your colleague? Why or why not? Aren't there any other alternatives? What would you suggest in this case?

6. Watch or remember *The Simpsons* "The Crepes of Wrath" episode (1990, S1 E 11) directed by Wesley Archer and Milton Gray. In this episode, Bart Simpson goes to France as a foreign exchange student. Can you analyze Bart's process of second language acquisition? What can Bart do at the end of his trip to France that he could not do at the beginning? Why is this possible? How can this be explained in light of the academic proficiency process? What strategies did Bart use to communicate in French?

7. A second-year student from Cambodia has written a paper worth 60 percent of the final grade. Although her ideas were interesting and reflected an understanding of the topics discussed in class, her professor failed her because the essay had many grammatical mistakes. The student does not understand why she did not get a better grade. In Cambodia, professors are regarded as substitute parents. Students never question their teachers. So, she does not ask her professor why she failed the essay. You are the department chair. The student decides to drop the course and asks for your authorization. What would you say to the student? Would you talk to your colleague? If so, what would you say? What can you do so that the student will not drop the course?

8. A colleague of yours teaches a course where students have to give presentations to external judges—mostly CEOs and managers from large corporations. He wants all his students to use "correct" English. He penalizes students who speak with regional or

218   Facilitating Deep Learning

foreign accents. Although most domestic students can control their regional accents, international students from South America cannot do anything about their accents. The external judges find the South American students' presentations quite interesting, but your colleague penalized these students with a low mark for speaking with a Spanish accent. The students are taking another class with you. They do very well, and you have good relations with them. They come to see you to talk about the situation in your colleague's class. They are very upset. What can you do? What would you say to the students? Would you talk to your colleague? If so, what would you say?

9. A Japanese student completing a four-year business administration degree in the United States is taking a course with one of your colleagues. The student reads English quite well and speaks English fluently. She is usually quiet in class. While giving a lecture on negotiating business deals, your colleague asks her the following question: "What do you think about the differences between negotiations in Japan and the United States?" The student looks embarrassed and does not answer. Your colleague tells you about this incident. Why do you think the student did not answer the question? What can your colleague do if he wants the student to contribute to the class discussions? What would you say to your colleague? Would you talk to the student if you knew her? If so, what would you say to her?

10. A fourth-year journalism student from Bolivia is always prepared for class and has very interesting questions that he thinks of while reading the assigned texts before class. His questions reveal a deeper understanding of the materials than the questions his fellow domestic students ask. Every time the student asks a question in class or makes a comment, his professor repeats the question or comment for the whole class. The professor does not do the same when the questions or comments come from domestic students. The student feels frustrated and blames himself for speaking with a strong accent. So, he decides not to participate in class any more. The student discusses this with you, the department chair. Why do you think your colleague repeats the student's questions? What can

International Students and Academic Proficiency

219

you do to help this student? What would you say to him? Would you talk to your colleague about this? If so, what would you say to your colleague?

TABLE 10.2 Placement test and other measures taken for international students at a small, undergraduate university.

With more students coming from the Middle East in the following semesters, the university designed a strategy to reach a compromise between campus constituencies that had differing views on what to do. The compromise consisted of raising the standards for admission for students from the Middle East and creating three types of courses: foundation, transition, and regular courses. Foundation courses are courses in general academic skills and in mathematics. Students are introduced to basic North American academic skills that they need to have in order to succeed in regular courses. The emphasis of the academic skills courses is on reading, writing, problem solving, critical thinking, and presentation skills.

The emphasis of mathematics foundation courses is on basic arithmetic operations and problems. Transition courses are dedicated courses for international students in the disciplines that are taught for more hours than the traditional three hour-a-week courses. The goal is to have more time to work with the materials and to have more time in class to work on teaching and learning activities. Teachers can also work on vocabulary and cultural issues that domestic students generally take for granted. Regular courses are traditional courses taken with domestic students and other international students.

In order to best recommend students the most appropriate type of course to take, the university designed two placement tests for all incoming international students: a literacy and academic skills assessment and a numeracy assessment. The former aims at evaluating general academic skills that students need in order to succeed in traditional university courses in North America. It simulates the types of activities that students have to do in most first-year courses in their majors, including watching a lecture, reading an article, writing an essay, solving a problem, and preparing a presentation. The numeracy assessment evaluates students' command of basic arithmetic competences. Before taking the placement test, students are encouraged to take a workshop where teachers discuss the expectations of the placement tests and go over basic North American test-taking strategies.

Literacy and Academic Skills Assessment

INSTRUCTIONS

Write your name neatly in capital letters on your test and booklet. Read all questions and instructions carefully. Write all answers in complete sentences for each section of the test.

Use your own words and complete all sections. Label your answers in the test booklet.

Hand in all test questions and booklets when you are finished.

Section One: Article (8 points total)

Read the article "The Arab World Wants its MTV" and summarize its main idea. (2 points)

Then, answer the following questions about the article. (6 points)

1. What is MTV's strategy for its new MTV Arabia channel?

2. Why are so many media groups going to the Middle East?

3. What does the author mean by MTV's localization strategy?

220   Facilitating Deep Learning

TABLE 10.2 *(Continued)*

Section Two: Lecture

INSTRUCTIONS FOR SECTION 2

You will view a video recording of a university lecture. During the viewing, take notes as if you were in an actual university class. Try and capture the key points of the lecture. You will use your notes to complete the written exercises below. You will view the lecture twice in a row and then will have one hour to complete the entire exercise.

Section Two, question one: Questions about the lecture (10 points)

Answer the following questions based on the lecture you have just watched. You can consult the notes you took while you watched the lecture. Use complete sentences.

1. What is the main objective of the lecture?

2. Why is MTV a good case study for international business?

3. What is MTV's target audience? How many viewers does MTV have around the world?

4. How much did MTV make in 2005?

5. What is MTV's business plan for the near future? What is their main goal for the near future?

Section Two, question Two: One minute-paper about the lecture (5 points)

Answer ONE of the following questions in full sentences. Your answer should be **one paragraph** in length. You will be marked on format and content.

•   What was the most surprising and/or unexpected idea expressed in the lecture?

OR

•   What interesting questions remain unanswered about the lecture's topic?

Section Three: Writing (8 points)

Write a one-paragraph introduction of an essay entitled "The successful MTV business model." You will be marked on explanations (content), format, and using complete sentences.

Section Four: Problem (12 points)

You are the project manager for MTV Arabia. Your group has to give a presentation to MTV's CEO about the plan for prime time programming. Everyone agreed to have his or her part of the plan drafted by the time your team met today. What would be an appropriate response to **each** of the following incidents at today's meeting?

Alex did not have his part ready. This is the first time he has not done his job on time.

Identify what you think is the problem.

a) How would you talk to the group member? What would you say to the group member that would be respectful and helpful to you and to the group member?

b) In general, how can you resolve the conflict that happens when someone does not do his/her part of the work?

1. Donald texted you saying that he had to miss the meeting because he was working on a report for MTV's vice-president.

2. Identify what you think is the problem.

a) How would you talk to the group member? What would you say to the group member that would be respectful and helpful to you and to the group member?

b) In general, how can you resolve the conflict that happens when someone does not do his/her part of the work?

International Students and Academic Proficiency

TABLE 10.2 *(Continued)*

Section Five: Presentation (5 points)

Prepare a PowerPoint-slide presentation entitled "The successful MTV business model." Use the information you learned from the article and lecture to help you. The presentation should have **at least** five slides. You must include a title and an outline in your answer. You can use the slides on the following paper or you can draw the slides in your exam booklet.

KEYWORDS

- academic proficiency
- ESL students
- international students
- language acquisition
- language learning
- second language
- teaching strategies

REFERENCES

Bailey, N.; Madden, C.; Krashen, S.D. Is There a "Natural Sequence" in Adult Second Language Learning? Language Learning, 1974, 24, 2, 235–243.

Clément, R.; Gardner, R. C.; Smythe, P. C. Motivational variables in second language acquisition: A study of Francophones learning English. Canadian Journal of Behavioral Science/ Revue canadienne des sciences du comportement, 1997, 9(2), 123–133.

Cummins, J. Cognitive/academic language proficiency, linguistic interdependence, the optimum age question and some other matters. Working Papers on Bilingualism 1979, 19, 121–129.

Faerch, C.; Kasper, G. Processes and Strategies in Foreign Language Learning and Communication. Interlanguage Studies Bulletin–Utrecht, 1980, 5, 47–118.

Faucette, P. *A Pedagogical Perspective on Communication Strategies: Benefits of Training and an Analysis of English Language Teaching Materials. Second Language Studies,*2001, *19, 2.*

Krashen, S. D.Second Language Acquisition and Second Language Learning; Prentice-Hall International: New York, 1988.

Krashen, S. D. The Case for Narrow Reading. Language Magazine, 2000, 3(5), 17–19.

Krashen, S. D.*The Input Hypothesis and its Rivals. I*n Implicit and Explicit Learning of Languages; Ellis, N., Ed.; Academic Press: London,*1994.*

Krashen, S. D. Why support a delayed-gratification approach to language education? The Language Teacher, 2004, 28(7), 3–7.

Krashen, S. D.; Brown, C. L. What is Academic Language Proficiency? Singapore Tertiary English Teachers Society Language and Communication Review, 2007, 6, 1.

Louis, R. M. Critical Performative Pedagogy: Augusto Boal's Theatre of the Oppressed in the English as a Second Language Classroom. Ph.D. Thesis, Louisiana State University and Agricultural and Mechanical College, 2002.

Pineau, E. L. Performance Studies across the Curriculum: Problems, Possibilities, and Projections. In The Future of Performance Studies: Visions and Revisions; Dailey, S. J., Ed.; National Communication Association: Annandale, VA, 1998.

Quan, K. Y. The Girl Who Wouldn't Sing.In Living Languages.Contexts for Reading and Writing.Buffington, N.; Moneyhun, C., Diogenes, M.; Eds.; Prentice Hall: Paramus, NJ 1997.

Ramisetty-Mikler, S. Asian Indian Immigrants in America and Sociocultural Issues in Counseling. Journal of Multicultural Counseling and Development, 1993, 21, 1, 36–49.

Richards, J.C. A Non—Contrastive Approach to Error Analysis.Journal of ELT, 1971, 25, 204–219.

Slocum, S. ESL Strategies. Facilitating Learning for Students Who Speak English as a Second Language; Alverno College: Milwaukee, 2003.

Ting, S.; Phan, G. Y. L. Adjusting Communication Strategies to Language Proficiency. *Prospect: An Australian Journal of Teaching/Teachers of English to Speakers of Other Languages (TESOL),*2008, 23, 1.

Vygotsky, L. Mind in Society: The Development of Higher Psychological Processes; Harvard University Press: Cambridge, MA, 1978.

Won, H. K. South Korean Students' Attitudes toward Americans. The Social Science Journal, 2005, 42, 2, 301–312.

PART IV
DEEP LEARNING AND EVALUATION

CHAPTER 11

EVALUATING TO LEARN

Everything that can be counted does not necessarily count; everything that counts cannot necessarily be counted.

— ALBERT EINSTEIN

CONTENTS

11.1 Introduction 226
11.2 Historical Development 226
11.3 Problems Associated with Summative Evaluation 228
11.4 Evaluating to Learn 230
11.5 Initial Evaluation 231
11.6 Simultaneous Evaluation 233
11.7 Retrospective Evaluation 237
11.8 Subjects Involved in Evaluation to Learn 238
11.9 Metacognitive Reflection and Self-Evaluation 240
11.10 Summary 246
Practice Corner 246
Keywords 249
References 249

11.1 INTRODUCTION

Evaluation is one of the most controversial issues in higher education. It has generated heated debate, mainly because of the consequences it implies. The results of evaluation have direct impact in the promotion of students, attrition, graduation, accreditation, access to graduate and professional schools, financial assistance, fellowships, and access to the job market.

I begin this chapter with a brief overview of the historical development of evaluation in order to show that summative evaluation and the grading system are relatively new phenomena in universities and colleges. This is followed by an analysis of the problems associated with summative evaluation. I will then explore the notion of evaluating to learn and its three phases: initial, simultaneous, and retrospective. For each phase, I will consider its main aspects, characteristics, instruments, and subjects involved in evaluation. Finally, I will explore the notion of metacognition and its role in the evaluating-to-learn process as well as the main metacognitive categories and tools to facilitate deep learning.

11.2 HISTORICAL DEVELOPMENT

The history of education shows that the grading system and summative evaluation as we know them today are relatively recent phenomena. Before the rise of the modern university, formal summative evaluation and grades were literally unknown. Socrates did not assign grades to Plato; Plato did not give grades to Aristotle. In Roman times, a "widely standardized and highly socially embedded web of educational practices could function, without formal examinations, by means of high levels of competition and other less formal means of assessment" (Morgan, 2001). The modern university is over 1,000 years old. For the most part of its history, teachers did not have to formally evaluate student achievement of educational goals. Teachers did not have to assign grades or fail students. The quality of the education students received was largely associated with the prestige of their professors.

Summative evaluation and grading developed with the Industrial Revolution in England. The first recorded evidence of summative evaluation by means of grades is linked to Cambridge University and William Farish, a professor of Chemistry. Farish began using letter grades to evaluate student papers in 1792. He modeled his grading system after the practice used at that time in factories to evaluate the quality of manufactured goods. The practice gradually extended to the rest of the university and Oxford.

In North America, teachers assumed the task of evaluating in the late 1800's. The current system was first adopted in 1897 at Mount Holyoke College. Harvard and Yale had begun using similar systems—albeit in isolated fashion—a few decades earlier. The grading system consolidated in the twentieth century. So, for the first 900 years of university education, there were no formal summative evaluation and grading systems.

Despite its relatively short existence, formal summative evaluation based on a grading system seems to be a permanent, unchangeable feature of the modern university. Teachers who do not adhere to this system are sanctioned by their university administrations. For example, teachers who do not follow grading policies have been denied tenure or have even been dismissed from the university. I remember that when I started to work in my current university, the division and department chairs gave me an Excel spreadsheet with the average grades in each department and told me to keep my grades within those averages. They stressed this throughout the year and repeated this process with every new faculty member. In my previous university, the department chair asked me to go to his office and told me about the importance of keeping grades within a certain range. When I went for reappointment, the tenure and promotion committee in my current university wrote me a letter saying that I was to be reminded of the importance of grades. I still do not know what the committee meant exactly. Senior administrators regularly press my department to discuss grade averages and to come up with an understanding of a common approach to grading students. This experience, which is quite common in many universities and colleges, shows that summative evaluation and grades are perceived as essential artifacts of the Instruction-paradigm.

11.3 PROBLEMS ASSOCIATED WITH SUMMATIVE EVALUATION

There are many serious problems with the evaluation system used in the Instruction paradigm. One of the most severe problems is that evaluation is disconnected from learning. In the last four decades, evaluation has come to be associated with accountability rather than with learning. Accrediting agencies and state—or provincial—governments across North America launched an assessment movement in order to evaluate the quality of educational institutions in a context of shrinking budgets and scarce public funds. This movement, which has had significant influences at the classroom level, is not concerned with quality learning (House, 1980). It is a system that ignores the multiple instances of evaluations that teachers do in the classroom on an everyday basis. It aims at obtaining information for the administration, government, and other stakeholders. This information is irrelevant for, and divorced from, the learning process.

The evaluation system has created a culture of surface learning. With a focus on summative evaluation and grades, it has given rise to a superficial learning orientation in most students, where their main goal is to obtain good grades at a minimum cost in terms of time and effort. Given the fact that examinations and other summative evaluation tools embed social problems, many students have had to resort to cheating and other nonacceptable practices in order to cope with the summative evaluation demands. The evaluation system has also created a culture of examinations, where teachers and students see the evaluation requirements as the most important aspects of the course (Sanjurjo and Vera, 1994). Many of these evaluation tools are arbitrary, and success depends on random factors such as when the test is administered. For example, Arthur Perlini and his colleagues (Perlini et al., 1998) found that test performance varies according to when a test is given to students. They found that students taking a class in the afternoon do better on a test when they take it at the beginning or in the middle of a class, whereas students taking a course in the evening do better on tests administered in the middle or at the end of the class rather than at the beginning.

Another problem with the evaluation system is that many teachers and students wrongfully believe that making evaluation tools more difficult improves the quality of education. Many perceive that courses using non-

Evaluating to Learn

traditional evaluation tools, such as the ones aimed at fomenting a process of discovery and construction of knowledge, and that lack final exams, grades, and term papers, among other artifacts of the Instruction paradigm, are not rigorous. Research studies show that summative evaluation does not improve learning. It is a myth that exacerbates the problem, as in most cases summative evaluation with a strong emphasis on grades and examination instruments tends to produce the opposite effect (Sanjurjo and Vera, 1994).

Another problem with the predominant approach to evaluation is the fact that it does not take into account individual needs in the learning process. In North America, it is customary for teachers to examine all students at the end of the course. Although every student has different time frames to learn, all students have to hand in a paper by the same deadline, have to write the midterm the same day, and have to take the final exam all together on the same day and in the same classroom. It is not possible, for example, for students to take the examination or show their achievement of the learning goals several years after having finished the course—a practice that is common in many South American universities. In these universities, students take exams when they are ready instead of right after the course and regardless of when other students in the same course take the exam. For some students, being ready can mean they can take the exam right at the end of the course. For other students who demonstrate the achievement of learning goals throughout the course, it means not having to take a final exam. But other students may need the whole summer to prepare for the exam. Others may need a few years to feel that they have achieved the goals and that they can demonstrate them in an exam. Long time frames have been associated with deep learning. Short time frames have little to do with the learning process. If rushed to demonstrate their learning through examinations and other evaluation instruments, students have no choice but to resort to surface approximations to learning. Short time frames for evaluation have little to do with learning and have a lot to do with the needs of the Instruction-paradigm institutions to move students quickly through their studies.

Another problem derived from the evaluation system with long-lasting adverse effects is the creation of reactance on the part of students. As discussed earlier, reactance is a phenomenon that occurs when students develop a strong resistance to learning. Students are exposed to a system that coerces them to study through grades and examinations. Once students end their higher education studies and are no longer coerced by grades, they will rarely try to learn academic, university-level materials for the sake of learning (Pollio and Beck, 2000). Human beings generally devalue those activities that they are obliged to do and overvalue those that are not allowed to do. Pollio and Beck (2000) argue that "learning not to learn may become the most lasting lesson of a college education."

11.4 EVALUATING TO LEARN

From a learning perspective, evaluation plays a fundamental role in the process of knowledge construction. The Instruction-paradigm university has neglected this aspect of evaluation since accreditation and accountability took over the field of evaluation. In order to analyze the role of evaluation in the construction of deep learning, once again we need to recall the conception of deep learning given earlier.

Deep learning takes place when a student is faced with an exciting situation, problem, or question, that creates a cognitive conflict derived from social interactions with peers, that the learner feels motivated to solve, and the learner makes nonarbitrary and substantive connections between the new knowledge (which must be within the learner's "zone of proximal development") arising from the situation, problem, or question and his or her existing cognitive structure. The learner employs higher-order cognitive and metacognitive skills, processes, practices, and competences while making these connections. If adequately and intrinsically motivated, the learner will change his or her cognitive structures so as to resolve the problem. In so doing, the learner will incorporate the new knowledge to his or her cognitive structure, which will produce a conceptual change. The learner will be able to use and apply the new knowledge to new and unfamiliar situations and see the connections to a larger framework. At the same time, at the social level, this process implies a change from one community of knowledge to another one or a move toward the center of a community of knowledge. For deep learning to occur, there must also be an awareness of this restructuring and conceptual change.

Evaluation becomes a continuing cycle of reflection about the processes carried out in the construction of deep learning (Sanjurjo and Vera, 1994). Deep learning requires the learner to reflect about his or her learning process and the resulting conceptual change. For this purpose, the learner must have information, that is, feedback, about the main phases of the learning process. The learner must also possess metacognitive skills and knowledge of categories of analysis to be able to use that information to reflect critically about the learning process. John Tagg (2003) uses the road sign metaphor to refer to feedback. He argues that in order to be effective, feedback needs to be like road signs that constantly provide useful information about the journey. The information that is needed to help advance the construction-of-knowledge process must be obtained before, during, and after the conceptual change. The information obtained during these phases of the learning process serves slightly different purposes and has different pedagogical foundations. Learners and teachers play an active role in each of these evaluation phases. In some cases, external, third-party evaluators can also provide useful feedback to the learner.

Evaluation as an essential part of the deep learning process comprises three phases: initial, simultaneous, and retrospective.

11.5 INITIAL EVALUATION

The learner's existing cognitive structure plays a determinative role in the construction of knowledge. Evaluation of the initial conceptions that students have is a necessary condition to begin with the deep learning process. We need to know our students' cognitive structures in order to plan the situations, problems, and activities that will help them construct knowledge in a profound way. In Lovell (1980)'s words,

> "in general, what the pupil knows today, what relevant anchorage he [sic] has, is the best single predictor of what he [sic] will know tomorrow as a result of your teaching… It is necessary for the teacher to try and establish the main ideas held by pupils at the time they begin to experience new material. Pupils hold many spontaneous strategies, misconceptions, and alternative frameworks. Teaching must be adjusted to the anchorage the pupil already holds."

Unless they come strongly motivated to learn our disciplines, students will not spontaneously connect the new knowledge to their existing cognitive structures. Students' evocation of their conceptual understanding is dependent on the students' current teaching and learning context. So, the challenge is to "bring to the foreground of students' awareness of learning the subject matter they are about to learn" (Prosser and Trigwell, 1999).

Although many of us try to get to know our students as well as possible, very few design a careful methodology to identify students'existing cognitive structure. The Instruction-paradigm institutions do not consider this an important aspect of the evaluation process. They do not give visibility to the evaluation of students'existing knowledge structures. An earlier study conducted on the analysis of course outlines used across the United States and Canada revealed that a negligible percentage of courses consider the analysis of student's initial ideas as part of the evaluation process (Hermida, 2011).

There are a number of ways to gather information to evaluate students' cognitive structures at the beginning of the academic term. One of the best methods is the clinical interview. This method consists of interviews to students conducted by their teacher on an individual basis. In clinical interviews, the teacher assigns some tasks to a student. Then he or she initiates an open dialog to find out about the student's knowledge structure. This interview is more effective if the teacher has a hypothesis about the student's relevant anchorage or a theory that the teacher wants to prove (Carretero, 2009).

There are many other alternatives to carry out initial evaluation. These include open-ended questions at the beginning of the class, votes, and written feedback memos (Filene, 2005). Written questionnaires can also help teachers find out about students' cognitive structures. We may ask questions about general principles of the discipline; we may describe problems and ask our students to write their explanations; or, we may ask students to draw or produce other visual representations of a problem. When accompanied by a biography, we may get enough information to contextualize the responses from the questionnaires in light of students' personal experiences. Concept maps are also a useful way to organize all of this information (Edwards and Fraser, 1983). As discussed earlier, concept maps are graphical tools for organizing and representing knowledge.

Evaluating to Learn

They include "concepts, usually enclosed in circles or boxes of some type, and relationships between concepts indicated by a connecting line linking two concepts" (Novak, 1984).

Alverno College in Milwaukee, Wisconsin uses videotaped performances of all students. A few weeks before the beginning of their first-year classes, students are asked to perform some activities while being videotaped. These videos are used by the teachers to gauge the initial cognitive structures of their students and by students themselves. Because students are videotaped again at different stages of their four-year studies, these tapes also help students and their teachers examine their progress (Loacker, 2000).

The learners themselves also need to recognize their initial conceptions in order to be able to change them eventually. So, it is important to help students identify and discuss these conceptions. Judith Stanley (2000), also from Alverno College, encourages students to reflect on and discuss some instances of their prior learning and asks them to deduce the standards by which they evaluate these instances of their previous learning.

11.6 SIMULTANEOUS EVALUATION

Students need to engage in an ongoing process of doing and thinking in order to construct meaningful learning. Donald Schön (1983, 1987) introduced the reflection-in-action concept in the context of professional education to refer to the way practitioners think about their professional activities while carrying them out. This process applies to other educational settings, even to nonacademic activities. Schön (1983) argues that

"when we go about the spontaneous, intuitive performance of the actions of everyday life, we show ourselves to be knowledgeable in a special way. Often we cannot say what it is that we know. When we try to describe it we find ourselves at a loss, or we produce descriptions that are obviously inappropriate. Our knowing is ordinarily tacit, implicit in our patterns of action and in our feel for the stuff with which we are dealing. It seems right to say that our knowing is *in* our action" (Schön, 1983).

The reflection-in-action process is an essential aspect of deep learning. It helps students advance in the process of the construction of knowledge.

Learners also need to be aware of the properties of objects, that is, empirical abstraction, and the actions and knowledge applied to the objects, that is, reflecting abstraction (Piaget, 1970). They also require information or feedback to guide their efforts. Effective feedback must be consistent, continual, and interactive (Tagg, 2003). Consistent feedback refers to common grounds for giving information to students about their performances. Continual feedback is information that is given on an ongoing basis and is connected with student performances. It is an inseparable aspect of the activities that students carry out while dealing with new and challenging situations. Feedback is interactive when it engages students in a permanent dialog. Interactive feedback does not occur if the teacher gives the information and students receive it passively.

Like in the initial phase of evaluation, teachers also need information about students' progress in order to provide them with adequate feedback to facilitate their learning processes. We have a wide array of different possibilities to obtain this information. Observation of student performance is the most useful source. Widely used in the first years of elementary education, teacher observation can provide substantial information about the student learning process also at the college and university levels (Maxwell, 2001). Observation permits teachers to carefully watch students while they engage in the performances of understanding. While observing, we may ask questions to students to get clearer insight of their cognitive activities. It is also important to document student progress. This may be done through observation notes, where we can write down examples of student performances and describe their learning incidents. Observation notes should not include judgments, but we may record questions and doubts so that we can come back later to those notes and use them to give new feedback to students. Observation notes should be written in a way that would permit students and other potentially interested parties to read them. Teacher observation can be incidental or planned. The former takes place during the students' performance of learning activities. The latter are specific activities that the teacher plans in order to observe some aspects of the students' learning process. Although planned observation may occasionally be useful to obtain some information, teacher observation should be predominantly incidental and embedded in the learning activities and the learning process. The most effective information comes from students' performance of the teaching and learning activities.

Evaluating to Learn   235

Evidence about learning might come from other sources, such as examinations, papers, projects, or even conversations between students and teachers (Bain, 2004). The role of these sources is to obtain evidence about student learning. And the role of teachers is to characterize and communicate evidence about the learning process rather than a grade or a score. As discussed in previous chapters, these activities should emulate real-world performances as closely as possible.

We must carefully use the information that we collect to help students advance in the construction-of-knowledge process. Errors are generally a very rich source that informs about the way learners construct knowledge. In many cases, they are the most revealing source of students' cognitive processes. So, instead of penalizing errors, for example, giving lower grades, taking points off, crossing out words from essays, or providing correct answers, as is frequently done in the Instruction paradigm, we should actively seek students' errors so as to get valuable information about their learning process.

Another important aspect of simultaneous evaluation is to provide students with feedback in ways that they can understand and process. In this respect, what we say does not count as much as how students perceive what we say (Kohn, 2008). The message received—not the message sent—is what will have the most significant effect on the students' attitude toward their learning processes. For example, a student once came to see me in my capacity of chair of the department. She was very upset because she told me that another professor had accused her of plagiarism. She showed me an essay that she had written. My colleague wrote on the essay that the student needed to paraphrase some paragraphs to conform to the writing style discussed in class. I asked the student for clarification, as I did not see any mention of plagiarism in my colleague's comments. The student insisted that those comments were meant as an accusation of plagiarism. I called my colleague to see if this was the case or if he had mentioned something about plagiarism to this student. My colleague was as surprised as I was because he had never meant to imply that the student had plagiarized. Apparently, the term paraphrase had triggered a previous experience with another professor where that professor had insisted that she needed to paraphrase ideas taken from other sources, or she would face plagiarism issues. We need to constantly check to ensure that what we want to communicate is what students actually understand. This is also especially important in the case of communication with international students. Students from other countries are not necessarily familiar with the way teachers give feedback in North America. A slightly negative constructive comment may be understood as a very negative criticism by students from certain cultures. Although this need for clarity may generally apply to any aspect of the teaching and learning process, because of the psychological implications that evaluation usually has, it is crucial in the communication of feedback. Table 11.1 contains—generally accepted—guidelines on how to give effective feedback that minimizes risks of erroneous perceptions.

TABLE 11.1 Characteristics of effective feedback.

Environment

Create a nice atmosphere to give feedback.

Don't embarrass your student by letting others hear your feedback to that student.

Performance

Focus on your student's performance and not on your student.

Refrain from giving advice. Give information about the performance.

Give feedback about your student's performance, not the motivations or reasons behind that performance.

Be specific when giving feedback and make specific references to your student's performance.

Always give positive feedback about some aspects of your student's performance.

Always give feedback to help your student improve some aspects of his or her performance.

Time

Give immediate feedback.

Give feedback embedded in the learning process.

Be brief when feedback is negative.

Don't be brief when feedback is positive.

Feedback receiver

Give feedback only when solicited.

Give your student opportunities to act on your feedback.

Take into account your student's needs.

Give feedback that your student can use.

Check to insure clear communication.

Be mindful of cultural differences in communication styles.

Evaluating to Learn

11.7 RETROSPECTIVE EVALUATION

A retrospective phase is also essential for the construction of deep learning. Retrospective evaluation helps the learner reflect about the learning process, that is, what he or she did and how, and about the end result of that process: the conceptual change. We need to help the learner engage in this reflective process. Retrospective evaluation means going back to the learning process with the aim of understanding it. It implies a permanent research attitude on the part of both students and teachers aimed at discovering and valuing all the—visible and invisible—processes involved in learning. This implies that when evaluating, we need to identify the most salient aspects, obstacles, attempts, achievements, and errors in the causes that played a factor in the learning process (Sanjurjo and Vera, 1994).

Learners and teachers also need to evaluate how the learner's cognitive structures changed. This is consistent with Piaget's postulates. Piaget (1954) argued that the learner must become aware of the restructuring of the cognitive structure. He referred to the process of becoming conscious about knowledge and about the ways in which learners know as "*prise de conscience.*" The learner goes through a series of intermediate phases in which he or she changes his or her ideas about the new phenomenon, but these changes do not yet constitute the learner's final conceptual change (Carretero, 2009). The learner must be able to reflect about these intermediate changes as well as the final change in the cognitive structure.

Retrospective evaluation is also consistent with Donald Schön's reflection-on-action theory, which consists of the reflection on the reflection-in-action process. The reflection-on-action process takes place in words. It is "an attempt to describe the knowledge that was generated and the conditions under which it was generated and the on-the-spot experimentation that was carried out" (Schön, 1995).

Furthermore, retrospective evaluation is also compatible with biological explanations of the functions of the brain. Cognitive neuroscience suggests that evaluation of one's own work, which engages the anterior cingulate region of the limbic cortex, is an essential aspect of the learning cycle (Zull, 2002).

There are many instruments that can help with retrospective evaluation. Virtually any instrument that facilitates the reconstruction of the steps taken toward the construction of knowledge can be used to evaluate the learning process and the transformation of cognitive structures. These include peer observation, teacher observation, group discussions, guided written questionnaires, journals, blogs, learning portfolios, videos, and collages, among many others. These instruments have in common that they permit an open dialog between the teacher and learner and/or between the learner and his or her peers. It is this dialog that will permit a critical reflection about the learning process and its result. This dialog also facilitates the learner's individual self-evaluation process.

Traditional exams, multiple-choice questions, papers, essays, and oral presentations about a disciplinary topic are the preferred instruments used in traditional formal summative evaluations in colleges and universities. Although widely used, none of these instruments permits a reflection about the learning process or conceptual changes. So, these instruments do not offer any significant use for retrospective evaluation.

11.8 SUBJECTS INVOLVED IN EVALUATION TO LEARN

The learner himself or herself is the subject that plays the most important role in evaluation. He or she needs to actively engage in the process of getting information and reflecting about the learning process and the resulting conceptual change. Self-evaluation is "the ability of a student to observe, analyze, and judge her performance on the basis of criteria and plan how she can improve it" (Alverno College Faculty, 2000). When self-evaluation is understood not as the bureaucratic act of giving oneself a grade but as the possibility of critically reviewing the processes carried out in the construction of learning, self-evaluation acts as a powerful tool to encourage deep learning (Sanjurjo and Vera, 1994). From a biological perspective, self-evaluation engages the areas of the brain that are connected to emotions. It has been suggested that when a learner evaluates his or her performance, he or she ends up owning it and feels in control of the learning process (Zull, 2002).

Evaluating to Learn

Teachers are also instrumental in the evaluating-to-learn process. We need to know our students' initial conceptions about our disciplines, the hypotheses, obstacles, and progress that students undergo, and the resulting conceptual change. We also play a very important role in helping students become proficient in the metacognitive process, which will be discussed later in this chapter.

Peers also play a fundamental role in evaluation, as they do in the whole deep learning process. Interaction with peers produces cognitive conflicts. Peers help negotiate meanings and contribute to the social aspect of learning. So, peers can also provide valuable feedback and evaluate the learning process. Peers are in a privileged position to learn about their fellow students' initial conceptions, as they generally know their colleagues and spend more time with them than their teachers. They also interact with fellow students during the teaching and learning activities. So they can give very useful information about the learning process, including the resulting conceptual change. Peers can also help their fellow students with metacognitive reflection.

External evaluators can also help learners—albeit to a lesser extent—with the evaluation of their learning processes. External evaluators can provide students with "real-life" evaluation. For example, my business department colleagues organize an annual case competition, in which students present their solutions to hypothetical cases to CEOs, directors, top managers, and other business people, who evaluate their analysis of the cases as they do when working for their corporations and other businesses. Working with external evaluators in authentic situations motivates students and gives them the perspective of professionals and other community members who help them with their performances of understanding. Because most of these professionals are not experts in university and college evaluation, their feedback and evaluation may not always be productive. In some cases, if they do not give feedback effectively, they can harm the students' learning process. For this reason, Alverno College has implemented a program to work with community members as external evaluators. Alverno trains interested community members in evaluation and monitors the quality of feedback that they give to students. Ken Bain, originally a history professor, also reports having used external evaluators (Bain, 1997). Bain worked with a history professor from another university,

240 Facilitating Deep Learning

who read and graded the papers written by Bain's students. Bain acted as coach to the students. He reports that these students produced papers that were among the best he has read in his teaching career. The value of these experiences with external evaluators lies in the fact that the teacher can act exclusively as a facilitator of the learning process.

Table 11.2 summarizes each phase of the evaluating to learn process.

TABLE 11.2 Evaluating to learn process.

Evaluation Phase	Initial	Simultaneous	Retrospective
Goal.	To obtain information about the learner's initial cognitive structure	To guide the learner in his/her learning process.	To reflect about the steps taken in the learning process and about the conceptual change.
Subjects.	Learner. Teacher. Peers.	Learner. Teacher. Peers.	Learner. Teacher. Peers. External evaluators.
Main instrument.	Interview.	Teacher observation.	Conversation about the learning process and conceptual change.
Other instruments.	Concept maps. Written questionnaires. Videotaped performances.	Conversations between teacher and students. Papers. Learning portfolio. Journal. Blog.	Peer observation. Teacher observation. Group discussions. Guided written questionnaires. Journals. Blogs. Learning portfolio. Videos. Collages.

11.9 METACOGNITIVE REFLECTION AND SELF-EVALUATION

Metacognition consists of reflecting about one's own learning process. Metacognition also implies monitoring one's learning process and being able to make changes along the way. In Perkins's words, metacognition

Evaluating to Learn

is learning the game of learning (Perkins, 2009). Metacognition ultimately leads to self-evaluation, which enables a process of lifelong learning. Teacher feedback and information are essential for student learning. But once students graduate, they do not have us to give them constant and ongoing feedback. Students need to learn how to reflect on their learning endeavors and to give themselves the information they need. Metacognition is the internalization of that feedback and information process. It is like an internalized geographic positioning system (GPS) that students create to give themselves the information they need to engage in the construction of deep learning. Students also need to recognize their knowledge limitations and what they need to learn in order to progress in their disciplines or professional fields. From a biological perspective, metacognition involves spindle cells and the anterior cingulate, which link the emotional and cognitive parts of the brain through the dorsal and ventral regions, respectively, of the anterior cingulate (Zull, 2011).

There are four key components to metacognition: awareness, knowledge, control, and emotion. Awareness refers to the process of learning about one's cognitive structure. It also entails learning how to set one's own learning goals. In college and university, teachers generally set those goals. Teachers tell students what aspects of a discipline or disciplines they need to learn. For example, if a student wants to become a historian, the university will have designed a curriculum that contains all of the concepts, facts, theories, research methods, and principles that students will need to master in order to graduate and become historians. But in order to be prepared for life outside university, students themselves need to learn how to set their own learning goals. Knowledge implies knowing about the learning process and knowing about one's own personal learning styles. Students need to learn about the process of knowledge construction and deep learning. They need to know the different cognitive development stages and how gender, race, and ethnicity influence knowledge. Control means monitoring one's own learning progress. It helps students correct themselves and make changes while they are engaged in performances of understanding. Emotion also plays an essential role in the process of thinking about one's own learning. James Zull (2011) argues that the spindle cells, which, as discussed earlier, act as a bridge between the emotional and the cognitive aspects of the brain, transform metacognition into an integrative process. "For metacognition we need to know what we think and how we feel about it; [and] we must know what we feel and what we think about that" (Zull, 2011). In practice, this means that as part of encouraging our students to reflect about their learning process, we need to help them recognize and focus on their emotions and feelings throughout that process. Table 11.3 summarizes the key components of metacognition and the strategies associated with each component of the metacognition process.

TABLE 11.3 Metacognition.

Components	Strategies
Awareness	Set goals about the learning process.
Existing cognitive structure.	Identify what you know about the problem or question.
Initial conceptions of the problem or question.	
Knowledge	Read and discuss about deep learning and the process of construction of knowledge.
Learning process.	
Individual and social construction of knowledge.	Be familiar with learning theories.
	Metacognitive questions.
Role of peers.	
Learning styles.	
Cognitive stages of development.	
Gender, race, and ethnicity and their influence on the learning process.	
Control	Metacognitive questions.
Monitor of one's learning progress.	Make corrections and changes while working on a problem or question.
Emotion	Recognize emotions and feelings throughout the learning process.
Role of emotions in the learning process.	
Feelings and emotions experienced as a result of the conceptual change, the move to a new community of knowledge, or the new position in a community of knowledge.	Reflect about feelings and emotions.
	Discuss feelings and emotions with peers and teachers.

The metacognitive reflection about the learning process must satisfy some conditions in order to be effective. First, learners have to recognize their initial conceptions. Because most of these conceptions are implicit, the learner has to reflect about them and get to explain them. Second, the

Evaluating to Learn   243

learner has to evaluate his or her conceptions and beliefs in light of the new conceptions that are being learned. Third, the learner has to reflect about whether or not he or she will restructure his or her initial conceptions (Carretero, 2009). Perkins (1992) puts forward the idea of the metacurriculum as a supplement to the existing curriculum. One of the main goals of the metacurriculum is to help students become effective learners. In this respect, we need to help students engage in the process of metacognition and help them reflect about metacognition itself. For this purpose, students need to acquire and develop metacognition tools and need to learn how to use them in their learning processes.

Metacognition tools are both general and discipline specific. General metacognition categories deal with how learners construct knowledge. A good way to help students reflect about their learning processes is through questions that they can ask themselves throughout the process. These questions can include the following with respect to any problem or question students are grappling with:

1) What do I know about this problem or question? What is my first reaction or gut feeling? How can I instinctively solve the problem or answer the question now?
2) What new information or knowledge do I need in order to solve the problem or answer the question effectively?
3) What conversations and discussions do I need to have with my peers about the problem or question?
4) What analysis do I need to do with the new information or knowledge?
5) How can I relate what I already know and the new information or knowledge? What connections can I make?
6) How can I solve the problem or answer the question now?
7) How do my gender, race, ethnicity, and other social factors influence my solution to the problem or answer to the question?
8) How does my new solution or answer differ from my original, gut-feeling, response?
9) What do I know now that I did not know before about the problem or question? What can I do now that I could not do before?
10) What do I know now about the discipline that I did not know before? What connections can I now make to the general framework

of the discipline? What connections can I now make to other disciplines?

11) How can I use what I now know to answer other problems or questions in the discipline? How can I transfer what I now know outside the discipline? How can what I now know help me solve everyday problems and answer everyday questions?

12) Where does this new knowledge place me within the discipline? What conversations can I now have with my peers and the discipline?

13) How has knowing what I now know impacted me? How does my solution or answer affect me and others? How have I felt throughout this process? What emotions have I experienced? Does knowing what I know now change my attitude toward other people I know outside the discipline or outside academia?

14) What new questions do I have now about the original problem or question? What new questions do I have now about the discipline?

15) What new personal goals do I now have about the discipline?

Discipline-specific metacognitive categories have to do with the way a discipline organizes and constructs knowledge, what questions the discipline asks, what method it uses to generate knowledge, what kind of conversation its knowledgeable members engage in, and what limitations the discipline has. It also deals with knowledge about the hidden structure of the discipline, that is, what Perkins refers to as uncovering the hidden game (Perkins, 2009). A good way to help students reflect about discipline-specific metacognitive categories is through questions. Table 11.4 shows some examples of metacognitive questions to assist in the reflection on university and college teaching. These are questions that we can all ask ourselves while preparing new courses or some aspects of new courses, particularly to reflect about whether or not we are creating a deep learning environment. These questions also give a general idea of how to formulate metacognitive questions in other disciplines.

Evaluating to Learn

TABLE 11.4 Metacognitive questions for teachers to develop a course.

The following metacognition questions aim at helping you reflect about your teaching practice, particularly about whether or not you are creating an environment conducive to teaching and learning. Not all questions will be relevant for you or for all teaching situations. You should discard those questions that are irrelevant. Ideally, you should gradually create new questions that will help you think about your own teaching so that you can use the standards of the Scholarship of Teaching and Learning discipline to recognize shortcomings and correct your reasoning as you go.

1. Do I know my students well enough? Do I know about their cognitive structures?

2. Have I created an exciting problem, question, or situation?

3. Does the problem, question or situation include new knowledge?

4. Has this new knowledge created a cognitive conflict?

5. Has this cognitive conflict arisen from social interaction with peers?

6. Is the problem, question, or situation motivating enough for students to try to solve the problem or answer the question?

7. Is the new knowledge arising from the problem, question, or situation within the student's zone of proximal development?

8. Am I encouraging students to make nonarbitrary and substantive connections between new knowledge arising from the problem or question and their existing cognitive structures?

9. Does the problem, question, or situation help students use higher-order cognitive and metacognitive skills, processes, and competences while making these connections?

10. Am I intrinsically motivating students? Am I helping my students play the whole game of the discipline?

11. Am I creating a safe and nonthreatening learning environment?

12. Have I helped my students produce a conceptual change? Have I helped them incorporate new knowledge to their cognitive structures?

13. Have I helped students reacculturate from one community of knowledgeable peers to another?

14. Have I helped students move from the periphery of a community of knowledgeable peers to the center?

15. Have I helped students use and apply new knowledge to new situations and contexts?

16. Have I helped students make connections to larger frameworks?

17. Is my course aligned? Are the learning goals consistent with the teaching and learning activities and student evaluation? Am I making room for oblique and indirect learning?

18. Am I helping students reflect about every aspect of their learning process, including the conceptual change?

19. Am I helping students deal with the feelings and emotions arising from their learning process?

20. Am I promoting metacognition?

21. Am I giving effective feedback?

22. Am I helping my students develop a wide array of skills and competencies? Am I helping my students read and write deeply?

246   Facilitating Deep Learning

11.10 SUMMARY

Despite being a relatively recent phenomenon in higher education, summative evaluation and a pervasive grading system dominate evaluation in today's universities and colleges. This practice has become associated with the assessment and accountability movement, which emerged in the United States in the last few decades.

The prevailing evaluation system is plagued with problems. First, evaluation is disconnected from learning. Second, there is a perception that making evaluation tools more difficult improves the quality of student learning, when this is clearly not so. Third, the system does not take into account individual needs and differences among students. Additionally, it may lead to student reactance.

Evaluating to learn is an approach that conceives of evaluation as an integral part of the deep learning process. This process necessitates constant information and reflection. The evaluating to learn approach consists of an initial phase aimed at getting information about the learners' cognitive structure; a simultaneous phase, which promotes reflection during the performance of learning activities; and a retrospective phase, which deals with reflection about the learning process and the resulting conceptual change.

Learners, teachers, peers, and external evaluators play a valuable role in evaluating to learn.

Another essential aspect of the evaluating to learn approach is metacognition. Metacognition is the practice of reflecting about, and monitoring, one's own learning process. It is a very useful strategy that permits the learner to make adjustments and implement changes to his or her own performances.

The next chapter examines another aspect of evaluation: teaching effectiveness in the context of a deep learning environment.

PRACTICE CORNER

1. Knowing your students' initial cognitive structure is essential to help them immerse themselves in a deep learning process. What

Evaluating to Learn 247

can you do to find out their initial conceptions about the main aspects of the discipline you teach?

2. Suppose you work in a university that has a rule that all courses must include a written three-hour final examination within the exam period. The rule states that final exams must be worth, at least, 25 percent of the final grade. You do not believe in quantifying knowledge. You do not believe in summative evaluations that are unrelated to the learning process. But you have to comply with this rule. What kind of evaluation task can you design that will help students learn deeply without infringing this rule?

3. Suppose you teach a large class of over 100 first-year students that meets three hours a week throughout a semester. You agree that teacher observation of students is the best source of obtaining information about student learning. How can you adequately observe your students' learning processes? Can you plan and design a system to implement teacher observation in this class?

4. Metacognition encompasses both general and discipline-specific categories, tools, and methods for reflection about the learning process. Students need to learn how to engage in metacognition. How can you help your students become proficient in metacognition? How can you help them master the general metacognitive categories? Can you think of metacognitive questions in your discipline or field to help students reflect on their learning processes and evaluate themselves?

5. After a course has finished and you have submitted final grades, a student sends you an email saying: "I am very upset with my final grade. I think I deserve an A. Anyway, can I write a paper to boost my mark up? I need to have, at least, an A–(80 percent) to have chances to get into law school." What do you do and why? What could you have done to prevent this situation?

6. You evaluate students following the standards model of assessment. Under this model, the teacher defines the standards that students should achieve at the end of the course in light of the intended learning goals. This model requires teachers to judge how well students' activities match the learning goals holistically and synoptically. It also requires teachers to assess students' performances

qualitatively and in their entirety—not by adding marks to their various parts. Students, however, are used to marks and quantitative assessment (measurement model of assessment). You asked your students to keep reflective journals and to compile portfolios with their best work. Most of the students who do not get an A complain that your evaluation is not fair and is not objective. What do you say? Some students appeal their grade. What are your arguments to defend your grades?

7. Your intended learning goals are aligned with your teaching and learning activities and with student evaluation. You ask your students to write a midterm test. You tell them that you will use the midterm to give them formative feedback so that they can improve their performance on the final. The results of the final are not better. What happened? What went wrong? Why?

8. You teach a course in which the intended learning goal is the mastery of the main theories in your discipline. In every class, students discuss a few articles on one theory in small groups. In the last 30 minutes, the whole class discusses the theory. For the final evaluation, you ask your students to do a very creative project. Students need to take pictures and create a photo album to illustrate one of the theories discussed in class. To your surprise, many students— even many of those who have actively participated in the discussion of the theories in class—did not do well. What do you think happened? Why? What can you do so that next time those students who did not do well on the project but who have actively participated in class will do much better?

9. You recognize the importance of the role peers play in the learning process, including their role in providing valuable feedback. But in your experience, when students have to evaluate other students, they have a tendency to be indulgent. Think about a course you regularly teach. Can you design an instance of peer evaluation for that course? How can you implement it effectively?

10. Brooke Shields (1985) writes about her experience taking exams at college: "Sometimes no matter how hard you've reviewed and studied, how well you've prepared, your professor might choose to pull a fast one on you. [...] You never know when a tricky pro-

Evaluating to Learn

fessor is going to throw a zinger at you." Analyze the "tricky professor's" evaluation strategy in light of the evaluating-to-learn approach. Does this strategy help create an environment conducive to deep learning? Can students learn deeply despite this type of strategy? Can you think of concrete examples of tricky exams? If students come to you for advice and ask you what they can do in a course with a "tricky professor," what can you tell these students?

KEYWORDS

- deep learning
- effective feedback
- evaluating to learn
- evaluation
- initial evaluation
- metacognition
- metacognitive questions
- peer evaluation
- retrospective evaluation
- self-evaluation
- simultaneous evaluation
- summative evaluation

REFERENCES

Alverno College Faculty. Self-Assessment at Alverno College; Alverno College: Milwaukee, 2000.

Bain, K. What the Best College Teachers Do; Harvard University Press: Cambridge, MA, 2004.

Bourdieu, P.; Passeron, J. C. Reproduction in Education, Society and Culture, 2nded.; Sage:London, 1990.

Carretero, M. Constructivismo y Educación; Paidós: Buenos Aires, 2009.

250   Facilitating Deep Learning

Edwards, J.; Fraser, K. Concept maps as reflectors of conceptual understanding. Research in Science Education, 1983, 13.1, 19–26

Filene, P. The Joy of Teaching. A Practical Guide for New College Instructors; University of North Carolina Press: Chapel Hill, 2005.

Freire, P. Pedagogy of the Oppressed; The Continuum International Publishing Group: New York, 1970.

Hermida, J. Student Assessment in Higher Education: An Evaluating to Learn Approach, Interdisciplinary Colloquium, Algoma University, Sault Ste. Marie, Canada, 2011

House, E. R. Evaluating with Validity; Sage Publications: Beverly Hills, CA, 1980.

Kohn, A. It's Not What We Teach; It's What They Learn. Education Week, 2008.

Loacker, G. Self-Assessment at Alverno College; Alverno College: Milwaukee, 2000.

Lovell, R.B. Adult learning; Croom Helm: London, 1980.

Maxwell, G. Teacher Observation in Student Assessment, 2001. http://www.qsa.qld.edu.au/downloads/publications/research_qscc_assess_report_4.pdf. (accessed Aug. 12, 2013).

Morgan, T. Assessment in Education: Principles, Policy and Practice, 2001, 8, 1, 11–24.

Novak, J.; Gowin, B. Learning How to Learn; Cambridge University Press: Cambridge, MA, 1984.

Perkins, D. Making Learning Whole. How Seven Principles of Teaching can Transform Education; Jossey-Bass: San Francisco, 2009.

Perlini, A.; Lind, D. L.; Zumbo, B. D. Context effects on examinations: The effects of time, item order and item difficulty. Canadian Psychology/Psychologie canadienne, 1998, 39(4), 299–307.

Piaget, J. The Construction of Reality in the Child; Basic Books: New York, 1954.

Pollio, H. R.; Hall, P. B. When the Tail Wags the Dog: Perceptions of Learning and Grade Orientation in, and, by Contemporary College Students and Faculty. The Journal of Higher Education, 2000, 71 (2), 84–102.

Prosser, M.; Trigwell, K. Understanding Learning and Teaching: The experience in higher education; Open University Press: Buckingham, 1999.

Sanjurjo, L.; Vera, M. T. Aprendizaje significativo y enseñanza en los niveles medio y superior; Homo Sapiens: Rosario, 1994.

Schön, D. Educating the Reflective Practitioner: Toward a New Design for Teaching and Learning; Jossey-Bass: San Francisco, 1987.

Evaluating to Learn

Schön, D. The Reflective Practitioner. How Professionals Think in Action; Temple Smith: London, 1983.

Shields, B. On Your Own; Villard Books: New York, 1985.

Stanley, J. Helping First-Year Composition Students Develop Self-Assessment Ability. In Self-Assessment at Alverno College; Loacker, G. Ed.; Alverno College: Milwaukee, 2000.

Tagg, J. The Learning Paradigm College; Anker Publishing Company: Bolton, MA, 2003.

Zubizarreta, J. The Learning Portfolio: Reflective Practice for Improving Student Learning; Jossey-Bass: San Francisco, 1990.

Zull, J.From Brain to Mind. Using Neuroscience to Guide Change in Education; Stylus: Sterling, VA, 2011.

Zull, J. The Art of Changing the Brain: Enriching the Practice of Teaching by Exploring the Biology of Learning; Stylus: Sterling, VA, 2002.

CHAPTER 12

STUDENT EVALUATION OF TEACHING: EVALUATING DEEP LEARNING

The only man who behaves sensibly is my tailor; he takes my measurements anew every time he sees me, while all the rest go on with their old measurements and expect me to fit them.

— GEORGE BERNARD SHAW

CONTENTS

12.2 The Instruction-Paradigm Student Evaluation of Teaching 254
12.3 Reliability Problems of Current Student Evaluation of Teaching 256
12.4 Teaching Evaluation and Deep Learning: A Scholarly Approach..... 261
12.5 Summary.. 266
Practice Corner... 267
Keywords 271
References... 271

12.1 INTRODUCTION

Universities and colleges have been relying on student evaluation of teaching (SET) to assess the effectiveness of their faculty for decades. Like the evaluation of students' work, the evaluation of teaching has very concrete effects on the lives of university and college teachers. SET results are mainly used for appointment, reappointment, tenure, and promotion. In most cases, they are the only data used for evaluation. Despite their importance, current SET instruments present severe validity problems, particularly because they have no correlation with student learning.

In this chapter, I will first examine the characteristics of the prevailing approach to student evaluation of teaching effectiveness in the Instruction paradigm. I will then analyze the biases and problems of the current approach. Finally, I will explore an alternative method for the evaluation of teaching effectiveness focused on the creation of a deep learning environment and based on a scholarly approach to evaluation under clear standards and multiple sources of data.

12.2 THE INSTRUCTION-PARADIGM STUDENT EVALUATION OF TEACHING

In one of the first job-search committees I participated on, we had to decide between two candidates (Alan and Chris) to bring in for a campus interview. It was a nontenure track position, so it was clear that teaching was the main factor for consideration. Alan was completing his Ph.D. at a prestigious university in southern Ontario, Canada. He had received full merit scholarships to fund his graduate studies. He was very active in his discipline. He had a few publications and conference presentations. He had also participated in several teaching and learning workshops during his master's and doctoral programs. He also presented a couple of papers on teaching writing to first-year students and attended a few teaching and learning conferences. During the summers, he taught as part-time faculty in his department. He taught five courses in this capacity. To me, he looked like a very good candidate on paper. Chris had finished his master's degree a few years before that search. He had not pursued doctoral studies. He had

Student Evaluation of Teaching: Evaluating Deep Learning 255

never published in his discipline. Neither had he participated in any teaching and learning workshop or conference. Like Alan, Chris had taught five courses as a part-time faculty in a small university. In my mind, it was clear that Alan deserved an invitation for a campus interview. If that did not work out, I wasn't sure Chris was worth interviewing. To my surprise, my colleagues in the search committee, all of whom had worked for years, even decades, at the university had a different take. They carefully compared the student evaluations submitted by Alan and Chris. Alan's were not bad. In a scale from 1 to 7, his average was around 6.50 for each category (clear course objectives, achievement of course objectives, accurate tests, fair grading, timely return of assignments, organized classes, availability, communication, open-mindedness, knowledge of subject matter, and instructor effectiveness). Chris's scores were a bit better. His average was around 6.65. In one particular category, knowledge of the subject matter of the course, Chris scored an average of 6.75 whereas Alan's average was around 6.30. My colleagues vividly argued that Chris was a far better teacher and that he knew a lot more than Alan about the discipline. At first, I honestly thought my colleagues were joking. When I sought clarification, they told me that they firmly believed that Chris was a better candidate than Alan because he outperformed Alan in every category. They were genuinely concerned that Alan did not know the discipline well enough. I urged my colleagues to consider Alan's whole file. Alan was a Ph.D. candidate, he had published in the discipline, and he had presented at several conferences. And the workshops he had taken, together with the publications in the field of the scholarship of teaching and learning, showed, at the very least, a commitment to a professional and scholarly approach to teaching, which was not evident in Chris's application. After heated discussions, except for me, all members of the search committee voted in favor of inviting Chris to interview. Needless to say, Chris was offered the position. He taught for our program for several years until the university decided to hire a tenure-track candidate.

The predominant practice of evaluation of teaching effectiveness reflects traditional conceptions of teaching and evaluation. Many authors, teachers, and administrators believe that it is possible and desirable to evaluate teaching effectiveness by means of instruments administered to students at the end of the course. These instruments, called student evaluations of teaching or SETs, require students to rate the effectiveness of the teacher in delivering the course. They generally include several questions or statements about different elements believed to be associated with good teaching, which students have to rate. For example, Herbert Marsh and his colleagues (1997) produced an SET instrument called SEEQ (Student Evaluation of Educational Quality). This widely used instrument comprises items classified into nine dimensions of teaching: learning, enthusiasm, organization, group interaction, individual rapport, breadth, examinations, assignments, and overall. Students have to give their opinion on each item or some selected items and rate them according to the following categories: Strongly Disagree, Disagree, Neutral, Agree, Strongly Agree. Marsh's SEEQ instrument is used in institutions across the Western world. Authors enrolled in the Instruction-paradigm approach argue that "SETs are the single most valid source of data on teaching effectiveness" (Marsh and Roche, 1997) and support SETs by acknowledging that they can provide powerful and useful information, provided evaluation is based on a systematic and careful approach involving all constituencies and achieving consensus on major issues (Theall and Franklin, 2001).

12.3 RELIABILITY PROBLEMS OF CURRENT STUDENT EVALUATION OF TEACHING

The predominant SET instruments have many reliability flaws. To say that student ratings are valid is to say that they reflect teaching effectiveness. However, SETs are plagued with reliability issues and are biased, or impose serious risks of bias (Clayson and Sheffet, 2009). One of the most serious reliability problems is that "minority faculty obtain significantly lower ratings than white professors" (Hamermesh and Parker, 2004). Similarly, students evaluate faculty who speak with a foreign accent more negatively than those who are native speakers of the official or predominant language in the jurisdiction of the university or college (Eisenhower, 2002; Llurda, 2000). Certain languages are subject to more negative stereotyping than others. This stereotype varies according to the general political climate in the country. For example, after the September 11, 2001 incidents in the United States, teachers speaking with an Arabic accent were less favorably evaluated than speakers of other languages. When there is a media and political campaign against illegal immigration in the United States, teachers whose first language is Spanish suffer more negative stereotyping, which is reflected in the SETs regardless of their actual effectiveness as teachers.

There is a long line of research studies showing that student ratings of educators depend largely on personality variables and not on pedagogical issues. These studies began with Naftulin and his colleagues'(1973) famous Dr. Fox experiment. These authors hired a professional actor to give a nonsensical lecture in the field of medicine to a highly educated audience, which included other professors, professionals, and graduate students in medicine and cognate disciplines. The actor, who looked intelligent, elegant, and distinguished, was introduced to the audience as Dr. Myron L. Fox, an authority in the field of applied mathematics to human behavior. Then the presenter shared Dr. Fox's impressive fabricated CV with the audience. The actor gave a very eloquent lecture, entitled "Mathematical Game Theory Applied to Physician Education," for one hour, followed by a 30-minute discussion period. He was very expressive, smiled, made frequent eye contact with the audience, and used face and hand gestures to accompany his talk. The lecture and his answers to the questions from the audience were completely senseless. They were full of contradictions, irrelevant examples, and ambiguity. He digressed all the time, told jokes, and used humor unrelated to the lecture. With his very dramatic style, Dr. Fox seduced his audience. No one realized that he was an actor. After the lecture and the discussion, the authors gave the audience an SET questionnaire with eight questions about Dr. Fox's teaching effectiveness, which also included room for open comments. The majority of the audience rated Dr. Fox very positively on every single question. Some members even commented that Dr. Fox analyzed the topic well. A minority even admitted having read Dr. Fox's inexistent publications. This clearly shows that nonverbal behavior, such as gestures, facial expressions, tone, and pitch, dramatically affects evaluations, and that SETs "respond primarily to minor aspects of a professor's classroom style; many of those behaviors reflect characteristics like race, gender, and class" (Merritt, 2008).

Another study is that conducted by Stephen J. Ceci, a professor of developmental psychology at Cornell University. After teaching for around 20 years, Ceci received a letter inviting him to participate in a teaching skills workshop to improve his teaching practice. His SETs were average, so he did not feel that he needed to take this workshop. But because he had no choice, he attended it. A professional media consultant with no knowledge of academia or teaching led the workshop. The media consultant helped the participants improve their presentation skills. Participants were taught how to sound more enthusiastic by varying pitch and using hand gestures when giving lectures. After finishing the workshop, Ceci decided to implement these tips to see if they could improve his SETs scores. He taught the same course he had taught many times before. And he taught it in exactly the same way, that is, same content, goals, lectures, book, and evaluation. He even taught the course on the same days and times as he had always done. The only difference was that he lectured with more gestures and more pitch variability, just as he had been advised in the workshop. At the end of the course, the SET results showed substantial improvement with respect to his previous courses (Williams and Ceci, 1997).

Another interesting factor in student evaluation of teaching is the "thin-slice" phenomenon (Ambady and Rosenthal, 1993). Students make a judgment of their teachers in the very first minutes of the first class. This judgment, which is based on the teacher's personality, seldom changes throughout the course. Another very interesting—and arbitrary—factor that strongly influences student evaluation of teaching is teachers' physical appearance. Teachers perceived to be physically attractive receive higher SET ratings than those who are perceived as unattractive. Those who are ranked as "hot" on ratemyprofessors.com or similar websites have better ratings than those who are not (Hamermesh and Parker, 2004; Riniolo, 2005). This phenomenon takes place with both deep and surface learners, as the attractiveness bias plays an important role in both types of students (Perlini and Hansen, 2001).

Another problem with the prevailing SET practice is that it focuses almost exclusively on teaching as an activity that takes place only in the classroom. Under this approach, teaching is usually associated only with course delivery. This is a very narrow conception of teaching. In fact, teaching is a process that goes beyond the classroom, which involves the following stages: (i) vision, (ii) design, (iii) enactment, (iv) outcomes, and (v) analysis (Shulman, 2004). Focusing on only one of these phases to determine the effectiveness of the whole process leads to a flawed evaluation

Student Evaluation of Teaching: Evaluating Deep Learning   259

process and to dubious results. It is the same as if we wanted to judge the effectiveness of an airplane; and we evaluated solely the way the engines work. The engines may work correctly, but if the fuselage is faulty, the airplane will fall down with catastrophic consequences. If we want to judge the reliability of an airplane, we need to judge the whole airplane and the whole process of construction of the airplane.

Another factor that influences SET ratings is the connection between grades and SET results. Students usually consider the grades that they expect to receive when evaluating the effectiveness of a teacher. Students form a mental comparison between how they expect to be graded with the grade they get or believe they will get. This comparison leaves students either satisfied or dissatisfied, thus influencing the ratings that they give to their teachers (Chambers and Schmitt, 2002).

Another problem with the reliability of SET instruments is that SETs are uni-dimensional. They do not evaluate those aspects of teaching that are not easily observable. As briefly mentioned earlier, pedagogy has four dimensions: (i) surface structure, (ii) deep structure, (iii) tacit structure, and (iv) shadow structure (Shulman, 2004). The surface structure of pedagogy is the set of behaviors that can be observed. For example, the surface structure of a traditional lecture reveals that the teacher explains facts, students take notes and ask questions, and the teacher answers those questions. The deep structure is the set of underlying intentions and goals that the observable behavior models. For example, the deep structure of the traditional lecture is that there is an expert, the teacher, who has the knowledge and transmits it to nonexperts, the students. The tacit structure refers to the values and dispositions that the behavior implicitly models. For example, the traditional lecture promotes a foundational conception of knowledge as a real entity that is not subject to collective negotiation. The shadow structure is the repressed pedagogy. It is what the pedagogy does not do. For example, the lecture does not promote student research or student collaboration. Most SET instruments focus on the surface structure and do not contain questions or statements about the other aspects of pedagogy, particularly the tacit and shadow structures.

Most SET instruments tend to reward Level 2 teaching rather than Level 3 (Biggs and Tang, 2007). Biggs classifies teaching into three different categories. Level 1 teaching consists of sorting students into good and bad.

Level 2 teaching focuses on teacher's performance. An effective Level 2 teacher is a teacher who masters the skills and the resources to perform well. For example, a good Level 2 teacher is a teacher who speaks clearly, projects his or her voice so that every student in the room can hear, and uses interesting visual aids. One can be a very good Level 2 teacher, but that does not mean that students will learn. Level 3 teaching focuses on what the students do. An effective Level-3 teacher is one who encourages students to actively engage in a process of discovery and construction of knowledge. The predominant SET practice conceives of teaching as Level 2. It focuses on what the teacher does instead of what the students do.

The weakest aspect of SET practice is that SETs have no correlation with student learning. In other words, high SET ratings do not necessarily mean that students have learned (Clayson, 2009). High SET ratings simply mean that the teacher's pedagogy conforms to the traditional role that predominates among students and in society in general. They also probably mean that the teacher is white, does not speak with an accent that suffers from negative stereotyping, and that the teacher's body language conveys positive messages to students. A high SET rating also probably means that the teacher is perceived as physically attractive. Conversely, low SET ratings do not mean that students have not learned. A low SET rating may simply mean that the teacher is not white, speaks with a foreign accent, and has body language that is perceived as negative. Or it may also mean that the teacher's pedagogy is not conventional. A high or a low SET rating may also mean that students had grade expectations that did not coincide with the grades they obtained in the course or that they expected to obtain. A low SET rating may also mean that the teacher promoted deep learning in a class where most students were surface learners. This is so because surface learners tend to judge teachers who promote deep learning quite negatively. At the same time, deep learners tend to judge teachers who promote surface learning negatively (Entwistle and Tait, 1990).

Another very serious problem with SETs has to do with the way tenure and promotion committees work and interpret SETs (McKeachie, 1997). Most committees lack sophistication and knowledge about the evaluation process of teaching (Theall and Franklin, 2001). Generally, these committees lack clear standards; decisions are made arbitrarily according to what their members think the standards of scholarly work should be at their institution. Moreover, committees tend to confuse data with evaluation. Many members usually think that SETs are evaluation of teaching. Students do not evaluate. They provide data, which tenure and promotion committees evaluate. So, in many cases, they automatically believe that low SET scores mean teaching ineffectiveness. Committees also tend to give negative information a disproportionate weight. So, for example, if most of the comments about a teacher are positive, but there are two or three that are negative, many committees have shown to focus on those negative comments rather than on the positive ones. Furthermore, committees tend to judge teachers who do not conform to the stereotype of good teaching as ineffective despite other evidence to the contrary (McKeachie, 1997). All of these problems are compounded because the work of the tenure and promotion committees tends to be private, confidential, and closed to the academic community. So, it is important to help tenure and promotion committee members to undergo a process of acculturation of evaluation of teaching from a learning perspective.

12.4 TEACHING EVALUATION AND DEEP LEARNING: A SCHOLARLY APPROACH

An efficient student evaluation program of teaching effectiveness must assess teaching effectiveness according to a learning perspective (Bain, 2004). So, the focus should not be on the methods that teachers use to teach their classes. The focus of SETs should be on whether or not teachers help students learn deeply. This does not mean measuring student learning to determine the effectiveness of teaching, as some students may learn even when the teaching is not effective (Biggs and Tang, 2007). The reverse is also true. Some students may not learn—for many different reasons—even when a teacher is effective. The key is whether the teacher created a motivating environment that is conducive to deep learning. For Bain, the fundamental question is: "Does the teaching help and encourage students to learn in ways that make a sustained, substantial, and positive difference in the way students think, act, or feel—without doing them any harm?" Bain (2004) breaks this question into four sub-questions:

"(i) Is the material worth learning? (ii) Are students learning what the course is supposedly teaching? (iii) Is the teacher helping and encouraging the students to learn (or do they learn despite the teacher)? and (iv) Has the teacher harmed the students (perhaps fostering short-term learning with intimidation tactics, discouraging rather than stimulating additional interest in the field, fostering strategic rather than deep learning, neglecting the needs of a diverse student population, or failing to evaluate students' learning accurately)?" (Bain, 2004).

These are all valid and relevant questions for an SET that focuses on teaching as a way of encouraging learning. Bain's set of sub-questions could be supplemented with other questions aimed at evaluating whether the elements of the deep learning process were present. These could include the following:

(i) Does the teacher expose students to appropriate social interaction that creates a cognitive conflict that students are motivated to solve?

(ii) Does the teacher encourage students to make connections between new knowledge and their existing cognitive structures?

(iii) Does the teacher promote a collective negotiation of meanings?

(iv) Does the teacher help students use higher-order cognitive and metacognitive processes and skills at both the individual and the group levels?

(v) Does the teacher help students reacculturate from one community of knowledgeable peers to another or move from the periphery of a community of knowledgeable peers to the center?

(vi) Does the teacher help students reflect about their learning processes and the resulting conceptual and social changes?

In turn, these sub-questions could be complemented with the following dealing with fundamental academic skills:

(vii) Does the teacher promote individual and collective deep reading?

(viii) Does the teacher promote individual and collective writing processes?

Although these questions may now seem too technical for students to understand, if we help students develop metacognitive categories as part of their learning and evaluation processes, students will be able to evaluate teachers' effectiveness and to answer these questions appropriately.

Like with any other research process, relying on only one type of data is not enough to reach reliable conclusions. It is useful to triangulate data, that is, to obtain data from multiple sources. For example, a fellow teacher could organize student small-group discussions where they carefully examine every aspect of the teaching and learning process (Merritt, 2008). The content of the discussions could then be communicated to the teacher in charge of the course, who could incorporate that feedback into future courses.

Data can also come from peer observation of teaching, provided that the peer observer understands teaching as the creation of a motivating environment that is conducive to learning. Another very important source for data is teacher self-evaluations. Teachers need to engage in the evaluation of their teaching along the same process analyzed for the evaluation of student learning. Like for students, the objective of teaching evaluation has to lead ultimately to teachers' self-evaluation of their own practice.

Additionally, because teaching exceeds the classroom enactment to include the course vision, and its design, outcomes, and analysis, a reliable and comprehensive evaluation of teaching effectiveness must seek data about all these other components of the teaching process. Students may not be in a position to evaluate them unless they share the whole process. So, these components may need to be evaluated with data from other sources. These may include presentations of the analysis of a course in a teaching and learning conference, the publication of an article about the vision for a course, and a written account of the design of a course, among others (Bolívar Botía and Caballero Rodríguez, 2008). Data can also come from the teacher's own reflections in his or her teaching portfolio or from a course portfolio. The course portfolio is a scholarly investigation into student learning at the course level—from its vision to the analysis of the teaching and learning process (Hutchings, 1998).

Teaching that promotes deep learning, conceived of as a process of working from a vision to the analysis involving inquiry into student learning, is often a scholarly activity. If it has the following three features, teaching also qualifies as scholarship. These features are: (i) public rather than private, (ii) susceptible to peer review and evaluation, and (iii) accessible for exchange and use by other members of the scholarly community (Shulman, 2004). So, if teaching qualifies as scholarship, then it must be evaluated like other types of scholarship. The following steps make up the essential aspects of the scholarly teaching process: (i) clear goals, (ii) adequate preparation, (iii) appropriate methods, (iv) significant results, (v) effective presentation, and (vi) reflective critique (Glassick, Huber, and Maeroff, 1997). These stages are similar to the five elements of teaching proposed by Shulman (2004). Clear teaching goals require a vision of the problem; the design demands adequate preparation anchored in the teaching and learning literature. The enactment of a course must be carried out through appropriate pedagogical methods. The learning outcomes are the results of the teaching enterprise, which must be analyzed—reflective critique in Glassick's words—and effectively communicated to peers and the academic community at large. Tenure and promotion committees should bear in mind these aspects of the scholarly teaching process and should evaluate its efficacy by discussing clarity, adequacy, appropriateness, and significance.

Table 12.1 outlines Glassick's and Shulman's approach to assessing scholarly teaching and includes examples of questions for evaluators to ask about the teaching practice.

TABLE 12.1 Criteria to assess scholarly teaching.

Glassick	Shulman	Questions
Clear teaching goals	Vision	Does the teacher define clear teaching goals?
		Are the goals adequately communicated to the students?
		Are the teaching goals appropriate for the students and the teaching context?
		Do the teaching goals reflect knowledge of students' needs and cognitive structures?
Adequate preparation	Design	Does the course reflect adequate preparation?
		Does the course reflect an adequate knowledge of the relevant teaching and learning literature?
		Does the course reflect adequate knowledge of the discipline's big questions and problems?
		Does the teacher plan interesting and motivating problems, situations, and questions for students to grapple with?
Glassick	**Shulman**	**Questions**

Student Evaluation of Teaching: Evaluating Deep Learning 265

TABLE 12.1 *(Continued)*

Appropriate methods	Enactment	Are the teaching and learning activities for the course appropriate to achieve the teaching goals?
		Does the teacher implement them effectively?
		Does the teacher create a safe and motivating environment so that students can engage in the proposed performances?
Significant results	Outcomes	Have the goals been met?
		Has the teacher created an environment that encouraged students to learn deeply?
		Have the students learned deeply?
		If students have not learned deeply, is it because the teacher has not created an environment conducive to learning or because of circumstances beyond the teacher's control?
Reflective critique	Analysis	Has the teacher analyzed his or her course? Has the teacher analyzed whether the teaching goals have been achieved?
		Has the teacher analyzed whether students have learned deeply or not?
		Has the teacher designed and implemented a classroom action research project to improve the learning outcomes in a future course?
Effective presentation	Public	Does the teacher share the results of his or her teaching with peers?
	Susceptible to peer review and evaluation	Does the teacher effectively communicate the results?
		Does the teacher actively seek peer review opportunities for the evaluation of the teaching?
	Accessible for use by others.	Is the teaching public? Are the teaching results public?
		Are the teaching results available for other teachers to use, build upon, and improve?

Based on Glassick, C. E.; Huber, M. T.; and Maeroff, G. I. Scholarship Assessed: Evaluation of the Professoriate; Jossey-Bass: San Francisco, 1997; Shulman, L. Professing the liberal arts. In Education and democracy: Re-imagining liberal learning in America; Orrill, R., Ed.; College Board Publications: New York, 1997; and Shulman, L. Teaching as Community Property. Essays on Higher Education; Jossey-Bass: San Francisco, 2004.

12.5 SUMMARY

The predominant approach to student evaluation of teaching reflects a nonconstructivist notion of learning and knowledge and a Level 2 conception of the teaching process. Furthermore, the predominant SET practice is full of biases and potential biases against minority teachers and all those whose teaching does not conform to the mainstream view of an effective teacher. SETs tend to respond to nonverbal behavior, such as gestures, body language, and facial expressions. Many of these behaviors are rooted in physiology, culture, personality, and habit, which are difficult to change and affect minority teachers more negatively than mainstream faculty. The most serious problem with SETs is that they do not take into consideration the learning aspect of the teaching and learning equation. By focusing exclusively on the teaching side, they do not provide any information about student learning.

An alternative approach to evaluating teaching effectiveness should focus on whether the teacher creates a deep learning environment. This does not mean that teaching effectiveness should be measured by assessing whether students actually learned or not, as there may be cases of students learning with an ineffective teacher and students not learning despite having an effective teacher. This means that the focus should be on whether the teacher has created an environment that is conducive to deep learning. For Bain (2004), the key question is: "Does the teaching help and encourage students to learn in ways that make a sustained, substantial, and positive difference in the way students think, act, or feel—without doing them any harm?" This question can be broken down in several sub-questions to reflect every aspect of the deep learning process.

Because teaching exceeds delivery in the classroom, evaluation of teaching effectiveness should evaluate the whole teaching process: vision, design, enactment, outcomes, and analysis.

Given the importance of SET for reappointment, tenure, and promotion, higher education institutions should promote a scholarly approach to the evaluation of teaching effectiveness with clear standards and multiple sources of data.

Student Evaluation of Teaching: Evaluating Deep Learning 267

The next chapter explores the connection between time and deep learning and focuses on intensive teaching formats.

PRACTICE CORNER

1. It is university policy to administer Student Evaluation of Teaching surveys at the end of every course. SETs are mainly used for tenure and promotion. One of your colleagues is in the third year of her tenure-track appointment. She is generally regarded as an excellent and conscientious teacher. She actively participates in educational development programs and regularly reads the literature on teaching and learning. Right before the administration of SETs, she asked her students to identify areas for improvement. Her SET scores were good, but not excellent. She applied for reappointment. Her tenure and promotion committee was concerned about her SET scores. The committee asked you to become her mentor and to discuss her SET scores. What can you do to help your colleague? What advice can you give her? What actions can you take?

2. The university's SET questionnaire includes the following statements for students to rate from 1 to 7: (i) the instructor was knowledgeable about the subject matter; and (ii) the instructor was able to communicate the subject matter effectively. What do you think about these statements? Are they appropriate for evaluating teaching effectiveness? Why or why not? Would you eliminate them from the SET questionnaire? Would you reformulate them? If so, how?

3. Your colleague decided to implement John Tagg's suggestion about comments on student papers. He decided not to assign any grade to students' papers throughout the term, because, like Tagg, he believes that students only pay attention to the grade and do not read comments and suggestions for improvement. So, he gave them only feedback without any grade. He asked students to act upon this feedback and resubmit their papers several times during the term. Your colleague was very happy with the results of this

practice, as students produced high-quality papers. However, he was shocked to receive very low SET scores. Students made the following comments: "I like to know all my grades not just find out my final mark." "Grades are arbitrary. You don't know your grade until the term is over." "The guy is nice but you have to work hard on the papers. If you don't you fail." What happened? Why do you think that students complained about this practice? What do the SET comments reflect? Why? What changes, if any, would you suggest to your colleague?

4. A recent hire in your department is a very hard working professor and scholar. She recently finished her Ph.D. and has already published two books and several articles in her base discipline. She is very demanding of her students. She believes she is very effective. At meetings and in informal gatherings, she often complains about her students' lack of adequate preparation for postsecondary studies. She received very low SET scores during her first year. Some students made the following comments: "This was the most miserable experience in all four years." "She is unapproachable. I am afraid to talk to her." "She made me cry when I went to her office to ask her about my grade." "She hates students. She is an awful prof." "She is too tough. She treats us as if we were Ph.D. students." You are the chair of the department, and you are worried about her SETs. You talked to her, but she dismissed your concerns by saying that the only reason why she got low SET scores is that she is very demanding and gives students low grades. She added that when students get low grades they tend to give low SET scores. You replied that everyone else had substantially higher SET scores in the department and that she should improve hers. She replied "Oh, that's only because other professors give away grades, that's how they get high SET scores." Why do you think your colleague reacted in this way? Is she right? Why or why not? What can you say to her? What advice can you give her? Students come to your office to complain about her teaching practice and marking quite frequently. What should you say to them?

5. John Biggs's questionnaire to gather evidence from student perception of teaching includes the following questions focused on

Student Evaluation of Teaching: Evaluating Deep Learning

constructive alignment (Biggs and Tang, 2007): Were the Intended Learning Outcomes (ILOs) clear? Did the Teaching and Learning Activities (TLAs) help students achieve the ILOs? Which did not? Did the Assessment Tasks (ATs) address the ILOs? Were the grading rubrics understood? In your opinion, does Bigg's questionnaire help assess teaching effectiveness understood as the promotion of a motivating deep learning environment? Without taking into account biases, could a traditional lecturer achieve a high SET score under Bigg's questionnaire? Without taking into account biases, could a teacher who successfully facilitates the creation of a deep learning environment obtain a low SET score under Bigg's questionnaire?

6. A group of students started the course two weeks after the beginning of the semester. One of the questions on the SET questionnaire asks students if the teacher anticipated and explained the learning outcomes during the first weeks of the course. The teacher did not want these students to answer this SET question. So, she went to her chair to discuss this situation. Her chair told her that the questions may not be changed and that these students had to answer the SET questions as everyone else. What do you think about the teacher's position? What would you do in her place? What do you think about the chair's response? What would you do?

7. A part-time colleague at a two-year college is on contract. He has very good SET scores and comments. However, a couple of students wrote the following comments "Worst professor ever!!! Very picky and unclear." "Very unorganized and very picky about what type of folder you use to turn in essays." His chair refuses to renew his appointment because of these comments. Do you agree with the chair? Why or why not? What would you do if you were the chair? Why? What would you do if you were the part-time teacher whose contract is not renewed because of students' comments? Why?

8. You have a policy of returning assignments, tests, and papers in the class immediately following the day students hand in the assignments or take the tests. One of the statements in the SET reads: "Required work was graded in time" You were sure that you would receive the highest score from every single student in this item.

To your surprise, some students did not rate you highly. You complained to your chair about this and offered evidence about your return policy for assignments and tests. The chair dismissed your comments and was upset with you because of your low SET score for that statement. Why do you think your students did not give you a high rating for that statement? What do you think of the chair's attitude? What, if anything, can you do now? What can you do to prevent students from giving you a low score next time you teach that course?

9. Remember or watch the school scenes from the film *The Easter Egg Adventure* (2004) directed by John Michael Williams. Suppose you are a student in Ms. Horrible Harriet Hare's class. Take the SET questionnaire used in your institution to evaluate Ms. Hare's teaching effectiveness. How would you rate her? An alternative to the traditional SET questionnaires that focus on what the teacher does in the course is to try to determine if the teacher has created an environment that is conducive to deep learning. What specific questions would you include to determine if a teacher has created a deep learning environment? How would you evaluate Ms. Hare's teaching using that questionnaire?

10. A questionnaire for the evaluation of part-time faculty includes the following:

EXPRESSION: Use of nonverbal behavior to solicit student attention and interest.

- Speaks in a dramatic expressive way.
- Moves about while lecturing.
- Gestures with hands or arms.
- Makes eye contact with students.
- Gestures with head or body.
- Tells jokes or humorous anecdotes.
- Effectively uses prepared notes or text.
- Smiles or laughs while teaching.
- Avoids distracting mannerisms.
  What do you think of these evaluation criteria? What are the implications of using these criteria? How can you improve the questionnaire?

KEYWORDS

- deep learning
- evaluating deep learning
- scholarly approach to evaluation
- scholarly teaching
- SET reliability problems
- student evaluation of teaching (SET)

REFERENCES

Ambady, N.; Rosenthal, R. Half a minute: Predicting teacher evaluations from thin slices of nonverbal behavior and physical attractiveness. *Journal of Personality and Social Psychology,* 1993,*64(3),* 431–441.

Bain, K. What the Best College Teachers Do; Harvard University Press: Cambridge, MA, 2004.

Biggs, J.; Tang, C.Teaching for Quality Learning at University;Open University Press: Maidenhead, 2007.

Bolívar Botía, A.; Caballero Rodríguez, K. Cómo hacer visible la excelencia en la enseñanza universitaria. Revista Iberoamericana de Educación, 2008, 46.8.

Clayson, D. E.; Sheffet, M. J.; Personality and the student evaluation of teaching. Journal of Marketing Education, 2006, 28, 149–160.

Delaney, J.; Johnson, A., Johnson, T.; Treslan, D. Students' Perceptions of Effective Teaching in Higher Education; Distance Education and Learning Technologies: St. John's, NL, 2010.

Eisenhower, K. American Attitudes toward Accented English. M.A. Thesis, McGill University, Montreal, Canada, 2002.

Entwistle, N.; Tait, H. Approaches to learning, evaluations of teaching, and preferences for contrasting academic environments.Higher Education, 1990, 19, 169–194.

Glassick, C. E.; Huber, M. T.; and Maeroff, G. I. Scholarship Assessed: Evaluation of the Professoriate; Jossey-Bass: San Francisco, 1997.

Hamermesh, D. S.; Parker, A. Beauty in the classroom: instructors' pulchritude and putative pedagogical productivity. Economics of Education Review, 2005, 24, 4, 369–376.

Herteis, E. M. (n/d). A Fine and Private Place: Making Teaching Visible.

Hutchings, P.; The course portfolio: How faculty can examine their teaching to advance practice and student learning. American Association for Higher Education: Washington, DC., 1998

Llurda, E. Effects of intelligibility and speaking rate on judgments of nonnative speakers' personalities, International Review of Applied Linguistics in Language Teaching. 2000, 38, 3–4, 289–300

Marsh, H.W.; Roche, L.A.; Making students' evaluations of teaching effectiveness effective. American Psychologist 1997,52, 1187–1197.

McKeachie, W. J. Student ratings: The validity of use. American Psychologist, 1997, 52(11), 1218–1225.

Merritt, D. Bias, the Brain, and Student Evaluations of Teaching. St. John's Law Review, 2008, 82, 235–287.

Naftulin, D.; Ware, J.; Donnelly, F. The Dr. Fox Lecture: a Paradigm of Educational Seduction. The Journal of Medical Education, 1973, 48, 630–5.

Perlini, A.; Hansen, S. Moderating Effects of Need for Cognition on Attractiveness Stereotyping. *Social Behavior and Personality: an international journal, 2001,* 29, 4, 313–321.

Riniolo, T. C.; Johnson, K. C.; Sherman, T. R.; Misso, J. A. Hot or not: Do professors perceived as physically attractive receive higher student evaluations? The Journal of General Psychology, 2006, 133, 19–35.

Shulman, L. Professing the liberal arts. In Education and democracy: Re-imagining liberal learning in America; Orrill, R., Ed.; College Board Publications: New York, 1997.

Shulman, L. Teaching as Community Property. Essays on Higher Education; Jossey-Bass: San Francisco, 2004.

Theall, M.; Franklin, J. Looking for Bias in all the Wrong Places – A Search for Truth or a Witch Hunt in Student Ratings of Instruction? In The Student Ratings Debate: Are they Valid? How Can We Best Use Them? Theall, P.; Abrami, L.; Mets, L. Eds.; Jossey-Bass: San Francisco. 2001.

Trigwell, K.; Michael Prosser, M. Improving the Quality of Student Learning: The Influence of Learning Context and Student Approaches to Learning on Learning Outcomes. Higher Education, 1991, 22, 3, 251–266.

Williams, W.M.; Ceci, S.J. How'm I Doing. Change, 1997, 13–23.

PART V

DEEP LEARNING AND TIME

CHAPTER 13

INTENSIVE TEACHING

The years teach much the days never know.

— RALPH WALDO EMERSON

CONTENTS

13.1 Introduction 276
13.2 Time and Deep Learning 276
13.3 Intensive Teaching and Deep Learning 277
13.4 Intensive Teaching and Other Advantages 279
13.5 Student Demographics 280
13.6 Motivation and Engagement 280
13.7 Active and Student-Centered Pedagogy 281
13.8 Learning Communities 282
13.9 Concerns 283
13.10 Summary 283
Practice Corner 284
Keywords 286
References 287

13.1 INTRODUCTION

Deep learning does not occur magically in short or arbitrary periods of time. It is a long process that requires multiple instances of grappling with problems, making connections, interacting with peers, and reflecting about new knowledge.

Some colleges and universities are experimenting with intensive teaching formats instead of the traditional scheduling format. In some cases, they use intensive teaching to structure and organize learning communities. In other cases, intensive teaching is used in conjunction with study abroad programs. Many universities and colleges use intensive teaching by scheduling courses during the summer, weekends, and evenings to allow nontraditional students the possibility of taking programs and courses that do not conflict with their work and family responsibilities (Danley-Scott, 2008). Intensive teaching models include a wide variety of scheduling formats where students take a course for more hours than they normally do in traditional courses.

Interestingly, traditional course schedule formats (60-minute-class three times a week, 90-minute-class twice-a-week, or 180-minute once-a-week sessions taught over a period of 13 to 15 weeks) are not based on any empirical research on student learning. Universities and colleges adopted the conventional schedules based first on intuition, then because it became customary, and recently as a result of standard norms imposed by accrediting agencies (Wlodkowski, 2003). But there is no pedagogical reason to justify the conventional schedule formats. They are simply artifacts of the Instruction-paradigm university, which teachers, students, administrators, and accrediting agencies simply take for granted (Tagg, 2003).

In this chapter, I will examine the connection between intensive teaching and deep learning. I will explore the benefits and advantages of intensive teaching as well as some concerns expressed about nontraditional scheduling formats.

13.2 TIME AND DEEP LEARNING

Deep learning is a long process that requires the learner to engage in a myriad of individual and collective instances of negotiation of meanings

Intensive Teaching

and reflection. It is not a simple or immediate process. It is a long journey of discovery and slow construction. Throughout this process, the learner experiences a series of intermediate phases in which he or she tries new ideas and explanations to respond to cognitive dissonances created by interaction with new knowledge. Neuroscience also supports the idea that changes in the brain, that is, the formation of neuronal networks of countless synapses, require multiple experiences along lengthy periods of time (Zull, 2011).

Think about skills that you learned deeply in your life, such as walking, speaking, playing a sport, writing, or playing a musical instrument. These learning processes took time; equally important, they extended over uninterrupted blocks of time. Lionel Messi, the world's greatest soccer player, four-time FIFA Player of the Year and Olympic gold medalist, and Manu Ginobili, a two-time NBA All-Star player and Olympic gold medalist, did not learn to play soccer and basketball, respectively, by playing 90 minutes twice a week over a semester or two while juggling multiple other learning activities. They learned by focusing on their sports most of the time for as long as possible. Soccer for Messi and basketball for Ginobili have always been their number-one priorities and main interests. I am not suggesting that we focus exclusively on one single activity for life or even at university. Apart from playing soccer, Messi went to school. And so did Ginobili, who also studied English as a second language in a language school as an extracurricular activity in Bahia Blanca, his hometown. But when a learner is trying to learn something deeply—a sport, an academic discipline, or any skill—he or she needs long and uninterrupted periods of time to delve into the deep learning process. Sitting in a classroom at predetermined times for a few minutes twice a week, followed by more sitting in another classroom to learn something different and disconnected to the previous class, does not help learners learn anything deeply.

13.3 INTENSIVE TEACHING AND DEEP LEARNING

Some universities and colleges have been increasing the time periods for courses. Students take courses that last the whole morning or even the whole day for several weeks and even months. During these blocks of time, students concentrate on taking only one course.

In terms of student deep learning, intensive teaching formats lead to better results than traditional scheduling formats (Kasworm, 1991; van Scyoc and Gleason, 1993; Wlodkowski, 1999). This is so because students and teachers have ample time to actively experiment with the discipline. They have time to explore topics, theories, and problems without being limited by artificial time constraints. Students are immersed in the discipline for a relatively long period of time. And during that time, this is all that they do in their academic lives. Geltner and Logan (2000) studied over 400,000 students who took conventional and intensive courses in a period of four years. They found better success in intensive courses than in traditional ones. Wlodkowski and his colleagues (1999, 2000) conducted several research projects where they compared students' learning achievements in courses taught in a traditional format with students' achievement in courses offered in an intensive format. The projects included courses in accounting, law, and philosophy with university undergraduate students who studied in English in the United States. After the end of the courses, students' performances were evaluated by experts in the field who were unrelated to the university. These were accountants, lawyers, business experts, and reputed philosophers who judged students' work as if they were produced by professionals or scholars. These independent evaluators found that students in the intensive-schedule-format courses achieved excellence in their respective fields and that these students attained deeper learning than their counterparts who took traditional-format courses. Wlodkowski and his colleagues wanted to see if this phenomenon was exclusive to university students who take courses in English. So, they replicated the same project with university students who study in Spanish in Puerto Rico. Wlodkowski and his colleagues found that those students who took courses in intensive scheduling modes also outperformed those who took part in conventional courses.

Intensive teaching formats can also give rise to significant changes in attitudes and behaviors—essential aspects of deep learning. Ray and Kirkpatrick (1983) compared students' knowledge, attitudes, and anxiety concerning sexuality for two groups of students—those who had taken a course on human sexuality taught intensively and those who had taken

Intensive Teaching   279

the same course taught traditionally. Whereas students in both courses understood the different types of sexuality and diverse gender conceptions explored in the courses, most students who took intensive courses changed their attitudes to embrace other forms of sexuality in their everyday lives. They became less biased. They showed more tolerance for different sexual groups. And they integrated students of different sexual orientations into their social circles. In contrast, only a minority of students who took a conventional scheduling course changed their attitudes.

A colleague taught Philosophy of Law in both intensive and conventional scheduling formats. The content of the courses, the goals, the teaching and learning activities, and the evaluation were identical. However, there was more uninterrupted time for class discussions and other activities in the intensive course. In both courses, my colleague discussed various notions of law with his students. He wanted his students to recognize that law is more than just what is traditionally associated with a positivist legal perspective (law as rules emanated from legislatures and courts). He wanted students to appreciate that law also comes from nongovernmental agencies such as the church, school, and the family and that the rules people adhere to when they play sports, wait for a bus, or talk to strangers on the street are also considered law. Both groups of students understood nonpositivist notions of law. But only some of the students in the intensive course adopted these notions as something meaningful for them. They embraced these nonpositive perspectives of law for their analysis and carried them in upper-year courses. Students in the regular course referred to situations of positivist law as "law" and to nonpositivist notions of law as "law for anthropologists" or "law for nonlawyers." One student even referred to these nonpositivist approaches as "all that crap." The longer uninterrupted time to explore, discuss, and experiment with these nonpositivist perspectives made the difference between both courses, as everything else was practically the same.

13.4 INTENSIVE TEACHING AND OTHER ADVANTAGES

Intensive course formats offer many other advantages such as a tendency to favor nontraditional students and to foster student engagement and teacher motivation. They also encourage the creation of learning communities and the adoption of active, student-centered pedagogies.

13.5 STUDENT DEMOGRAPHICS

Although all or most students have evidenced important success in terms of deep learning in intensive teaching formats, the students who tend to benefit the most are students who are considered nontraditional and marginal (Messina, 1996). Intensive modes promote deep learning in all age groups (young and mature) and in all ethnic backgrounds: aboriginal, white, Latino, African American, and Asian, among many others. It also strongly benefits students whose first language is not English or the language of instruction, as immersion in a language has proved to help students improve their language and academic skills. Students who transferred from two-year colleges, returning students, and immigrants also experienced more successful and deeper learning experiences in intensive courses than in traditional scheduling modes. Intensive teaching formats facilitate accessibility and learning opportunities for—part-time and full-time—students from nontraditional backgrounds and with lower incomes (Wlodkowski, 2003). Intensive teaching models have also proved to have more positive effects on student retention than conventional scheduling modes.

13.6 MOTIVATION AND ENGAGEMENT

Intensive teaching formats also increase student motivation and engagement. Teachers are also more motivated when they teach intensive courses, as this facilitates the elaboration of longer—than-usual projects and out-of-class activities. Anyone who experienced having to stop a very interesting class discussion because it was time to leave the classroom and make room for a new class knows that sometimes it is important to let students have ample time before they engage in a lively discussion. Once students are engaged, the discussion should develop uninterruptedly without any time constraints.

Many universities and colleges use intensive teaching modes to take their students abroad. They teach entire courses off-campus. Students learn not only by taking courses in another country but also from the whole experience of living in a foreign culture. For example, a drama teacher from a university in Los Angeles, organized an entire program around theater companies formed by students from different countries. He complements acting courses in Los Angeles with international experiences in Japan, Europe and Latin America. As part of their program, every cohort of students takes formal acting classes abroad. Students also audit workshops and showcase a play abroad. And, most important, they see foreign plays and interact with foreign drama students, professors, and professional actors. Additionally, the university invites some of these professors to Los Angeles to continue with some of the projects initiated abroad. These experiences are not limited in terms of traditional scheduling formats. It is the learning experience that dictates the time students need to make the most of these initiatives and projects. For example, when students go see a play abroad, they stay until the play is over, regardless of how long it takes. Furthermore, they usually meet the actors and directors after the play; in many cases they all go have dinner together and linger on for hours talking about the play and their acting experiences. These very rich learning projects cannot be done when teachers and students have to abide by rigid schedules and when students are taking other courses.

13.7 ACTIVE AND STUDENT-CENTERED PEDAGOGY

Intensive scheduling models discourage teaching through traditional lectures. So, in order to keep students' engagement, most teachers employ active and deep learning teaching methods, such as group projects, creative class activities, collaborative learning, experiential learning activities, and problem solving (Sainsbury, 2008). Adoption of active pedagogies also includes assessment practices that are aligned to active and student-centered teaching methods (Lee and Horsfall, 2010). When we adopt this student-centered approach to teaching and assessing, students tend to have more positive learning experiences in intensive courses than in conventional scheduling formats. Some teachers see the intensive format as an opportu-

282 Facilitating Deep Learning

nity to experiment with creative and active pedagogies (Sainsbury, 2008). For example, a colleague in a two-year college taught an intensive course on the history of indigenous peoples. She asked students to research the way different indigenous peoples eat. Students had to find out the main foods, eating habits, and nutrition patterns of different peoples. For this purpose, students lived for a few days in some selected reserves across North America and learned about foods while having meals and by listening to stories told by elders. When they came back, they had to cook authentic meals and explain the group's eating habits.

13.8 LEARNING COMMUNITIES

Intensive teaching tends to construct similar social relations as those formed in learning communities (Brown, 1992). As discussed earlier, a learning community is a group of students and teachers who associate themselves for a common purpose: learning. In learning communities, students can negotiate their meanings interdependently by conversing with other students and teachers. In attempting to understand others' meanings, students try to fit these understandings into their own knowledge structures (Cross, 1998). Learning communities also enhance the quality of student learning (Shulman, 2004), as they foster collaborative thinking (Bruffee, 1999) and break down traditional professor-student relationship models (Richmond and McCroskey, 1992).

Students in intensive courses and programs have more possibilities to interact with one another. They discuss readings, comment on class activities, and study together. They are also in a better position to provide more meaningful feedback about their peers' learning processes. Students tend to regard intensive scheduling course formats, particularly when the whole program is made up of intensive courses, as a supportive learning environment. In most cases, the success of intensive teaching also has to do with the socialization activities that teachers encourage outside formal instruction, which may include an innumerable array of activities, such as dances, picnics, meals, movies, sports games, travels, and shopping, among many others (Buzash, 1994). This creates a cohesive and relaxed atmosphere, which is indispensable for learning. A stronger bond is formed between

Intensive Teaching

teacher and students "when they meet every day rather than just two or three times a week" (Austin and Gustafson, 2006).

13.9 CONCERNS

Some traditional Instruction-paradigm academics are concerned with the quality of intensive-teaching programs. They argue that programs based on intensive or accelerated formats are second-class programs. They usually hold that in accelerated programs there is insufficient time to cover the most important aspects of the discipline and that they sacrifice depth and breadth. Other critics stress that there is inadequate time for reflection and analysis of the materials in accelerated courses (Traub, 1997). Most of the criticisms of intensive teaching scheduling modes come from opinions that lack empirical support. Moreover, these criticisms revolve exclusively around accelerated courses, which is only one type of intensive teaching.

Although intensive teaching formats do not necessarily guarantee quality, there is nothing in the format itself that disallows quality learning. On the contrary, it offers the possibility for engaging in creative, active, and student-centered pedagogies without the limits of artificial time schedules, particularly when intensive courses extend over long periods of time (Tagg, 2003).

13.10 SUMMARY

The traditional semester-length course schedule formats are not based on any empirical research on student learning; there are no pedagogical reasons to justify these conventional scheduling formats. They are used mainly as a matter of tradition in the Instruction paradigm.

Intensive teaching presents several pedagogical advantages over conventional scheduling formats. First, with respect to student learning, intensive teaching leads to the same or better results than traditional scheduling modes. This has been clearly shown in empirical studies carried out in virtually every single discipline at every educational level. Second, although intensive teaching has proved to be beneficial for all types of

284 Facilitating Deep Learning

students—young and mature, mainstream and nontraditional—it tends to benefit nontraditional and marginal students—mature, aboriginal, Latino, African, Asian, international, immigrant, part-time, and at-risk—the most, because they can benefit from intensive teacher-student contact and can concentrate on one course at a time. Third, intensive teaching promotes learning communities or, at least, similar social relations as in learning communities. Fourth, intensive teaching also favors motivation, student engagement, retention, and active, student-centered pedagogies.

The success of intensive teaching formats depends on the recognition of the advantages and the possibilities that they offer. When intensive teaching formats are not accompanied by active and student-centered pedagogies, such as when teachers resort mainly to lectures with little or no student involvement and traditional assessment practices, intensive teaching may not produce deep learning results. Thus, in order to ensure a successful learning experience for all students, it is necessary to emphasize teaching pedagogies that make the most of intensive course and program formats.

The next chapter explores the main characteristics of the Learning paradigm. It offers a brief overview of the goals, structure, and methods needed to create higher education organizations focused on deep learning.

PRACTICE CORNER

1. Think of a course you are currently teaching. How would you adapt it to offer it in an intensive format? What changes would you make? What aspects of the course would you keep intact? Why?
2. Some critics of intensive teaching argue that survey introductory courses are not fit to be taught in intensive scheduling formats. What do you think? How would you respond to these critics?
3. A colleague noticed that there is practically no research on whether undergraduate thesis courses can be effectively taught in intensive formats. She wants you to help her design a research project to assess whether thesis courses can be taught in intensive and compressed formats. What will be the most important aspects of the

Intensive Teaching

research design? How can you evaluate whether thesis courses can be taught effectively in intensive formats?

4. One of your colleagues has to teach an intensive course for the first time. She usually assigns ten books to her students per term. She does not think that students can read ten books in a one-month intensive course, even if this will be the only course students will be taking. Your colleague is familiar with the literature on intensive teaching and deep learning. She knows that students taking intensive courses do as well or even better than students in traditional semester courses. But she is not convinced that this applies to her discipline and courses. She comes to you for advice. What can you say to her? What advice can you give her? Does she need to make some changes to her course? If so, what changes? Would she need to make changes to her course in order to achieve deep learning even if she continued to teach a traditional-scheduling-format course?

5. Your university is considering moving to a block plan, that is, a scheduling system where all courses are taught intensively, and students take only one course at a time. A group of colleagues approaches you for advice. Your colleagues are worried because they do not know how to teach in the new system. What advice can you give them? How can they adapt their courses to teach in the block plan?

6. Another group of teachers vehemently opposes the block plan. These colleagues approach you because they want your support in opposing the block plan. They think that only traditional students will do well in this format. They also argue that international students who speak English as a second language will not be able to take courses in the block plan. They fear these students will drop out. What do you think of their arguments? What will you say to them?

7. The editor of a teaching and learning journal has asked you to contribute a one-paragraph analysis on the most salient literature findings about the relation between intensive teaching and deep learning. The editor would also like you to think of examples of

classroom activities that make the most of intensive formats. Write this paragraph and the examples.

8. A colleague of yours teaches theater performance. He has been asked to teach a course intensively (three hours a day for four evenings a week over a month). He doubts that he can teach students how to act in a compressed format. He comes to you for advice. What would you say to your colleague?

9. In the book *On Your Own*, Brooke Shields (1985) writes about how she had to juggle her studies and work commitments when she studied at Princeton. "It's not unusual for me to be studying while [working]. There are so many demands to be met and time is always limited." Can higher education students who have some work responsibilities benefit from intensive scheduling formats? Are there any drawbacks? Are they better off in conventional semester classes? What about students who work full time and can only take one or two courses per semester?

10. Austin and Gustafson (2006) argue that "there is a better bond between teacher and student when they meet every day than just two or three times a week." Do you agree? Why or why not? Assuming that this assertion is true, does it have any impact on the deep learning process? Why or why not?

KEYWORDS

- **deep learning**
- **engagement**
- **intensive teaching**
- **learning communities**
- **non-traditional scheduling**
- **time**
- **traditional scheduling**

REFERENCES

Austin, A.; Gustafson, L. Impact of Course Length on Student Learning. Journal of Economics and Finance Education 2006, 5.1. 26–37.

Bain, K. What the Best College Teachers Do; Harvard University Press: Cambridge, MA, 2004.

Brown, D. Teaching Literature in the Intensive Weekend Format. Annual Meeting of the College English Association, 23rd, Pittsburgh, PA,1992.

Bruffee, K. Collaborative Learning: Higher Education, Interdependence, and the Authority of Knowledge, 2nd ed.; The John Hopkins University Press: Baltimore and London, 1999.

Buzash, M. Success of two-week intensive program in French for superior high school students on a university campus. Annual Meeting of the Central State Conference on the Teaching of Foreign Languages, Kansas City, M.O, 1994.

Cross, K. Why Learning Communities? Why Now? About Campus, 1998, 3, 4.

Danley-Scott, J. Teaching the Extended Length Class. Western Political Science Association, 2008.

Kasworm, C. Rethinking the acts of learning in relation to the undergraduate classroom. Proceedings of the Project for the Study of the Adult Learner Symposium. Normal: Illinois State University, College of Continuing Education and Public Service, 1991.

Lee, N.; Horsfall, B. Accelerated Learning: A Study of Faculty and Student Experiences Innovative Higher Education, 2010, 35, 191–202.

Messina, R. Power package: An alternative to traditional course scheduling. ERIC Document Reproduction Service, No. ED 396787, 1996.

Ray, R.; Kirkpatrick, D. Two time formats to teaching human sexuality. Teaching of Psychology, 1983, 10, 84–88.

Richmond, V, P.; McCroskey, J. C. Power in the Classroom: Communication, Control, and Concern; Lawrence Erlbaum: Hillsdale, NJ, 1992.

Sainsbury, M. Intensive Teaching of Graduate Law Subjects: McEducation or Good Preparation for the Demands of Legal Practice? Journal of the Australasian Law Teachers Association, 2008, 1, 247.

Shields, B. On Your Own; Villard Books: New York, 1985.

Shulman, L. Teaching as Community Property. Essays on Higher Education; Jossey-Bass: San Francisco, 2004.

Tagg, J. The Learning Paradigm College; Anker Publishing Company: Bolton, MA, 2003.

Traub, J. Drive-thru U: Higher education for people who mean business. New Yorker, October, 114–123, 1997.

van Scyoc, L.; Gleason, J. Traditional or intensive course lengths? A comparison of outcomes in economics learning. Journal of Economics Education, 1993, 24, 15–22.

Wlodkowski, R. J. Motivation and diversity: A framework for teaching. In Motivation from within: Approaches for encouraging faculty and students to excel; Theall, M., Ed.; Jossey-Bass: San Francisco, 1999.

Wlodkowski, R. J., and Westover, T. (1999). Accelerated courses as a learning format for adults. The Canadian journal for the study of adult education. 13, 1–20.

Wlodkowski, R. J.; Kasworm, C. E. Accelerated Learning for Adults: The Promise and Practice of Intensive Educational Formats; Jossey-Bass: San Francisco, 2003.

FINAL PART
A NEW PARADIGM

FINAL PART

A NEW TARADUCA

CHAPTER 14

THE LEARNING PARADIGM

The golden rule: Do what you want your students to do. Be what you want your students to be.

— JOHN TAGG

CONTENTS

14.1 Introduction 292
14.2 The Learning Paradigm 292
14.3 Summary 298
Practice Corner 299
Keywords 302
References 302

14.1 INTRODUCTION

Discontent with the results of the Instruction paradigm and an understanding of the deep learning process have created a unique opportunity to move away from the Instruction-paradigm universities and colleges to a new form of higher education organizations fully focused on student learning (Buckley, 2002). The Learning paradigm is a model that describes these ideal organizations (Tagg, 2003). In contrast to the Instruction paradigm, the main purpose of the Learning paradigm is to produce learning at all levels. In learning institutions, students, teachers, administrators, and other relevant stakeholders work together to create deep learning environments.

In this chapter, I will analyze the main characteristics of the Learning paradigm, and I will contrast its elements with the characteristics of the Instruction paradigm. The goal behind this exploration is to show that developing learning institutions is a possible—albeit not easy—endeavor. The best way to achieve this goal is through embracing every aspect of the deep learning process in our own classrooms.

14.2 THE LEARNING PARADIGM

The Learning paradigm refers to a model of universities and colleges that does not predominate in our society. It is a model that those of us who want to help our students engage in deep learning can work toward in our quest for transforming our teaching practices and our institutions. It is a utopia of sorts, but a possible one.

In contrast with the Instruction paradigm, the sole purpose of the Learning paradigm is to produce learning, that is, "to produce environments that encourage students to discover and construct knowledge for themselves, to make students members of communities of learners that make discoveries and solve problems" (Barr and Tagg, 1995). In learning organizations, everyone works toward the same objective. So, every member of the institution helps students learn deeply and meaningfully.

Additionally, everybody—and not just students—is engaged in learning. Teachers learn how to be better teachers. Administrators learn how to better lead their institutions. Information Technology (IT) staff learn how

The Learning Paradigm

to improve technology in higher education. This is also in sharp contrast to the Instruction paradigm. In the Instruction paradigm, teachers' learning is hidden from their students. For example, teachers tend to teach courses within their areas of expertise. When they are assigned to teach a new course outside their expertise, they do not always make explicit the fact that they do not know all the aspects of the new course topic. They learn in their offices or at home. They try to prepare ahead of classes. They do not learn in front of their students, let alone with their students or from students. Not knowing the discipline that one teaches is seen as a sign of weakness and lack of professionalism, not as an opportunity to model learning for our students. In the Learning paradigm, learning becomes visible. Teachers learn together with their students. Teachers provide meaningful opportunities to negotiate and construct knowledge together. They also provide role models for their students, as teachers are mature and experienced learners. Even if teachers do not know a certain discipline, theory, or topic, they have experience in learning academic issues. They have a wide repertoire of metacognitive skills. They know the challenges and difficulties in academic learning processes. So, when teachers learn the same materials together with their students, they provide students with a unique learning experience.

Another way for teachers to learn and to make their learning visible to their colleagues and the whole academic community is through engaging in scholarly teaching and the scholarship of teaching and learning. This is an approach where teachers immerse themselves in teaching in the same way they approach research in their base disciplines (Glassick, 1997). As discussed earlier, this entails selecting clear goals aimed at producing learning. This approach requires us to be familiar with the theoretical perspectives in the teaching and learning field. It also calls for conducting research to improve our teaching practice by following appropriate methods for the collection of data, which leads to significant results. One method to conduct research and to systematically examine our teaching practice is classroom action research (Table 14.1 outlines the main aspects of classroom action research, and Table 14.2 describes the steps to be followed in order to conduct classroom action research). A scholarly approach to teaching also entails communicating and sharing results with peers and students. Scholarly teachers also engage in a reflective process and contin-

294   Facilitating Deep Learning

ually test and evaluate their projects. Scholarly teaching is "making transparent the process of making learning possible" (Trigwell et al., 2000). When we follow a scholarly approach and also make our teaching public, subject to peer review, and available so that others can build on it, we engage in the scholarship of teaching and learning, which gives maximum visibility to the learning process (Shulman, 2004).

TABLE 14.1   Classroom action research.

Notion	A method of gathering data about one's teaching practice.
Goals	To improve one's teaching practice. An opportunity to maximize student learning.
Use of research results	To improve teaching practice by making changes to one's classes.
Validity	Triangulation of data.
Focus	Practical significance of research results.
Effects	Ownership of one's teaching practice. Collaboration between students and teachers in the teaching process. Frequent improvement in the quality of student learning.
Dissemination of research results	Research results may be communicated in teaching and learning workshops, presented at teaching conferences, and informally shared with colleagues.

Based on Mettetal, G. The What, Why and How of Classroom Action Research. Journal of the Scholarship of Teaching and Learning 2001, 2, 1.

TABLE 14.2   Steps to conduct classroom action research.

Step	Content
Observation of and reflection about one's teaching practice.	Knowledge of strengths and weaknesses of one's teaching practice.
Formulation of a research problem.	Research problem must be an aspect of one's teaching practice that may be improved.

The Learning Paradigm

295

TABLE 14.2 *(Continued)*

Step	Content
Formulation of preliminary hypothesis.	Tentative answers to the research problem.
Literature review.	Knowledge of learning theories.
	Knowledge of theories, strategies, and best practices that deal with the selected research problem.
Research design.	The methodology and procedure to conduct the research.
	Quantitative methods.
	Qualitative methods.
	Combination of qualitative and quantitative methods.
Data collection.	Multiple sources of data collection: student performances, teaching and learning activities, surveys, observation, student reflections, course portfolio, videotape of classroom teaching, journals, and student interviews.
Data analysis.	Analysis of collected data through varied techniques and procedures.
	Theories identified in the literature review.
Implementation of results.	Change to the teaching practice.
Evaluation of implemented results.	New classroom action research to evaluate whether the implemented changes improved the teaching practice and the quality of student learning.
Dissemination of results.	Presentations to colleagues to help them reflect about teaching and learning and find potential solutions to similar problems.

Based on Mettetal, G. The What, Why and How of Classroom Action Research. Journal of the Scholarship of Teaching and Learning 2001, 2, 1.

In the Learning paradigm, the institution itself also learns. All members engage in research about the institution's goals, the implementation of these goals, and the learning experiences of students, teachers, and administrators, among other equally significant institutional aspects. The research process is open. All members are encouraged to participate in various capacities. And the results of these research initiatives are widely communicated. Most important, the results are implemented and periodically evaluated so as to improve the overall quality of education. Again, this contrasts with the way in which the Instruction-paradigm universities and colleges work. In the Instruction-paradigm institutions, faculty and administrators engage in a series of actions for which they are clearly not prepared. For example, during the first year of my tenure-track appointment in my current university, I had to be a member of a search committee. I did not know how to short-list, interview, and select the best candidate. I must admit that my senior colleagues did not know, either, even if they had participated in dozens of searches. We all conducted these searches as we have seen others do in the past, much like many teachers teach in the Instruction-paradigm university. I later learned that there are theories, strategies, and techniques to hire personnel. There are hundreds of books and thousands of articles written about hiring. What's more, you can do research about different hiring alternatives. For example, you may implement a certain selection alternative, then hire somebody, and evaluate whether that choice was an effective one. If it was not, you can go back to the drawing board for the next hiring opportunity, make changes to the hiring method, and implement them. Then you can communicate the results of the research process so that other search committees can review them and build upon them. In the learning-paradigm university, the organization makes better-informed decisions in fairer processes, as members engage in a process of learning not only how to teach better but also how to do other tasks more effectively.

The pedagogy in the Learning paradigm is open and diverse. Any method that helps students discover and construct knowledge is a valid one, including but, not exclusively, teaching. Students learn by having freedom and flexibility in setting their own goals and by negotiating meanings

The Learning Paradigm

with their peers. The role of the teacher is to encourage and facilitate student learning by creating opportunities and environments that are conducive to deep learning. In this respect, students can engage in a wide variety of projects. If, for example, while embarked on a project, students find that they need to learn certain disciplines or topics, such as statistics, a foreign language, or business concepts, they may learn by reading books in the library and discussing them with a teacher or other peers, they may take a formal course taught by a teacher, or they may become immersed in a culture where the foreign language is spoken.

The Learning paradigm has a flexible structure and organization. Any structure that helps create a learning environment is welcome. The structures of the Instruction paradigm, for example, courses, semesters, traditional teachers, credits, and grades to name a few, may not be necessary in the Learning paradigm. Teachers are conceived of as designers of learning environments, whose main goal is to "study and apply best methods for producing learning and student success" (Barr and Tagg, 1995). In the Learning paradigm, universities and colleges are "boundary-free. They [are] less a place and more a range of opportunities" (Zull, 2011). In Chapter 1, I referred to the Instruction-paradigm university as a factory assembly line conveyor belt that moves students along until they graduate. The metaphor for the Learning-paradigm university is the sculptor's studio, where a sculptor patiently carves and models stones and other materials to make unique sculptures. The student is the sculptor. The stones, the other materials, the sculpting techniques, the models, the books the sculptor reads for inspiration, and all other resources the sculptor employs in the creation of the artwork represent the artifacts of the Learning paradigm. In the Instruction paradigm, one of the benchmarks of success is student graduation rates. In the Learning paradigm, the learning process itself, that is, the process of discovery and construction of knowledge, is at the same time its goal and the benchmark for success.

Table 14.3 summarizes the main differences between the Instruction paradigm and the Learning paradigm.

TABLE 14.3 The instruction paradigm vs. the learning paradigm.

The Instruction Paradigm	The Learning Paradigm
Focus on teaching.	Focus on learning.
No visibility of teachers' learning.	Maximum visibility of teachers' learning. Scholarship of teaching and learning.
Surface learning.	Deep learning.
Foundational notion of knowledge.	Non-foundational notion of knowledge.
Transmission of knowledge.	Individual and social construction of knowledge.
Distributional curriculum made up of courses.	Learning environments.
Summative evaluation.	Evaluating to learn.
Final (summative) evaluation.	Initial, simultaneous, and retrospective evaluation.
Grades.	Metacognition.
Rigid structure and organization.	Flexible structure and organization.
Uniform credit hour-courses.	Intensive teaching and long time periods.
Teacher as expert.	Teacher as designer of learning environments.
Coverage.	Discovery.
Individual learning.	Individual and collaborative learning.
Lecture (including, lecture conventions and recitation conventions).	Any method that helps students learn. Student performances.
Success equals graduation.	Success equals learning.
Factory assembly line conveyor belt metaphor.	Sculptor's studio metaphor.

Based on Tagg, J. The Learning Paradigm College; Anker Publishing Company: Bolton, MA, 2003.

14.3 SUMMARY

The Learning paradigm is a model that describes the ideal higher education institution. The goal of the Learning paradigm is to produce learning.

The Learning Paradigm

Every member of the Learning-paradigm university or college works to help students learn. At the same time, every member is engaged in learning. For example, teachers learn together with students. They act as experienced role models for students. Teachers also give visibility to their teaching practice by following a scholarly approach to teaching and by engaging in the scholarship of teaching and learning.

Unlike in the Instruction paradigm, there is no signature or predominant pedagogy. Any method that helps students learn is a valid one. This may or may not include teaching courses. Similarly, the structure of the Learning-paradigm institutions is very flexible. Learning organizations do not need many of the artifacts of the Instruction paradigm, such as grades, courses, traditional teaching, lectures, and standardized practices.

PRACTICE CORNER

1. Suppose you apply for the position of director of the Teaching and Learning Centre at your institution. The search committee would like you to answer the following questions: (i) As the new director, what can you do to help promote a culture of deep learning? (ii) How can you adopt some elements of the Learning paradigm across campus? and (iii) What advice can you give to teachers who would like to implement some or all of the aspects of the deep learning process in the classroom in a university or college that is hostile to teacher innovation?

2. John Tagg (2003) advanced the notion of orientation as a distinctive from approach. An orientation to learning can also be deep or surface. Tagg characterizes the notion of orientation as the general tendency to take either a deep or a surface approach to studying and learning. According to Tagg (2003), an orientation is "not the product of a single course or teacher but of [students'] overall experience over many years of schooling and of the expectations founded on that experience." Like with the surface approach, most university and college students today have a surface orientation to learning.

VP Academic has just read John Tagg's analysis of the distinction between orientation and approach. He is concerned with the fact that Tagg has found that surface orientation "is the default setting for academic learning regardless of the subject and content." VP Academic understands that only a change in the paradigm can modify the orientation. But he wants you to help him think of specific measures to gradually shift the surface orientation of the university toward a deep learning orientation. What can you do? What strategies can you suggest in order to achieve this very ambitious goal?

3. Analyze your institution's mission and vision statements. Can you identify any elements of the Learning paradigm? If so, what specific actions can you take in your department to implement these elements?

4. Your new president wants you to implement a pilot two-year program based on the Experimental College in your own institution. How can you design this program in a way that will engage students and be meaningful to them?

5. In higher education, governments and accrediting agencies sometimes hijack good ideas and initiatives. They appropriate those ideas and denaturalize them, using them for their advantage and for purposes that have little to do with the goals behind these ideas and initiatives. This was the case with the notion of learning outcomes and assessment, among many others. What can we as members of the academic community of knowledgeable peers do to protect the Learning paradigm ideas from possible appropriation?

6. Remember or watch the film *Accepted* (2006) directed by Steve Pink about a high school graduate who cannot gain admission to any school and ends up creating his own university. Can you identify any elements of the Learning paradigm? Do you think that South Harmon Institute of Technology's students take a deep approach to learning? Why or why not? If so, what do the students learn deeply? What is their motivation? Can you identify elements of the unschooling movement? What is the role of the teacher?

The Learning Paradigm

7. The editor of a teaching and learning journal has asked you to contribute a one-paragraph analysis on the characteristics of the Learning-paradigm university and the challenges of implementing learning-centered changes in current higher education institutions. What would your paragraph include?

8. Your institution wants to adopt a learning community program for all incoming first-year students: national, domestic, full time, and part time. You chair the committee charged with designing and implementing the program. How would you design the program? Would you implement only one very large learning community or more than one? If the latter, how would you form the learning communities? What are the advantages and disadvantages of homogeneous learning communities? What are the advantages and disadvantages of heterogeneous learning communities?

9. Barr and Tagg (1995) argue that teachers' role is to "study and apply best methods for producing learning and student success." What does this mean in practice? Can you think of effective methods for producing student learning and success? Can some of these methods be implemented in existing Instruction-paradigm institutions? Or is a radical change in paradigm needed?

10. As part of the 2011 Princeton Commencement's Class Day Address, Brooke Shields (2011) said to graduating seniors: "This university doesn't just teach you about subjects, it teaches you how to have independent thought, how to take direction and give it, how to engage in heated debate. [...] You are leaving here not so much changed, but rather, revealed. The education you have received was intended to develop your character and teach you the imperative of integrity." What elements of the Learning paradigm do you see in this address? Are there any elements of the Instruction paradigm? If so, can you identify them? If you had to give a commencement address in a Learning-paradigm university, would your address be similar to this one?

KEYWORDS

- action research
- deep learning
- Instruction paradigm
- learning organizations
- Learning paradigm
- surface learning

REFERENCES

Barr, R.; Tagg, J. From Teaching to Learning—A New Paradigm for Undergraduate Education. Change 1995, 13.

Buckley, D. P. In Pursuit of the Learning Paradigm: Coupling Faculty Transformation and Institutional Change. Educause Review 2002, 28–38.

Mettetal, G. The What, Why and How of Classroom Action Research. Journal of the Scholarship of Teaching and Learning 2001, 2, 1.

Shields, B. Class Day Remarks. News at Princeton, May 30, 2011. http://www.princeton.edu/main/news/archive/S30/67/81I02/ (accessed Aug 12, 2013).

Shulman, L. Teaching as Community Property. Essays on Higher Education; Jossey-Bass: San Francisco, 2004.

Tagg, J. The Learning Paradigm College; Anker Publishing Company: Bolton, MA, 2003.

Trigwell, K.; Prosser, M. Improving the quality of student learning: the influence of learning context and student approaches to learning on learning outcomes. Higher Education 1991, 22, 251.

Zull, J. From Brain to Mind. Using Neuroscience to Guide Change in Education; Stylus: Sterling, VA, 2011.

FINAL SUMMARY

The instruction-paradigm universities and colleges are not achieving the goals that they are supposed to attain. They have become fossilized bureaucracies. They are focused on teaching, regardless of whether this leads to meaningful learning or not. For this purpose, they have created a wide array of artifacts such as classrooms, exams, grades, courses, lectures, schedules, labs, syllabi, degrees, departments, disciplines, and even teachers. This giant bureaucracy increasingly needs more students and more artifacts to subsist.

The instruction paradigm's fixation with teaching has given rise to the preeminence of the lecture as the signatory pedagogy. The lecture revolves around the teacher, who is at the center of the course. The teacher's main role is to transmit information to students, whose task is reduced to taking down notes and reproducing this information later in exams, papers, and other forms of evaluation.

In the last few years, growing numbers of voices expressed their profound discontent with the Instruction paradigm's disregard for student learning. Studies show that most university and college students learn superficially. They soon forget what they learn. They cannot apply it to other situations or contexts, and they cannot make connections to larger frameworks. Students' lives are not transformed when they take a surface approach to learning. Their brains do not experience any significant change. In some cases, years of instruction in higher education even lead to reactance to anything academic. University and college graduates refuse to read academic texts and to follow university writing styles unless forced to do so in their professional lives.

Deep learning is the answer to higher education's performance problem. Deep learning is learning for life. It is a transformational process of constructing knowledge, which can then be applied to new, unscripted problems, even in completely different settings.

304   Facilitating Deep Learning

In order to learn deeply, students need to be faced with an exciting situation, problem, or question. While dealing with this situation, problem, or question, together with their peers, students must experience a cognitive conflict, that is, a discrepancy or dissonance between the new knowledge arising from the situation, problem, or question and their own cognitive structures. Students must recognize that they cannot explain this conflict with their existing cognitive structures. So, in order to solve this conflict, students must employ nonarbitrary and substantive connections between the new knowledge (which must be within the learner's zone of proximal development) and their existing cognitive structures. These connections require higher-order cognitive and metacognitive skills, processes, and competences at both the individual and collective planes. As a result of these connections, students must change the way they see the situation, problem, or question. This new way of seeing the situation or problem becomes part of their cognitive structures. In other words, this produces a conceptual change. This change has a correlation in the students' brains. The deep learning process rewires the brain by forming new connections between neuronal networks. At the same time, at the social level, this process leads one of the two following changes: a reacculturation from one community of knowledgeable peers to another or a movement from the periphery of a community of knowledgeable peers to the center. The deep learning process also requires ongoing evaluation and self-evaluation and awareness of both the social and the conceptual changes. Additionally, it requires a motivating, stress-free, and exciting environment, where students feel safe to interact with the new knowledge individually and with their peers.

The deep learning process calls for freedom for students to develop their own curriculum around their own interests and goals. The unschooling movement provides a theoretical and practical framework to implement this freedom in a way that helps students develop intellectually. This places teachers in a new role. It displaces them from the center of the teaching system; it gives them the role of facilitators of the whole deep learning process. Their role changes from transmitting information to creating environments that are conducive to deep learning. In this role, teachers create situations, projects, and challenges so that students will engage in a multitude of experiences. Many types of performances such as dia-

Final Summary

305

logs, questions, cases, student teaching, and out-of-class projects can help create these problems and situations. These performances have in common that students are the center of all activities. Teachers act as coaches who facilitate this process and teach with their mouths shut. Consequently, there is no need for lectures and other traditional artifacts of the Instruction paradigm.

When the object is to help students become part of a discipline, it is important to re-create the whole world of that discipline, where students can try out all the activities that disciplinary experts usually engage in, including those activities that are not traditionally considered strictly academic. This offers students the whole picture of the discipline and not just an artificially selected fraction. Playing the whole game of the discipline also foments the social aspect of learning. Learning is both an individual and a collective process. Students need to engage in collective negotiations of meaning and come to appreciate the fact that they need to construct knowledge individually and together with their peers and other members of the discipline they are trying to join. This will help them cross over communities of knowledgeable peers or make a move from the periphery of a community of knowledge to its center.

All academic and professional disciplines share some features in the way they communicate and interpret thought both orally and in writing. In order to become full members of the communities of knowledgeable peers of the disciplines they want to enter, students need to master the general and specific categories of analysis, reading and writing styles, and strategies to communicate thought in writing and to interpret academic texts. The teaching of reading and writing should not be disconnected from the general deep learning process. On the contrary, it should be an integral part of the journey of construction of knowledge and deep learning.

There is a strong connection between diversity and deep learning. The cognitive conflict—one of the essential aspects of the deep learning process—is produced through social interaction with peers who are at different cognitive stages of development. The more diverse the learner's peers are, the richer and deeper the connections that may result in conceptual change can be. But diversity alone does not automatically give rise to these rich connections and deeper conceptual change. This may only be achieved through the creation of deep learning environments, where we place diversity at the forefront of our teaching. Student diversity is the first component of the inclusive deep learning environment. But it requires other essential aspects. First, it calls for the explicit incorporation of diverse knowledge modes into the classroom experience, which implies recognizing, valuing, and including a wide array of worldview perspectives in our classes as well as helping students adopt diverse expressive styles. Second, it calls for internationalizing students' education, which, in turn, requires internationalizing the university and college curricula, designing integrated study abroad programs, and preparing students culturally to move from ethnocentric to ethnorelative stages. Third, it also entails plurilingual education, that is, helping students learn the disciplines in different languages. One of the most difficult challenges of the inclusive deep learning environment is teaching students who pursue higher education studies in their second or a foreign language. These students need longer periods of time to become academically proficient than native-language-speaking students. They also need a series of strategies that respect the natural order in the process of language acquisition and the rejection of common practices that hinder this process such as forcing students to produce output in the target language and the overcorrection of errors.

The deep learning process also needs plenty of information. Students need to receive and obtain information about every stage of the learning process. In this respect, metacognition, that is, the practice of reflecting on one's own learning, provides students with the most effective tools to monitor their own learning and to introduce changes throughout the whole process. Metacognition helps students engage in a process of reflection and self-evaluation for life. Student peers, disciplinary experts, and professionals also play a role in furnishing information about the learning process. Teachers are instrumental in accompanying students' learning process by actively observing and providing feedback all along. Teachers also need to receive information from students and other sources about their teaching efforts. All this requires a radical shift in the focus of evaluation from summative to truly formative.

Finally, deep learning endeavors require long and intensive periods of uninterrupted and dedicated time, where students and teachers embark together on the process of construction of knowledge without arbitrary and artificial scheduling constraints.

Final Summary

When all these changes are implemented, they will help transform the current universities and colleges from institutions obsessed with teaching to organizations focused exclusively on deep learning.

EPILOGUE

A couple of years ago, practically ten years since I started to teach full time, some students asked me if I could teach a course in space law in the following semester. They wanted to learn about something that was in the news at that time. The local newspaper had run some stories on the recent collision of two satellites. The article talked about the possibility of a piece of space junk falling in the city and the likelihood of destroying property and even killing people. The stories also discussed the legal implications of damages caused by space objects. The newspaper had interviewed me and quoted me in one of the stories. Students told me that they wanted to learn more about space law.

Despite the fact that I wrote my doctoral dissertation on space law, I had not been able to teach a full course in space law in any of the universities I have worked for, because it is perceived as a highly specialized area of the law. However, I managed to sneak in a couple of texts and some topics related to outer space in some of my courses. My current and previous full-time positions have led me to specialize in other legal areas, particularly criminal law, which is what I have been mainly teaching all these years.

When these students asked me if I could teach a course on space law, my initial, almost instinctive, reaction was to tell them that I could do so only after my sabbatical leave, as I needed time to review the content that I had forgotten and to catch up with new developments in the discipline. Students were visibly disappointed. For several days, I also felt disillusioned with myself. But at that time, I believed that it would be irresponsible to teach a course without adequate content preparation.

A few days later, students came to me again and insisted that they wanted me to teach that course. I remembered the panic I had experienced when I had to cover my supervisor. After more careful reflection, I also remembered my quest for deep learning. So, I made a deal with my students. We would learn together. They would even teach me. I would facilitate their learning by creating situations, problems, and questions that would challenge their preconceived ideas. We would create a safe and motivating environment to play the whole game of space lawyers. Basically, I promised them, and especially myself, that I would keep my mouth shut during the whole course.

This book, which you have just read or which you are about to read (if you are like me and like to start reading the end of a book first), tells the story of this course and other similar endeavors.

APPENDIX

APPENDIX I: A PROMISING SYLLABUS

INTRODUCTION TO LEGAL STUDIES

Prof.: Dr. Julian Hermida
Course number: JURI 1105 A E
Teaching hours: Tuesdays and Thursdays 1 pm
Term: Fall and winter

JOURNEY OF DISCOVERY

This is an exploratory journey of discovery into the fascinating world of law. In this journey, we will walk around the different meanings of law, its functions, roles, and elements. We will immerse in the exploration of law across different legal traditions and cultures. We will venture into the fertile contributions of social sciences to the legal studies discipline and into the rich theoretical jurisprudential debates. As if this weren't exciting enough, this voyage will also take you to walk through the main legal traditions present in Canada—common law, civil law, and aboriginal law. We will examine the tensions among these traditions as well as the efforts for coexistence.

For most of you, this is the very beginning of a long journey into the study of law, which—in many cases—will last a lifetime. For others, this will be the entire journey, but I am sure you will encounter numerous situations and issues with enormous legal implications no matter what you do in life.

For all of you, this journey will give you the theoretical lens to analyze virtually any legal issue from a unique and comprehensive perspective. You will be able to see the big picture in any legal situation. You will learn to generate your own solutions to legal problems, to identify and evaluate the political and social implications of your proposed solutions, and to compare these solutions to those offered in other legal traditions and cultures. These will be the journey outcomes—what you will take out of this voyage of high adventure, if you actively engage in it.

WHAT WE WILL DO IN OUR JOURNEY OF DISCOVERY

We will do a myriad of exciting activities, that will include group discussions, Socratic dialogs, cooperative group problem solving, games, analysis of video segments depicting scenes relevant to legal and justice issues, debates, construction of web sites, interpretation and production of audio-visual materials, group presentations, and analysis of legal and sociolegal texts from all over the world. I have also prepared reading guides to help you navigate through the texts and to help you focus on the fundamental issues of each text.

A CONVERSATION ABOUT YOUR LEARNING AND DISCOVERIES

Throughout our journey of discovery, we will stop several times so that we can talk about your learning. I will be providing you with formative feedback along the way. There will be plenty of opportunities to experiment, try, fail, and receive formative feedback in advance of and separate from summative evaluation. I will also help you develop the metacognitive tools and strategies so that you can assess your own learning progress.

By the end of this journey, you will show me what you have taken out of it, what you have learned, and how your thinking has changed. I will be particularly interested in seeing how well you have achieved the journey outcomes. I will want to see how well you can analyze legal issues from a comprehensive—historical, spatial, and theoretical—perspective, how well you can generate solutions to legal problems, how well you can identify and evaluate the political and social implications of those solutions, and whether you can compare these solutions to those offered in other legal traditions and cultures. I will want to see if you can do all this in a way that shows creativity, originality, and critical thinking skills, ideally beyond information given in the course.

Appendix

313

Because you have different learning styles, are in different positions of knowledge development, and perform optimally with different formats of assessment, you are free to choose the type and format of evidence you want in order to prove your learning and its quality. For example, you are free to prepare a portfolio where you will include evidence of your best work, write a research paper, make oral presentations, produce audiovisual materials, write a reflective journal, write a case and offer a solution, or show me the achievement of the journey outcomes and their quality by your active participation in class, or by talking to me in my office. You may, of course, use any combination of these possibilities, or even something else. But remember, I will not be assessing your portfolio itself, or paper, or journal, or whatever else you may want to supply. What I will be looking at is whether and how well you have achieved—and can perform with respect to—the intended learning outcomes of this journey of discovery.

I will assess the evidence you will show me holistically and synoptically. I will make a judgment about whether you have attained the intended journey outcomes, and if so—to what level. I will assess your evidence qualitatively and in its entirety—not by adding marks to its various parts. I will be interested in knowing how well you have learned and not how much. My judgment—like any judgment or assessment—will be subjective, but let me assure you that it will not be arbitrary. It will be based on my expertise as both a legal scholar and a teacher, not unlike a juror at a film festival judges films, or a curator judges pictures for a museum exhibition.

ITINERARY

Fall

Class	Topic	Readings
Class 1	Introduction and orientation	
Class 2	Concepts of law Nature and function of law Types and functions of law Social control Dispute resolution Social change	The syllabus and the course website. Positivism (pages 5 to 10 from Canadian Law book).

Classes 3, 4 and 5	Concepts of law Sociological and anthropological concepts of law. Elhrich, Malinowski, and Weber.	An analytical map of the social scientific approaches to the concept of law by Tamanaha
Classes 6, 7, 8 and 9	Legal traditions The three main legal traditions in Canada Common law Civil Law Aboriginal Law	Mixed Jurisdictions by Tetley
Class 10 and 11	Conceptual divisions of law	The Conceptual Divisions of Law (pages 38 to 40 from Canadian Law book)
Class 12 and 13	Sources Conflict of sources	The Sources of Canadian Law (pages 40 to 46 from Canadian Law book)
Classes 14 and 15	Criminal Law across legal traditions and cultures.	Criminal Law (pages 333 to 344 from Canadian Law book)
Class 16 and 17	Constitutional Law Constitutionalism Constitutional movements	Constitutional Law (Chapter 4 from Canadian Law book)
Classes 18, 19 and 20	Contracts Formation Interpretation rules Breaches	Convergence of common law and civil law contracts by Julian Hermida
Class 21, 22, 23 and 24	Prostitution Legal responses	Prostitution and Male Supremacy by Andrea Dworkin

Winter

Class	Topic	Readings
Classes 1, 2 and 3	Torts and extracontractual responsibility	Torts (Chapter 7 from Canadian Law book)

Appendix

Classes 4 and 5	Legal reasoning and legal methods The doctrine of *stare decisis*.	Precedent in Past and Present Legal systems by Lobingier
		Law & Geometry by Hoeflich
		Logic for Law students: Thinking like a lawyer by Ruggero J. Aldisert et al.
Class 6, 7 and 8	Family Law Same sex marriage	Family Law (Chapter 8 from Canadian Law book)
		The Halpern Transformation: Same-Sex Marriage, Civil Society, and the Limits of Liberal Law by F.C. DeCoste
Classes 9, 10, 11, 12, 13 and 14	Immigration Legal responses	Evaluating Canada's New Immigration and Refugee Protection Act in its Global Context by Dauvergne
Class 14, 15 and 16	Corporations	New Principles for Corporate Law by Greenfield
Class 17, 18, 19, 20 and 21	Interpretation rules	Statutory Interpretation in the Courtroom, the Classroom, and Canadian Legal Literature by Stephen F. Ross
		Chapter 3 from Canadian Law book.
Classes 22, 23 and 24	Sexual harassment Legal responses across legal traditions and legal cultures.	What is Sexual Harassment? From Capitol Hill to Sorbonne by Abigail Saguy
Class 25	Feedback	

RESOURCES

I have selected the following textbook to help you navigate through this journey of discovery: Canadian Law: An Introduction by Neil Boyd, 4th edition, Thomson Nelson, 2006, ISBN 0-7747-3574-0. But, please note that you can read from any other introduction to law or legal studies book.

You will also need to read all the articles listed above deeply. You are responsible to get them from the Library databases. You must read these texts and any other text that you may find necessary to prepare to participate in class.

A web site is available at http://www.julianhermida.com. You will be able to explore and consult the reading guides, class activities, journal articles, and other useful information.

I am here to guide you all throughout this journey of discovery. Think of me as your expedition experienced companion, that is, someone who has traveled this route several times before, but is still amazed at the wonders discovered along the route.

RULES AND POLICIES

This exploration may only be successful if you engage in it; and if you work honestly and enthusiastically. Since this is a collective exploration, you also need to follow certain rules and policies so that the learning process will be fair to all. Here are the rules and policies. They may sound strict. They are. But, trust me, they have been conceived so that this exploration is as smooth and productive as possible.

ATTENDANCE POLICY

Your presence and participation in every class are an essential part of the learning process for you and your classmates. I firmly believe that the class constitutes a unique learning environment; and most of what you will learn takes place in class, not in solitude. You will learn collaboratively with your colleagues and with my guidance.

Appendix

FILM COPYRIGHT

If you decide to show a video in class for a class activity, you must make sure that the university has the copyright to show that video in class, even if it is only an excerpt. This includes videos that you may find online and DVDs that you rent or own. Currently, the university is subscribed to Audio Cine Films and Criterion Pictures, two licensing organizations. The university has also acquired rights to show some films from the National Film Board. BEFORE showing a film in class, please make sure that you will be able to show it without infringing copyright law. If in doubt, please ask me. You can also check with the library.

ACTION RESEARCH

In order to improve my teaching practice and to enhance student learning, I always conduct classroom action research. For this purpose, I will collect some information about the course and your learning. Sometimes, I will ask you to complete surveys, questionnaires, or other instruments. These are anonymous and voluntary. Your responses will be kept strictly confidential. Other times, I will use your class work as evidence. In all cases, the information will be reported in general terms without specific reference to individual responses or actual names. If you do not wish to participate in the research projects or you do not want to complete surveys, questionnaires, or other instruments, simply let me know as soon as possible. You will not be penalized for this at all. If you have any questions or concerns about my action research projects, please contact me. Please note that surveys, questionnaires, and other instruments that I will specifically use for action research projects will be anonymous; and they will not be considered for any grade in the course. For further clarification, whether you decide to complete these instruments or not, and your responses to these instruments in the event that you do decide to participate, will never be taken into account for grading purposes.

318 Facilitating Deep Learning

APPENDIX II: SOLO TAXONOMY

Implementation of the SOLO taxonomy to assess the learning goals of a course:

Evaluation Criteria for Class Participation

Pre-structural

The student does not participate actively in most classes. The student does not show that he/she has read the assigned texts. The student does not participate in an appropriate manner that contributes to class discussions and does not show a positive attitude toward his or her classmates, the teacher, and the activities. The student does not work in small groups and does not volunteer to lead activities, debates, and debriefs. The student seldom asks questions in class.

The student's responses to the class activities contain irrelevant information; and they miss the point. The responses have no logical relationship to the question. The student gives bits of unconnected information. The responses have no organization, and make no sense. The student does not make connections to the theoretical issues, readings, class discussions, and class activities done throughout the course. The response to the class activities does not show an understanding of the issues dealt with.

Unistructural

The students participates actively in some classes. In some classes, the student shows that he/she has read the assigned texts. The student sometimes participates in an appropriate manner that contributes to class discussions and shows a positive attitude toward his or her classmates, the teacher, and the activities. The student works in small groups, but does not always volunteer to lead activities, debates, and debriefs. The student sometimes asks useful questions that contribute to the development of the class and fosters collective understanding or usually asks simple questions that do not contribute to the development of the class.

The student's responses to the class activities contain one relevant item, but they miss others that might modify or contradict the response. There is a rapid closure that oversimplifies the issue or problem. The student makes simple and obvious connections to some of the theoretical issues, readings, class discussions, and class activities done throughout the course, but the significance of the connections is not demonstrated. In most class activities, the student can identify and list the issues or questions presented in class. The response to the class activities does not show an understanding of the issues dealt with, or it demonstrates only a very superficial understanding.

Appendix

Multi-structural

The student participates actively and meaningfully in most classes. In most classes, the student shows that he/she has read the assigned texts and that he/she has reflected about the required readings. The student participates in an appropriate manner that contributes to class discussions and shows a positive attitude toward his or her classmates, the teacher, and the activities. The student works productively in small groups and volunteers to lead activities, debates, and debriefs on most classes. The student generally asks useful questions that contribute to the development of the class and fosters collective understanding.

The student's responses to the class activities contain several relevant items, but only those that are consistent with the chosen conclusion are stated, and the significance of the relationship between connections is not always demonstrated. Closure in the class activities is generally selective and premature. The student makes a number of connections to theoretical issues, readings, class discussions, and class activities done throughout the course, but the meta-connections between them are missed, as is their significance for the whole. In most class activities, the student can enumerate, describe, combine, and list the issues or questions presented in class. The student uses some of the relevant data.

Relational

The student participates actively and meaningfully in every class. The student shows every class that he/she has read the assigned texts quite deeply and that he/she has critically reflected about the required readings. The student participates in an appropriate manner that contributes to class discussions and shows a positive attitude toward his or her classmates, the teacher, and the activities. The student works productively in small groups and volunteers to lead activities, debates, and debriefs in every class or in most classes. The student asks useful questions that contribute to the development of the class and fosters collective understanding.

The student makes connections to theoretical issues, readings, class discussions, and class activities done throughout the course. In general, the student demonstrates the relationship between connections and the whole. In every class activity, the student can focus on several relevant aspects, but these aspects are generally considered independently. Response to the class activities is a collection of multiple items that are not always related within the context of the activity. In all class activities, the student is able to classify, compare, contrast, combine, enumerate, explain causes, and analyze the issues or questions presented in class. The student uses most or all of the relevant data, and he/she resolves conflicts by the use of a relating concept that applies to the given context of the question or problem.

320 Facilitating Deep Learning

> **Extended abstract**
>
> The student participates actively and meaningfully in every class. The student shows every class that he/she has read the assigned texts deeply and that he/she has critically reflected about the required readings. The student participates in an appropriate manner that contributes to class discussions and shows a positive attitude toward his or her classmates, the teacher, and the activities. The student works productively in small groups and volunteers to lead activities, debates, and debriefs every class. The student asks useful questions that contribute to the development of the class and fosters collective understanding.
>
> The student makes connections not only to theoretical issues, readings, class discussions, and class activities done throughout the course but also to issues, theories, and problems beyond information arising from class. In every class activity, the student shows the capacity to theorize, generalize, hypothesize, and reflect beyond the information given. The student even produces new relevant hypotheses or theories. In every class, the student can link and integrate several parts, such as class activities, readings, class discussions, and theories, into a coherent whole. The student links details to conclusions and shows that he/she understands deeply the meaning of issues and problems under analysis. The student questions basic assumptions and gives counter examples and new data that did not form part of the original question or problem.

Evaluation Criteria for the Paper

> **Pre-structural**
>
> The paper contains irrelevant information. It misses the point. The paper has no logical relationship to the selected topic. It deals with bits of unconnected information. It has no organization. It makes no sense. The student does not make connections to the theoretical issues, readings, class discussions, and class activities done throughout the course. The paper does not show an understanding of the issues dealt with in class. The paper does not follow the required writing style.

> **Unistructural**
>
> The paper contains one relevant item, but it misses others that might modify or contradict the position taken. There is a rapid closure that oversimplifies the issue or problem. The student makes simple and obvious connections to some of the theoretical issues, readings, class discussions, and class activities done throughout the course, but the significance of the connections is not demonstrated. The student can identify and list the issues or questions discussed in class. The paper does not show an understanding of the issues dealt with, or it demonstrates only a very superficial understanding. The paper minimally follows the required writing style.

Appendix

Multi-structural

The paper contains several relevant items, but only those that are consistent with the chosen position are stated, and the significance of the relationship between connections is not always demonstrated. Closure is generally selective and premature. The student makes a number of connections to theoretical issues, readings, class discussions, and class activities done throughout the course, but the meta-connections between them are missed, as is their significance for the whole. The student enumerates, describes, combines, and lists the issues or questions presented in class. The student uses only some of the relevant data. The paper follows only some aspects of the required writing style.

Relational

The paper is a collection of multiple items that are not always related within the context of the selected topic. The student classifies, compares, contrasts, combines, enumerates, explains causes, and analyzes the issues or questions presented. The student uses most or all of the relevant data, and he/she resolves conflicts by the use of a relating concept that applies to the given context of the selected issue. The student makes connections to theoretical issues, readings, class discussions, and class activities done throughout the course. In general, the paper demonstrates the relationship between connections and the whole. The student focuses on several relevant aspects, but these aspects are generally considered independently. The paper follows most aspects of the required writing style.

Extended abstract

The paper makes connections not only to theoretical issues, readings, class discussions, and class activities done throughout the course but also to issues, theories, and problems beyond information arising from class. The student shows the capacity to theorize, generalize, hypothesize, and reflect beyond the information given. The student even produces new relevant hypotheses or theories. The student can link and integrate several parts, such as class activities, readings, and theories, into a coherent whole. The student links details to conclusions and shows that he/she understands deeply the meaning of issues and problems under analysis. The student questions basic assumptions and gives counter examples and new data that did not form part of the original question or problem. The paper follows the required writing style.

Evaluation Criteria for the Presentation

Pre-structural

The presentation contains irrelevant information. It misses the point. The presentation has no logical relationship to the selected topic. The presentation deals bits of unconnected information. It has no organization, and it makes no sense. The student does not make connections to the theoretical issues, readings, class discussions, and class activities done throughout the course. The presentation does not show an understanding of the issues dealt with in class.

Unistructural

The presentation contains one relevant item, but it misses others that might modify or contradict the position taken. There is a rapid closure that oversimplifies the issue or problem. The student makes simple and obvious connections to some of the theoretical issues, readings, class discussions, and class activities done throughout the course, but the significance of the connections is not demonstrated. The student can identify and list the issues or questions discussed in class. The presentation does not show an understanding of the issues dealt with, or it demonstrates only a very superficial understanding.

Multi-structural

The presentation contains several relevant items, but only those that are consistent with the chosen position are stated, and the significance of the relationship between connections is not always demonstrated. Closure is generally selective and premature. The student makes a number of connections to theoretical issues, readings, class discussions, and class activities done throughout the course, but the meta-connections between them are missed, as is their significance for the whole. The student enumerates, describes, combines, and lists the issues or questions presented in class. The student uses only some of the relevant data in the presentation.

Relational

The presentation is a collection of multiple items that are not always related within the context of the selected topic. The student classifies, compares, contrasts, combines, enumerates, explains causes, and analyzes the issues or questions presented. The student uses most or all of the relevant data, and he/she resolves conflicts by the use of a relating concept that applies to the given context of the selected issue. The student makes connections to theoretical issues, readings, class discussions, and class activities done throughout the course. In general, the presentation demonstrates the relationship between connections and the whole. The student focuses on several relevant aspects, but these aspects are generally considered independently.

Appendix

Extended abstract

The presentation makes connections not only to theoretical issues, readings, class discussions, and class activities done throughout the course but also to issues, theories, and problems beyond information arising from class. The student shows the capacity to theorize, generalize, hypothesize, and reflect beyond the information given. The student even produces new relevant hypotheses or theories. The student can link and integrate several parts, such as class activities, readings, and theories, into a coherent whole. The student links details to conclusions and shows that he/she understands deeply the meaning of issues and problems under analysis. The student questions basic assumptions, and gives counter examples and new data that did not form part of the original question or problem.

Evaluation criteria for the take-home evaluation and for the test

Pre-structural

The student's responses to questions and problems contain irrelevant information. The responses miss the point. They have no logical relationship to the question. The student gives bits of unconnected information. The responses have no organization, and make no sense. The student does not make connections to the theoretical issues, readings, class discussions, and class activities done throughout the course. The response to the questions and problems does not show an understanding of the issues dealt with.

Unistructural

The student's responses to the questions and problems contain one relevant item, but they miss others that might modify or contradict the response. There is a rapid closure that oversimplifies the issue or problem. The student makes simple and obvious connections to some of the theoretical issues, readings, class discussions, and class activities done throughout the course, but the significance of the connections is not demonstrated. The student can identify and list the issues or questions discussed in class. The response does not show an understanding of the issues dealt with, or it demonstrates only a very superficial understanding.

Multi-structural

The student's responses to questions and problems contain several relevant items, but only those that are consistent with the chosen conclusion are stated, and the significance of the relationship between connections is not always demonstrated. Closure is generally selective and premature. The student makes a number of connections to theoretical issues, readings, class discussions, and class activities done throughout the course, but the meta-connections between them are missed, as is their significance for the whole. The student can enumerate, describe, combine, and list the issues or questions presented in class. The student uses some of the relevant data.

324   Facilitating Deep Learning

Relational

Response to the questions or problems is a collection of multiple items that are not always related within the context of the exercise. The student is able to classify, compare, contrast, combine, enumerate, explain causes, and analyze the issues or questions presented. The student uses most or all of the relevant data, and he/she resolves conflicts by the use of a relating concept that applies to the given context of the question or problem. The student makes connections to theoretical issues, readings, class discussions, and class activities done throughout the course. In general, students demonstrate the relationship between connections and the whole. The student can focus on several relevant aspects, but these aspects are generally considered independently.

Extended abstract

The student makes connections not only to theoretical issues, readings, class discussions, and class activities done throughout the course but also to issues, theories, and problems beyond information arising from class. The student shows the capacity to theorize, generalize, hypothesize, and reflect beyond the information given. The student even produces new relevant hypotheses or theories. The student can link and integrate several parts, such as class activities, readings, and theories, into a coherent whole. The student links details to conclusions and shows that he/she understands deeply the meaning of issues and problems under analysis. The student questions basic assumptions and gives counter examples and new data that did not form part of the original question or problem.

Based on Biggs, J.; Tang, C. Teaching for Quality Learning at University; Open University Press: Maidenhead, 2007.

APPENDIX III: FIRST DRAFT OF CHAPTER 7

The purpose of including this appendix with the very first draft of a chapter is to show that all first drafts look messy and confusing. This draft is full of spelling, grammar, and punctuation mistakes. Some sentences are incomplete. Many bibliographical references are missing. Some ideas are taken verbatim from books and articles. Most students' papers look like this draft.

Appendix   325

6. DEEP WRITING

    a.   Writing to learn and learning to write
    b.   Media literacy

INTRODUCTION

Writing has been traditionally relegated to the margins of university and college instruction until the 1970's. Academic writing was a pervasive activity, but teachers did not pay any attention to the writing process in their classes. They simply requested students to write exams and occasional projects without actually teaching students how to write. Teaching writing was the responsibility of college composition and English classes for first-year students.

With the Writing Across the Curriculum movement in the 1970's and 1980's in the United States, the United Kingdom and other countries, writing became the focus of much attention in higher education. Today, many teachers usually refer to writing as an essential skill that students need to master. Few, however, actually teach writing in a way that helps students learn how to write in a deep way. Still fewer teachers help students write to learn deeply.

In this chapter, we will examine the importance of producing written work as an essential aspect of the discovery and construction of knowledge. We will also discuss what teachers can do to help students learn how to write in their disciplines in a profound way.

WRITING TO LEARN DEEPLY

Janet Emig has argued that writing constitutes a unique mode of learning. She claims that "writing serves learning uniquely because writing as a process-and product possesses a cluster of attributes that correspond uniquely to certain powerful learning strategies. Higher cognitive functions, such as analysis and synthesis, seem to develop most fully only with the support system of verbal language—particularly, it seems, written language."

326   Facilitating Deep Learning

Emig's claims gave rise to a movement known as Writing to Learn. Its main tenet is that writing enhances learning (Durst and Newell). While this proposition is quite attractive, empirical research has not demonstrated the validity of this claim (Ackerman, 1993; Newell, 1998). While there are some studies that show that in certain specific circumstances writing can help improve the learning process, there are other studies, sometimes even conducted by the same researchers that show contradictory results (Klein, 1999).

Klein (1999) identified four models on the connection between writing and learning:

- Point of utterance model: writers spontaneously generate knowledge without planning and revision.
- Forward search model: writers externalize ideas in text, then reread the text, and make new inferences based on the text.
- Genre model: writers use genre structures to organize relationships among discursive elements of the text, and connect elements of knowledge. "A genre is distinguished by a rhetorical intention, expressed through discourse elements that form particular relationships with one another." Each discipline implements genre in its own distinctive way, with different norms about discursive elements.
- Backwards search model: writers set rhetorical goals. They derive content subgoals from rhetorical goals, and problem-solving goals from content goals.

Klein (1999) argues that "point of utterance allows writers to generalize their existing concepts to new instances, but not to change these concepts. Forward search increases the coherence of lengthy and complex texts, and may help writers to construct relationships among ideas." The backward search model explains the creation rhetorically good writing. Students must negotiate three conditions for genre to lead to learning. First, the student may or may not adopt the goal of composing a text in a given genre. Second, the student may or may not implement a strategy involving higher-order cognitive skills, to realize this goal. This strategy may or may not generate new knowledge. Similarly, Gonyea and Anderson (2009) find that "the genre-based theory and the problem-solving theory both identify the reorganization of existing knowledge as one mechanism by which writers create knowledge. The forward search model also suggests that examining relationships already expressed in text provides the impetus for

Appendix

developing the new relationships that the writer will next record." Gonyea and Anderson (2009) do not find any evidence that the point of utterance model promotes learning. Bereiter and Scardamalia identified two models of the writing process: knowledge telling and knowledge transformation:

- Knowledge telling: The basic steps include the mental representation of the writing task, the generation of topic identifiers, and the use of these topic identifiers as cues to retrieve information through a process of "spreading activation." The writer tends to retrieve and write down all the ideas she has, until the use of the cues is exhausted. At the same time, the writer draws on appropriate identifiers of discourse knowledge to match the task (e.g., opinion essay). The knowledge-telling model, while appropriate for routine writing tasks, does not foster the generation of new knowledge, because it relies on already established connections between content elements and readily available discourse knowledge.
- Knowledge transformation: When writers engage in the knowledge transforming model of writing, they increase their knowledge acquisition through content processing and discourse processing interaction. In the content space, the problems of knowledge and beliefs are considered, while in the discourse space, the problems of how to express the content are considered. The output from each space serves as input for the other, so that questions concerning language and syntax choice reshape the meaning of the content, while efforts to the express the content direct the ongoing composition. It is this interaction between the problem spaces that provides the stimulus for reflection in writing. The dynamic relationship between the content space and the rhetorical space in the knowledge-transforming model illuminates why writing is such a critical part of learning.

The inconclusiveness of research on the relation between writing and learning demonstrates that writing in itself is not an essential aspect of the discovery and construction of knowledge. This conclusion is supported by those studies that found deep learning where there is not an instance of production of knowledge in writing (Marton & Saljo, 1976).

The existence of some studies that do show that under certain circumstance writing positively influences learning merits analysis. Klein (1999) argues that when writing, particularly genre writing, is articulated as a cognitive strategy, such as in the genre model and in some types of the backward search model, students may profit from writing to learn deeply. Similarly, Bereiter and Scardamalia (1987)'s knowledge-transformation model may contribute to learning. Bazerman (2009) also argues that "it is not simply the act of writing that leads to learning. [...] Learning takes place because of the practices that are engaged as one produces the text. The produced text itself is not that relevant." So, while it may not be affirmed that all writing leads to learning or that there may be no deep learning without an instance of production in writing, these arguments show that writing, when writing is embedded in a constructivist process, it may enhance the learning quality.

So, what teachers can do in our classrooms to use writing to enhance the learning process?

There are various writing formats and types of texts that have shown to enhance learning. But learning can profit from writing if writing takes places within the deep learning context and process we have discussed. This implies that in order to be effective, a writing task must create a cognitive conflict, i.e., new knowledge presents the learner with a conflict that the learner is motivated to solve. To do so, the learner makes – nonarbitrary and substantive—connections between new knowledge, which must be within the learner's "zone of proximal development", and the learner's prior cognitive structure. While doing so, the learner resorts to higher order cognitive and metacognitive skills, processes, and competences. So, for example, a few years ago, I was invited to lead an educational development workshop in Buenos Aires, Argentina. I mentioned the importance of including an instance of writing production in our classes. Flavia showed me some research results reported in the literature indicating that writing does not lead to learning (those which I cited earlier, but which at that time I ignored). I mentioned to Flavia that there were other studies showing the opposite results. I also promised her that I would look into the article she told me about and that I would report the results of my research back to the workshop participants. So, I had a problem that I was very motivated to solve. I read the articles that Flavia gave me. While reading them, I made notes. My notes were not verbatim. I wrote the gist of each articles, and I made connections to the articles I had read and my own experience as a teacher and educational developer. While making these connections, I critically evaluated the research findings, I challenged the authors' claims, I

Appendix

329

compared the research findings, I formulated some hypotheses, and I came up with some preliminary theories. I wanted to report back my analysis of the research findings and my theories to the workshop participants. So, I wrote workshop notes, following a style that I find interesting to communicate to teachers in educational development events. While writing my analysis and conclusions, I went back to the articles. After I finished the notes, I reread them. I noticed some inconsistencies. I called Flavia and had a discussion. I also had conversations with other colleagues. Then, I felt that I needed to read some research studies, which Flavia had not given me. I revised the text again and incorporated the ideas I had while discussing and reading the new material. I finally came up with my new understanding of the problem, that is, writing does not always enhance learning, but it may do so if writing is embedded in the construction of deep learning process. This conclusion is consistent with Gonyea and Anderson (2009), who argue that "writing that contributes most substantially to learning is the writing that engages students in deep learning activities." Bazerman (2009) also suggests that short written assignments done twice or three times a week are more effective to learning than the traditional essay assignment, which is long and which students have to submit at the end of the course.

In a study of the attitudes and activities of Harvard University students, Richard Light postulates that students value good writing and suggestions to improve it. Courses that emphasize writing.

In his book, Light recommends the following strategies for students to improve their (Reread LIGHT)

Teachers respond to most writing as if they were a final draft, thus reinforcing an extremely constricted notion of composing. Their comments often reflect the application of a single ideal standard rather than criteria that take into account how composing constraints can affect writing performance. Furthermore, teachers' marks and comments usually take the form of abstract and vague prescriptions and directives that students find difficult to interpret. These comments rarely seem to expect students to revise the text beyond the surface level. These responses to texts give students a very limited and limiting notion of writing, for they fail to provide students with the understanding that writing involves producing a text that evolves over time. Teachers need to develop more appropriate responses for commenting on student writing. They need to facilitate revision by responding to writing as work in progress rather than judging it as a finished product.

It is not the amount of writing that matters when it comes to achieving the higher-order learning outcomes. Instead, it is the amount of writing that promotes deep learning.

TEACHING STUDENTS HOW TO WRITE ACADEMIC TEXTS

In this section, we will discuss the process of how to help our students learn to write in the disciplines we teach. Here, the writing is the specific target as opposed the considerations made in the previous sections, where the target was to learn the discipline, and writing was a means to enhance the quality of the learning process.

In general, we want our students to learn to write effectively so that they can become better communicators and so that they can become familiar with the discursive conventions of the discipline we teach (Klein, 1999).

Students learn how to write by using the same processes that students resort to for learning other competences, skills, and processes. But, writing—like many other complex processes—presents also some specific issues, which need to be taken into account. We will explore both general and specific considerations. In order to deeply learn how to master disciplinary writing, students need to be faced with a problem or situation, where their current disciplinary literacy level is not sufficient to solve the problem or to effectively deal with the situation they face. Additionally, students need to be motivated to do something about this conflict. The challenge, that is, learning to write at the new disciplinary level must be within the students' zone of proximal development. While working to solve this conflict, students need to make -nonarbitrary and substantive—connections between the new writing genre and style and their current writing style. This process must encourage students to use higher order cognitive and metacognitive skills, processes, and competences. Students need to also to negotiate meanings collectively with their peers. They also need to reflect about the process of the construction of their new disciplinary literacy and the

Appendix 331

resulting conceptual changes. For example, a colleague of mine teaches Space Law at the undergraduate level. His students were motivated to discuss the new legal regime for private space transportation, particularly for space tourism purposes. The government announced a law reform process and invited presentations to discuss a new legal framework for the regulation of private space transportation. The students were eager to influence the process. So, my colleague encouraged them to make a written presentation. The students worked hard on the content and submitted their report to the government. The space office contacted the students. Officials were impressed with their work, but told them that their presentation was rejected, because it did not comply with many—discursive—formalities. Their teacher explained to the students that their writing style did not coincide with the style usually used for law reform initiatives. So, students decided to resubmit their presentation. They asked their teacher for presentations to other law reform processes. Students deconstructed, analyzed, and discussed the language style of these presentations. Students compared them with format and style of their original presentation. They made changes. They read them several times. They made revisions and discussed their changes. Then, they gave a new draft to their teacher. Students expressly asked the teacher to comment on the language of the presentation. The teacher gave them feedback, which students incorporated. Then, students submitted the new version of their proposal, which was accepted. Finally, the teacher helped students reflect about their learning process. Students reconstructed every step they took until they submitted the new version of the proposal. They even reflected about the conventions of law reform presentations related to Space Law matters.

We will now break down the process of helping our students to write in a number of steps and analyze each of these steps.

THE PROBLEM OR SITUATION

Expert academic writers generally engage in writing in order to find a solution to a problem (Bean, 1996). Designing a problem for our students to solve is one of the most important elements of teaching writing. The problem has to attract students' attention. Students need to care enough to want to resolve the problem.

The problem has to lead students to recognize that their existing literacy skills and knowledge is not sufficient to solve the problem or face the situation. Klein (1999) argued that students may or may not adopt the goal of composing a text in a given genre. Students may not engage in the process of learning to write for several reasons. First, the problem may not deal with a situation where students realize that they need to change the way the write. This happens when, for example, a teacher assigns students a situation where they have to resolve a problem or express their opinions, or even research a theory. These are all issues, which may lead to student learning if appropriately embedded in the deep learning process, but students will not necessarily change the way they write to solve a problem, express their opinion, or research a theory if the task in question does not help them see that they need to change the way they write. Students tend to believe that they can already write clearly and effectively. After all, they have been writing since they were in grade school. So, the problem or situation must lead them to discover that the way they write is in fact ineffective to accomplish the task in question.

Second, the problem may not be motivating enough for students to want to engage in a process of changing their writing. Recall that Ken Bain (2004) argues that students will embark in a deep learning process if they face a problem, question, or situation that they find significant, intriguing or beautiful. Students need to come to understand for themselves the importance of changing their writing. For example, when I taught grade 10 English as a foreign language in South America in an all boys high school, I designed an activity where students were matched with pen pals from the US. Those boys that were matched with girls found that their writing was not enough to impress girls. As several students told me later, in their minds they all wanted to impress those girls. So, they worked hard at improving the way they wrote in English.

Third, the new level of writing may be outside the students' zone of proximal development. In a first-year college course, students, who still write as high school students, may not all of a sudden write like experienced disciplinary experts. This literacy level is completely outside their zone of proximal development. We as teachers need to carefully evaluate

Appendix

the writing level of our students and take them gradually to higher levels within their zone of proximal development.

Fourth, the cognitive conflict does not arise from social interaction. Students need to come to the realization that their writing capabilities are not effective to deal with the situation or problem through interaction with their peers. When the conflict is perceived as purely individual or exclusively as something induced by the teacher, it will not produce the desired effect of encouraging students to embark in a deep learning process to change their approach to writing.

Fifth, the problem or situation is not clear for students or it gives too many instructions that it restricts students' freedom to engage in meaningful writing. Katherine Gottschalk and Keith Hjortshoj (2003) argue that we need to define boundaries clearly. "Good assignments clearly define the boundaries within which students are free to write. Writers must have some freedom to take positions, develop ideas, and choose language that communicates what they have to say. Freedom becomes meaningful and constructive only within boundaries, and unclear boundaries tend to restrict freedom by making every move seem potentially a wrong move." Gottschalk and Keith Hjortshoj (2003) caution us about the inclusion of counterproductive clarifications in writing assignments. They argue that "teachers often obscure the boundaries of an assignment by offering suggestions, hints, examples, and clarifications that imply a hidden agenda and thus qualify the freedom that they have previously defined. Students should know where your role as the teacher ends and where their roles, choices, and responsibilities as writers begin."

Finally—and this applies to every single step of the teaching writing process—the teacher did not create a theory-Y climate. An encouraging and trusting environment is essential for any learning endeavor. If teachers do not care about their students, if they do not trust that they can achieve the fullest potential, and if they do not hold very high expectations of their students, then students will probably not embark in the challenging deep learning process.

- Collaborative learning
- o Collective negotiation of meaning
- o "Assignments should create real occasions for students to read and respond to another's work."

334   Facilitating Deep Learning

o   A community of writers: Dialogue on paper.
o   Students will talk to each other not only in the classroom but through the exchange of written texts.

HIGHER-ORDER COGNITIVE PROCESSES, SKILLS, AND COMPETENCES: ENCOURAGING REVISION

Expert writers engage in several cognitive activities while writing. After having identified a problem, expert writers obtain data from other sources, interview people, talk to colleagues, make notes, write several drafts, reread their drafts, revise, and make new revisions (Bean, 1996). These activities usually imply that writers resort to higher-order cognitive skills, such as reading critically, analyzing, applying, evaluating, and theorizing. Expert writers also edit their drafts, but they do so generally do so when they consider that their drafts are ready to be published. Editing for spelling, punctuation, grammar, and even sentence structure does not require the use of higher-order cognitive skills and competences.

We need to encourage students to engage in the process of critically analyzing the problem, finding a solution, writing, rereading, revising, and reformulating their ideas in writing, because this is the process that expert writers follow to write effectively. Students need to learn how to embrace this process in order to be able to write effectively.

The problem with many students is that they tend not to engage in this process. Students tend to consider that their first draft is the last one. And this draft is ready to be handed in to the teacher, who after all will know what it means. So, students' first and only draft usually looks like the first draft of expert writers, i.e., there is no clear solution to the problem, thoughts are disconnected, the organization is poor, and there are many editing problems. The main difference is that the first draft of expert writers is a draft that only the writer reads. And it is a draft that will undergo several layers of revisions in ideas, focus, structure, organization, and even spelling and grammar.

So, it is very important to help students to understand the importance of rereading and making extensive revisions. How can we do this? First, we need to bear in mind that there are two kinds of revisions: (i) personal revi-

Appendix

sions, where the expert writers revise their drafts before submitting the article to an editor for publication, and (ii) editor or reviewer mandated revisions, where the expert writer has to incorporate the suggestions and make the changes indicated by the editors and reviewers. According to Nancy Sommers, "most experienced writers revise their work extensively as a malleable substance before they submit a complete draft." Once expert writers feel that their work is ready for the readers to read, they submit it for publication. In academia, most publications need to be peer reviewed. And in commercial literature, most publications have to be approved by several editors. Peer reviewers and editors usually offer many suggestions for changes. After all, it is their job to do so. Many expert writers are reluctant to introduce these changes. Not because they are nonsensical—although anyone who has submitted a manuscript to a journal or publisher knows that in many cases they are—but because the expert writer feels that he or she has decided that the text is done. He or she had finished the text before, when he or she sent it for publication. Nancy Sommers refers to this moment as the point in which the text solidifies. At this point, the text is no longer malleable. It is solid. Except for a few typos here and there, expert writers refuse to revise the text. Most still do, of course, as otherwise their texts will not be published. But, they do so reluctantly without much effort, and in many cases, without resorting to those higher-order cognitive and metacognitive processes that they did resort to while revising their texts before the solidified. "Student writing, by contrast, solidifies at the moment it hits the page. The student has never lingered in the first stage of writing during which revision usually takes place for experienced writers." This problem is compounded by the type of suggestions we usually offer our students for revision. Nancy Sommers vividly exemplifies this process: "when we simply give students the opportunity to revise their papers without little guidance, they tend to make only cosmetic changes. When we offer detailed suggestions, students confine their revisions to the changes we recommend, leaving us in the awkward position of evaluating the fruits of our own labor. Peer reviews from other students often yield superficial revisions." So, Sommers proposes delaying that sense of completion of the student submission. Again, how can we do this? How can delay this feeling that the text is prematurely finished?

336   Facilitating Deep Learning

Fink (1999) suggests creating a dialog on paper between the student and the teacher and among students themselves (Fink, 1999). John Tagg (2003), who was an English teacher at Palomar Community College, separates the grade from the comments on his students' papers. He believes that if he gives student a grade accompanied by comments on their students' paper, students look at the grades and not the comments; or they read the comments superficially without acting upon them, particularly if the grade corresponds to their expectations.

The key to this problem is in the kind of feedback we give our students.

TEACHER'S FEEDBACK

o   The proper place for grading is at the end of the process of reading and responding to student papers, not at the beginning. This process should begin with reading.
o   Teaching with your mouth shut.
o   Joseph Williams: Most teachers look for and find errors in student writing. They are automatically on the lookout for sentence-level errors.
o   Sometimes it is easier to notice and comment on sentence-level errors than on the more substantive problems of a student's essay.
o   Some of the "errors" that so greatly alarm us in student writing are not absolute matters of right and wrong but are determined only by taste and discipline—they are actually matters of style.
o   Studies show that students aren't making more mistakes (Robert Connors and Andrea Lunsford).

When responding to finished papers, let the writers know how well their papers worked and offer suggestions that might be useful in future projects.

When responding to drafts, open these versions of the papers to revision, with guidance for making improvements.
- Illuminate the apparent argument and structure of the draft.
- Offer comments about strengths and about further possibilities.
- Identify fundamental limitations and problems.
- Leave the task of solving those problems with the writer.

Appendix

METACOGNITION

- The recursive nature of learning to write
  - o Learning to write is not a linear progression. When students start to write in a new difficult subject, they may run into trouble with sentence structure, with the use of vocabulary, even with control over basic sentence correctness. Immediate and primary attention to errors or to stylistic choices may not solve the problem.
  - o Writing effectively is simply a process students have to relearn, even at the sentence level of grammar and style. They don't need to be immediately belabored about error: they need practice with their new subjects.
  - o "Ask students to assess their own papers or to give you comments on what they think about their papers."

BIBLIOGRAPHIC REFERENCES

Meiers, M. (2007). Writing to learn. *Research Digest*, 2007 (1). Retrieved from http://www.vit. vic.edu.au.

Bazerman, Charles. (2009). Genre and Cognitive Development: Beyond Writing to Learn. Pratiques No. 143/144.

Gottschalk, Katherine and Hjortshoj, Keith. (2003). The Elements of Teaching Writing. Boston, MA: Bedford/St. Martin's.

INDEX

A

Abandoned pet, 85
Aboriginal issues, 181
Academic probation, 37
Academic proficiency, 179, 204–215, 221
Academic skills, 65, 170, 176, 260, 280
Accrediting agencies, 53, 228, 276, 300
Actual learning, 7, 53
Actual violations, 160
Adequate preparation, 193, 264, 268
Airplane fuel, 3
Allopathic conception of medicine, 189
American physicians, 130
Analogy pursues, 23
Annual case competition, 239
Anthropologists, 156, 279
Antirequisites, 7
Architecture program, 52
Arduous texts, 119
Art deco architecture, 59
Artifacts, 2, 8, 10, 65, 227, 276, 297, 303, 305
Artificial scheduling constraints, 306
Artificial time constraints, 278
Artwork, 297
Asian ethnicity, 38
Assembly line, 7, 297
Astronomical fees, 5
Atomistic, 6, 7
Attitudinal resources, 193
Audiovisual materials, 134, 312, 313
Authentic meals, 282
Authentic situations, 239
Authoritative, 128
Automobile accident, 60
Aviation industry, 129

B

Backward-search model, 141, 161

Banking education, 80
Belabored, 337
Benchmarks of success, 7, 297
Biological perspective, 143, 238, 241
Biological research, 87
Bloom's taxonomy, 26
Bodily memory, 25
Boundary-free, 297
Brain's sensory cortex, 24
Budgetary issues, 157
Business experts, 278
Bureaucratic apparatus, 4

C

Cafeteria employees, 190
Catastrophic consequences, 259
Cavalier journeys, 187
Central participation, 98
Cerebral cortex, 36, 56
Classic experts, 101
Clear teaching goals, 264
Clinical interview, 191, 232
Cluster of attributes, 142, 312
Cognitive blind spots, 7
Cognitive strategy, 141, 161, 327
Coherence of lengthy, 326
Collaborative learning, 100, 106, 109, 281, 333
authority of knowledge, 100
higher education, 100, 106–109, 158, 281, 333
Collective planes, 94, 120, 135, 304
College composition, 142, 325
College education, 3, 134, 230
College game, 8
Commercial literature, 152, 335
Committee meetings, 6
Comparative campaign, 119
Complete surveys, 317

340   Facilitating Deep Learning

Complex texts, 326
Comprehensible input, 30, 209, 213, 215
Conduct empirical research, 157
Consonance, 52, 133
Construction-of-knowledge process, 231, 235
Constructivism, 28, 65
Constructivist scholars, 23
Contemporary philosophy, 126
Content-processing, 144
Context-based learning theories, 65
   curriculum cohesion, 65
   diverse pedagogies, 65
   learning communities, 65, 79, 94, 101, 104, 108, 276, 282, 301
Contextual relativism, 97, 102
Contextual societies, 175
Contradictory messages, 160
Controversial issues, 226
Conventional scheduling modes, 280
Conveyor belt, 7–9, 297
Corporeal, 25
Correctional officers, 84, 85
Counterproductive, 151, 333
Critical analysis, 26, 61
Critical part of learning, 327
Critical thinking, 27, 174, 205
   self-corrective thinking mode, 174
   self-directed, 174
   self-disciplined, 174
Critiquing, 102
Cross-listed courses, 6–7
Cross-cultural awareness, 188
Cross-cultural experiences, 25
Cultural adaptation, 192, 193
Cultural background, 171, 177
Cultural communication expert, 171
Cultural literacy, 127
Cultural miscommunication, 181
Culture of surface, 8, 17, 228
Curator judges, 313
Curriculum movement, 142, 325

D

Dedicated workshops, 192

Deeper levels of learning, 162
Developmental phases, 23
Disproportionate weight, 261
Disciplinary colleagues, 52
Disciplinary committee, 182
Disciplinary concepts, 117
Disciplinary expert readers, 125
Disciplinary experts, 5, 36, 136, 150, 162, 305, 332
Disciplinary jargon, 6
Disciplinary literacy, 147, 148, 337
Disciplinary perspective, 170
Discourse knowledge, 143, 327
Discourse-processing interaction, 144
Discrepancy, 304
Discursive elements, 143, 326
Discussing clarity, 264
Disproportionate weight, 261
Dissonance, 22, 277, 304
Distributional curriculum, 6
Diverse backgrounds, 23, 170
Diverse perspectives, 170, 177
Doctoral dissertation, 309
Doctoral programs, 254
Drawing board, 296
Dynamic relationship, 144, 327
Dysfunctional families, 124

E

Education organizations, 284, 292
Educational component, 187
Educational developers, 66, 171, 190
Educational programs, 54
Effective readers, 132
Effective tools, 306
Elementary school, 25, 26
Emotion hub, 36
Emotional information, 175
Emotional trauma, 39
Emphasize writing, 147, 329
Encyclopedias, 125
Energy-efficiency metrics, 148
Epistemological beliefs, 32, 34
Epistemological orientation, 24
Epistemological spectrum, 95

Epistemology, 94, 95
Error analysis, 214, 215
Error-free papers, 213
Ethnocentric, 192, 198, 199, 306
Ethnorelative perspective, 189, 193
Ethnorelative stages, 192, 193, 198
European integration, 187
Evacuation, 2, 3
Evaluation criteria, 270, 318, 320, 322, 323
Eviscerated, 6
Excessive teachers, 162
Exciting environment, 304
Expert academic writers, 149, 331
Expert writer, 151–161, 334, 335
Explicit formulation, 64
Explicit incorporation, 306
Exploratory journey, 311
Extensive formal education, 67
Extensive revisions, 152, 334
External constraints, 56
External evaluators, 239, 246
Extrapolating aspects, 26
Extrinsic motivation, 37, 43

F

Facial expressions, 257, 266
Factory assembly line conveyor belt, 7, 297
Faulty expectations, 22
FIFA Player, 277
Film festival judges films, 313
Financial assistance, 226
Financial constraints, 157
Financial crises, 121
First-year college course, 150, 332
Flexibility, 53, 296
Foreign programs, 190
Formal education, 66, 67, 86, 187
Formal language, 207
Forward-search model, 161
Fossilized bureaucracies, 303
Foster evaluation, 123
Francophone quebeckers, 205
Frontal cortex, 36, 42, 194

Fructiferous, 32
Frustration, 4
Fullest potential, 151, 333
Fundamental assumptions, 7
Fundamental issues, 4, 8, 64, 125, 312

G

Gender stereotypes, 181
Gender violence, 58
Generalization processes, 193
Genre model, 143, 144, 161, 326, 327
Genre writing, 327
Genre-based model, 144
Geographic positioning system, 241
Giant bureaucracy, 303
Goals of universities, 2
Good assignments, 151, 333
Grade expectations, 260
Grade-point averages, 205
Grading machines, 155
Grading system, 226, 227, 246
Graduation rates, 297
Grammatical errors, 207

H

Hard sciences, 95
Hidden agenda, 151, 333
Hierarchical social, 106
Highest degree, 170
Higher-order cognitive skills, 26
application, 26, 29, 78, 102, 117, 124, 129, 134, 147, 155, 255, 329
extrapolation, 26
theorization, 26, 102
Hire personnel, 296
History course, 182
Home curriculum, 190–193
Home-campus curriculum, 188, 198
Homogeneous, 176, 205, 301
Homogeneous social backgrounds, 176
Host institution, 191, 192
Human panic, 3
Human sexuality, 71, 278

I

Iceberg, 117
Ideal higher education, 298
Illegal immigration, 257
Immigration reforms, 58
Impenetrable, 6
Imported goods, 26
Individual learner, 23
Individualism, 107, 108, 110, 176
Institutional constraints, 42, 157
Institutional mission, 63
Institutional outcomes, 51
Instructive graders, 155
Insurance companies, 2
Integrative cortex, 20, 24–26
Intellectual challenge, 22
Intellectual skills, 4
Intensive teaching formats, 267, 276, 278, 280, 284
Intercultural issues, 188
Intercultural resources, 193
Interdependent fashion, 104
Intergovernmental organizations, 148
Internalization, 180, 241
International telecommunication union, 148
Internationalization, 186–189, 198, 200
Internationalizing students, 306
Internet translation, 190
Interpersonal communication skills, 206
Interpret academic texts, 305
Intrapsychological, 28
Intrinsic interests, 54
Intrinsic motivation, 37, 43
Investment organizations, 2
Inward-looking fashion, 175
Irrelevant data, 6
Islamic scholars, 130
Italian neorealist films, 59

J

Joint enrollment, 6
Journey outcomes, 312, 313
Jurisprudential debates, 311

K

Knowledge construction, 17, 19, 24, 230, 241
Knowledge diversity, 175
Knowledge transformation, 144, 327, 328
Knowledge-telling model, 143, 327

L

Labeling theory, 60, 61
Lack of professionalism, 293
Landmark buildings, 105
Language acquisition, 30, 204, 207, 210, 213–217, 306
Law reform initiatives, 331
Learner's zone, 20, 41, 145, 304
Learning community, 66, 98, 101–104, 282, 301
Learning endeavor, 118, 151, 241, 306, 333
Learning equation, 266
Learning orientations, 8
Learning paradigm, 5, 284, 292, 296–301
Learning portfolios, 238
Learning profoundly, 132
Learning quality, 328
Learning-outcome-based, 52
Legal framework, 331
Legal scholar, 156, 313
Legal traditions, 311, 312
Lengthy discussion, 146
Lexical meaning, 215
Liberation education, 80, 88
Library databases, 316
Licensing organizations, 317
Limbic cortex, 237
Linear discursive, 175
Linear exposition, 175
Literacy level, 147, 150, 330, 332
Literacy skills, 149, 332
Logical alternative, 3
Logical relationship, 318, 320, 322, 323
Low-anxiety situations, 209
Lower-order skill, 27
Ludicrously unattainable, 195

343 Index

M

Malleable substance, 152, 335
Management firms, 2
Marginal activity, 133
Margins of university, 142, 325
Medical schools, 189
Medieval europe, 124
Medieval universities, 186
Memory limitations, 314
Menstruating, 182
Mental models, 23
Mental paradigms, 23
Mental representation, 143, 327
Metacognitive skills, 20, 133, 145, 148, 159, 230, 293, 304, 328, 330
Meta-connections, 319, 321–323
Mirror neurons, 29
Modern university, 226, 227
Motor cortex, 25
Multicultural context, 189
Multiculturalism, 38
Multinational corporation, 78
Multitude experiences, 304
Museum curator, 118
Museum exhibition, 313
Myriad array, 79

N

Naïve theory, 27
Native Spanish speakers, 181
Native tongues, 172
Native-language-speaking students, 306
Negative environment, 37, 38, 213
Neuronal networks, 20, 31, 59, 194, 277, 304
Neuroscience, 29, 36, 55, 237, 277
Nonacademic activities, 154, 233
Nonarbitrary, 19, 30, 41, 102, 120, 135, 145, 230, 304, 328, 330
Non-ESL students, 210
Nonlawyers, 279
Nonlinear process, 162
Nonlinguistic information, 208
Nonnative speakers, 34, 137, 204, 207
Nonnative-speaking students, 204

Nonpositivist notions, 279
Nonreligious students, 172
Nonsensical, 152, 257, 335
Nonthreatening environment, 20, 213
Nontraditional students, 170, 174–179, 276, 279
Nonverbal behavior, 193, 257, 266, 270
Nonverbatim basis, 30
North American soil, 3
Number-one priorities, 277
Nutrient-dense regimen, 57
Nutrition patterns, 282

O

Oblique learning, 57, 69
Obscure trivia, 6
Observation skills, 193
Obsessive focus, 17
Occasional projects, 142, 325
Occupy Wall Street movement, 120
Olympic gold medalist, 277
Ongoing composition, 144, 327
Open-ended questions, 18, 232
Oral presentations, 238, 313
Original presentation, 148, 331
Outcome-based education
Overcorrection of errors, 51–53

P

Paralinguistic symbols, 97
Patient's symptoms, 130
Patriarchal, 174
Pedagogical debate, 62
Pedagogical foundations, 231
Pedagogical perspective, 30, 36, 216
Pedagogical point, 23
Pedagogical practices, 131
Pedagogical roots, 65
Pedagogical stance, 3
Pedagogical vocabulary, 53
Pedagogy dimensions, 132
Peer reviewers, 152, 154, 335,
Penalizing errors, 235
Peripheral participation, 30, 104
Pervasive activity, 142, 325

344   Facilitating Deep Learning

Pervasive grading system, 246
Piaget's postulates, 28, 237
Piecemeal solutions, 4
Plagiarism complaint, 182
Playing soccer, 154, 277
Plenty of information, 306
Plurality of languages, 179, 186, 194, 195
Plurilingual education, 171, 179, 186, 188, 195, 200, 204,306
Point of utterance model, 143, 161, 326, 327
Positivist legal perspective, 279
Postsecondary level, 195
Potential biases, 266
Powerful learning strategies, 142, 325
Preconceived ideas, 310
Preconceived notions, 55
Predominant goals, 8
Predominant knowledge mode, 173, 174
Predominant notion, 50
Predominant pedagogy, 5, 299
Preeminence, 303
Prefrontal cortex, 194
Preliminary theories, 146, 329
Preponderant role, 8
Prerogatives, 62
Presentation skills, 258
Private space transportation, 331
Privilege teaching, 5
Problem-solving goals, 144, 326
Problem-solving theory, 326
Procrastinate, 54
Professional communities, 116, 117
Professional conference, 156
Professional fields, 108, 116, 135, 194, 241
Professional media, 258
Program formats, 284
Pythagoras, 95

Q

Question basic assumptions, 3
Quick mental reactions, 27

R

Radical cultural, 188
Radical deconstruction, 80
Radical shift, 106, 306
Reacculturative conversation, 106
Real learners, 84
Real occasions, 333
Real-life situation, 85
Recitation conventions, 105, 110
Reconstructs evidence, 174
Recursive nature, 337
Reference books, 125
Reflection-in-action process, 233, 237
Reflective abstraction, 35
Reflective journal, 193, 248, 313
Reformulating, 152, 334
Re-imagining liberal, 265
Relaxing atmosphere, 209
Reliable conclusions, 263
Relevant anchorages, 81
Reliability flaws, 256
Remedial teaching, 181
Remedy comprehension, 128
Repress nonmainstream backgrounds, 179
Rereading, 128, 152, 334
Research endeavor, 107
Research findings, 84, 146, 328
Research study, 18
Restructuring, 35, 103, 230, 237
Retrocede, 160
Retrospective, 226, 231, 238, 246
Retrospective evaluation, 237, 238
Reviewers, 152–155, 335
Revising, 152, 153, 163, 334, 335
Rhetorical intention, 143, 326
Rhetorical space, 144, 327
Rich theories, 189
Rigid schedules, 281
Routine practices, 7
Routine writing tasks, 143, 327

S

Sabbatical leave, 309
Salta's society, 60
Scheduling course formats, 282

Index

Scheduling formats, 276, 279, 281, 283, 286
Scholarly teachers, 293
Scholarly teaching process, 264
adequate preparation, 193, 264, 268
clear goals, 264, 293
significant results, 264, 293
Sculptor's studio, 297
Second-class programs, 283
Seldom plan, 87
Self-evaluation process, 238
Self-imposed fiefdoms, 6
Semester-length course, 283
Seminal work, 5
Sentence-level errors, 160
Series of projections, 23
Sexual orientations, 279
Short written assignments, 329
Shrinking budgets, 228
Signatory pedagogy, 303
Single cultural perspective, 173
Single discipline, 2, 283
Single ideal standard, 147, 329
Skill-building hypothesis, 208
Slow construction, 277
Soccer-intensive culture, 154
Social consensus, 29
Social construction, 94–107
Social crisis, 120
Social influence, 102
Social interaction, 19, 102, 119, 150, 171, 176–179, 230, 262, 305, 333
Social level, 20, 28, 41, 101, 103, 107, 230, 304
Social media, 89, 120, 121, 137
Societal hierarchical, 60
Societal problems, 4
Socratic dialogs, 312
Socratic method, 81, 82, 85
Somber situation, 3
Sophisticated processes, 95
South Tower, 2
Soviet union, 118
Space law, 309, 310, 331
Space objects, 309
Spiral curriculum, 63

Spiral process, 24
Spreading activation, 143, 327
Stairwells, 2, 3
Stakeholders, 3, 84, 148, 228, 292
Standardization processes, 148
Standardized practices, 299
Status quo, 4, 8, 209
Stereotype threat, 38, 43
Stereotyping, 36, 38, 81, 193, 256, 260
Strategic learner, 17
Stress-free environment, 36
Strongly disagree, 256
Student conference, 156
Student success, 297, 301
Student's relevant anchorage, 232
Student-centered activities, 86, 87
collective writing, 86, 262
debates, 62, 86, 87, 125, 311–319
role-playings, 86
Student-centered pedagogies, 280, 284
Student-generated mapping, 24
Stylistic choices, 337
Subject-matter content, 215
Substantial information, 234
Substantive revisions, 155
Summative evaluations, 65, 238, 247
Superficial revisions, 153, 335
Superficial understanding, 318, 320–323
Superordinate, 128
Supranational levels, 53
Surface learner, 17, 258, 260
Surface-level errors, 160
Surface-structure errors, 160

T

Tacit structure, 132, 259
Taxpayers, 7
Teacher-centered lecture, 5
Teacher-directed, 24
Teachers embark, 306
Teaching models, 60, 276 280
constructive alignment, 60, 71, 97, 133, 269
misalignment, 60
Teaching strategies, 177, 200, 210, 216

Technical aspects, 4
Technicalities, 53
Tenure-track appointment, 267, 296
Tenure-track candidate, 255
Terrorist attacks, 2, 129
Text solidifies, 153, 335
Theory-Y climate, 333
Top-notch professors, 86
Tourist excursions, 188
Traditional essay assignment, 329
Traditional lecture, 9, 86, 105, 259, 281
Traditional scheduling format, 276, 278, 281, 285
Traditional scheduling modes, 280, 283
Traditional-format courses, 278
Transformational process, 303
Triangulate data, 263
Truly formative, 306
Trusting environment, 151, 333
Truth legitimizing, 7

U

Unclear boundaries, 151, 333
Unconscious repertoire, 130
Undergraduate criminology curriculum, 189
Undergraduate level, 331
Underlying intentions, 132, 259
Uniform practices, 8
Unilingual, 194, 195, 205
Unique learning experience, 293
Unique ways, 25
United Airlines, 2
University-level materials, 230
Unmanageable, 37
Unscripted problems, 303
Unstated context, 127
Upper-year courses, 63, 279

V

Vague prescriptions, 147, 329
Vague standards, 52
Ventral regions, 241
Verbal language, 142, 325
Verbatim, 146, 324, 328
Visual representations, 232
Vociferated, 205
Voluntary, 317

W

Weigh evidence, 174
Well-reputed writers, 159
Whimsical, 26
White-collar job, 3
Wide array, 23, 79, 83, 157, 177, 179, 213, 234, 303, 306
Workshop participants, 42, 89, 146, 328, 329
World Trade Center, 2, 3
engineering firms, 2
government departments, 2
insurance companies, 2
law firms,2
transportation companies, 2
Worldview perspectives, 173, 179, 306
Works of literature, 6, 105
destroyed, 6
eviscerated, 6
Writers resort, 334

Y

Yield superficial revisions, 153, 335

Z

Zone of proximal, 29, 30